PRAISE FOR *TRUTH & LIES*

"Mark Bowden and Tracey Thomson give us a front row seat to understanding nonverbal communication and human behavior."
—TONYA REIMAN, behavioral analyst and author of *The Body Language of Dating*

"The cluttered space of body language clickbait continues to grow, but *Truth & Lies* clears a path to clarity and focus."
—SCOTT ROUSE, body language analyst and military interrogation trainer

"A thoroughly insightful read, packed full of useful information to put to immediate and practical use. Let Mark and Tracey guide you to success and increase your awareness of other people."
—CRAIG JAMES BAXTER, author of *Behind the Mask*

"If you've ever wondered what selfies say, why people 'ghost,' and how to detect the signals of deception in the physical and digital world, then *Truth & Lies* is the definitive, nonverbal communication book of this generation."
—JAMIE MASON COHEN, handwriting analyst for criminal profilers and TEDx speaker

"Fascinating, revealing and, at times, unsettling, *Truth & Lies* explains the nuances of body language to help you better understand the complexities of human behavior and discover what people are really thinking."
—VICTORIA STILWELL, principal at Positively and author of *It's Me or the Dog*

Truth & Lies

Also by Mark Bowden

Winning Body Language: Control the Conversation,
Command Attention, and Convey the Right Message
without Saying a Word

Winning Body Language for Sales Professionals:
Control the Conversation and Connect with Your
Customer without Saying a Word

Tame the Primitive Brain: 28 Ways in 28 Days
to Manage the Most Impulsive Behaviors at Work

TRUTH &
LIES

What People Are Really Thinking

Mark Bowden
and Tracey Thomson

HarperCollins Publishers Ltd

Published by HarperCollins Publishers Ltd

First edition

HarperCollins books may be purchased for educational, business, or sales
promotional use through our Special Markets Department.

HarperCollins Publishers Ltd
2 Bloor Street East, 20th Floor
Toronto, Ontario, Canada
M4W 1A8

www.harpercollins.ca

Library and Archives Canada Cataloguing in Publication information is available
upon request.

ISBN 978-1-44345-209-0

Printed and bound in the United States

23 24 25 26 27 LBC 12 11 10 9 8

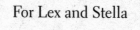

For Lex and Stella

Everything we see is a perspective, not the truth
—Falsely attributed to Marcus Aurelius (author unknown)

CONTENTS

INTRODUCTION

WE CAN ALL RECALL EXAMPLES when our sense of what another person was thinking turned out to be the truth. Equally so, there have been times when we were so sure we were reading another person right only to discover, after the fact, how dead wrong we were. Sometimes, we learn the hard way that we were purposely lied to and cannot believe we did not see it for even one moment . . . until it was too late. Chances are that no matter the case, we were relying to some extent on correctly reading another's body language.

We are inundated through news and social media with clickbait, articles and guides on how to read body language, which attempt to make it quick and easy for us to glance at someone and deduce their most secret thoughts. For example, they've crossed their arms, so obviously they don't like what I'm saying. They've pointed their feet elsewhere—clearly, they are more attracted to someone else in the room. They scratched their nose, so they're a no-good liar.

The problem is that while some of the time our "quick read" of someone's body language may correctly uncover the truth about what they are thinking, all too often our readings and interpretations prove incorrect in the moment and we get it horribly wrong. On a good day there is only about a fifty-fifty chance of being correct.

Having said that, people who are truly practiced at the skill of reading and interpreting body language have found that by following tried and trusted processes, they can be far more effective at deducing what people are really thinking.

HERE IS A STORY from someone whose job it has been, in the interest of public safety, to always get the reading right: to examine behaviors, make an informed judgment from them, and then test how accurate his judgments are to uncover the truth of the matter. Read on and ask yourself how much you would trust your current body language reading skills in this situation, where stress and the stakes are high, in order to catch a murderer.

Our colleague and friend Paul Nadeau is a former police detective with twenty-five years of investigative background, including homicide, and was a trained polygraph examiner—in other words, a professional lie detector. Paul describes the polygraph as an instrument that can detect the "slightest physiological changes in someone's body; changes that can occur when someone is anxious giving a deceitful answer to a clear question." As the polygraph examiner, Paul had to record and analyze the stress shown when answering questions to determine which ones the examinee may have lied about.

Paul notes that, of course, individuals who agree to take a polygraph examination may indeed already be in quite an anxious state, particularly if they are being investigated by the police. Someone in Paul's position understands that if a person being questioned is immediately attached to a polygraph, there is every chance of getting a "false positive" result—they might look like a liar, even when they are not.

"Before hooking any suspect up to the instrument, I would first take some time to bring the examinee to a calmer state, putting them at ease. But that's not all. I would also be watching every movement made by the examinee. Taking mental snapshots of that person's physicality; looking for changes—especially as we move onto talking casually about the subject matter under investigation."

Paul shared with us one real-life situation, a homicide case where a gang member had been found in a rival gang's territory stabbed to death, with three deep knife wounds to the heart. The theory was that the gang was sending a powerful message: Do not trespass on our turf—or else! The suspects were any and all of the rival gang's members. Unsurprisingly, each gang member denied committing the murder, and each of them was requested by the police to take a polygraph test.

It was Paul's task to interview and give polygraph tests individually to the entire rival gang, any of whom could be the murderer, and all of whom denied any involvement. But then there was rival gang member number six, whom Paul describes as displaying body language that felt to him cocky and argumentative. "His chin was up and pushed out defiantly. He looked down his nose at me with a lopsided snarl. He hated all cops and had no respect for them." Right off the bat, Paul, a veteran of interrogation and lie detection, put the suspect at ease by leaning in and confiding that he too felt much the same way about the officers he worked with. This tactic paid off in that the gang member warmed to him and they got to making small talk.

Once they were involved in more relaxed banter, the gang member chatting about his family and girlfriends, Paul noted that he was at this point openly displaying a true smile, with no seemingly defensive postures. Paul was effectively establishing an understanding for himself of this individual's most normal behavior in the interview situation when in a relaxed state.

The crucial moment of body language interpretation happened when Paul purposely and abruptly shifted the conversation to the topic of the homicide. "His eyes left mine, his head turned away and his arms crossed. Although he answered 'no' to being involved, his verbal answers were inconsistent with what his body language was now broadcasting to me . . . the more I asked about his involvement, the more he leaned back into his chair—uncomfortably so."

This extreme change in body language was all Paul needed to see to have a strong suspicion that this guy was guilty.

To test his theory, Paul confronted him with a powerful question: "You didn't intend to *kill* him. You just wanted to teach him a lesson—'Don't come back!' Otherwise, I'm sure you would have stabbed him much more than three times. Isn't that the way it happened?"

The gang member dropped his head into his hands and turned away from Paul, hiding his face. He confessed then and there to the murder and was later convicted in court.

For Paul, taking mental snapshots of the behavior as he went through this interrogation, creating moments when a change in body language would stand out, as well as evaluating whether the suspect's words were consistent with the body language he saw, and taking the moment to test his conjecture, made him a "human lie detector"—he had no need for the polygraph.

Of course, this was Paul's job as a law enforcement professional, an essential service in ensuring public safety. Paul was highly skilled and well practiced in his system for reading body language with accuracy.

Wouldn't it be incredibly useful if you could emulate Paul's level of expertise in getting to the truth in your everyday life, without going through the detective training, and without coming across as an interrogator? For example, what if you understood as Paul did the suspect's lopsided snarl, looking down his nose, jutting chin: All his facial expressions that indicate arrogance and contempt, a powerful feeling of being "above" Paul and the cops. Then, if you knew to empathize with the person and find their baseline of relaxed behavior for that situation, to instigate a change in the situation that might reveal a notable change in body language, and to—finally—test the findings for accuracy, eliciting displays of shame and even guilt—well, that skill would surely prove useful, instead of your acting solely on a hunch and going with a knee-jerk reaction to another's body language.

ALYSON SCHAFER, A HIGHLY RESPECTED parenting expert, told us a story that highlights just how important it is to put aside those knee-jerk reactions we can have to nonverbal behavior, to hold off on making wrong and possibly even catastrophic assumptions based on those reactions, instead taking the time to investigate situations more thoroughly to get to the truth.

One afternoon as she and her eight-year-old daughter walked their usual route home from school, Zoe started behaving "very weird." "She suddenly seemed very anxious. This came across for me in her hypervigilance—she was constantly checking out everyone around her." Alyson asked her if anything was wrong, and Zoe replied, "No, nothing." But her answer did not ring true to Alyson.

Over the next few days, Alyson saw Zoe repeatedly behaving like this. She also noticed that Zoe was continually stopping to retie her shoelaces. To parents of young children, Alyson's first response will be familiar: She took it to be the behavior of a dawdling child. However, Alyson made a conscious decision to set aside her initial assumption and also try to keep her annoyance at bay. Instead of saying "Hurry up!" she decided to keep a more open mind and gently investigate what was clearly a change from the norm in her daughter's behavior.

Though Zoe kept insisting everything was OK, Alyson noticed that with this response, Zoe would quickly look away from her and move on. The evidence was mounting for Alyson that her daughter's continued evasive behavior meant something was up.

On the next journey to school together, instead of using words to ask if there was a problem, Alyson used her own body language to get through to Zoe, just as she was going to crouch down to retie her laces: "I interrupted by waving my hand over her chest and tummy [where many people feel their anxiety or tension], wiggled my fingers as I moved my hand in fluttery circles, and asked, 'Do you want this feeling to go away?' She immediately looked me right in the eyes and replied, 'Yes!'

"I told her I knew someone [a therapist] she could talk to who would help her get those feelings to go away. She was thrilled."

We were intrigued by Alyson's story, and we asked what was going on. Alyson relayed to us the event that had triggered the unusual behavior:

"The day this all started, as we were on our usual morning walk to school and approaching the lights where we'd cross the street, a woman came out of her house and suddenly fell to the ground in front of us—and then started throwing up! She was holding keys and pointing and saying something in a language I did not understand. I quickly told Zoe to stay put, took the keys and entered the house she seemed to be pointing at. Once inside, I yelled loudly for help. It turned out that the woman's daughter lived in the house. She came running out with me to help her mom. Once her mom was settled, she sent us on our way—assuring us that everything was OK."

While Alyson felt very happy to have helped a neighbor and largely forgot about the event, for her young daughter it proved to be extremely traumatic; the woman's being so sick and the feeling of panic at being powerless to help triggered a response of acute anxiety in Zoe. Her changed behavior reflected a new hypervigilance to make sure no one else around her was randomly going to be that ill. And the shoelaces? Retying her shoes was a strategic maneuver to avoid passing that house, by delaying until the traffic light turned red, thus forcing them to walk on the opposite side of the street from the house.

For us, this story shows some smart thinking by Alyson in taking a little extra time to observe the situation, to suspend her own judgment about her daughter's actions—rather than assuming that Zoe was just dawdling—to be mindful of what was going on in the moment, and then to test her theory that there really was a problem by using her own body language to more powerfully and directly communicate.

How easy is it to emulate Alyson's decisions and suspend your judgment, to hold off on the easy route of the knee-jerk reaction and remain curious about behaviors you see? How can you learn to be as observant, thoughtful and objective in your everyday life, to determine whether the behavior of others that has a direct impact on you is meant to have that impact or is just their normal way of being? In other words, how can you get a baseline of behavior for someone that lets you know when something important or extraordinary is happening, so you can reply in a way that is understandable, as well as make assumptions that are closer to the truth?

When we incorrectly read body language signals, we are likely to make false assumptions about others and what they intend toward us, and as a result we stand a good chance of disappointment or perhaps experiencing serious consequences.

HERE'S A STORY ABOUT how we put ourselves and our body language out into the world via social media, what signals we send and how much truth we reveal about ourselves in the way our posts are received. It may very well ring true for you too.

Cathryn Naiker is a stand-up comedian and comedy writer who works with our organization. One afternoon, she decided that would be the day she would start online dating.

Having just changed her look with a cool new haircut, she staged a photo shoot, for which she wore an equally cool-looking dress and held a fake cocktail. The dimmed atmospheric lighting made it look as if she were living it up at an after-party. She even had a photo taken of her on an exercise bike with mocktail in hand—like "Look at me, I'm crazy!"—to showcase herself in a twenty-something-fun-girl-looking-for-love-and-adventure profile.

Once done, she filled out the lengthy dating website questionnaire. "Questions came up like: Do you exercise? The truth is I don't, but I didn't want people to think I was lazy! Plus I just took a picture of myself on an exercise bike in a dress with a cocktail . . . So let's even that out with saying 'sometimes' and other embellishments of the facts."

Once she had created the perfect profile showing a version of herself that she felt did basically represent her—though admittedly a version that reflected how she *wanted* to be seen—she started to make contact with her best suitors.

Cathryn eventually came across one guy who showed potential. He was the same age and seemed to enjoy parties as much as she did. He had a picture of himself on his profile as the best man at a wedding, his arms around family. "His face reflected an easy attitude—a gentle smile, no stressed-out lines of tension. He appeared calm, fun-loving, confident and outgoing. And his physical description said 'Athletic.' I instantly thought, *This guy is perfect for me!*" They agreed to meet.

When Cathryn saw her date face to face, she was shocked. "He did not look like his photo—at all! He was much heavier, not only his body but in his face too. Also, where his profile picture's gentle smile had been now sat a forced grimace showing off a great deal of dental hardware to correct his teeth. But perhaps most disconcerting was that he was at least three inches shorter than the 'six feet' he listed himself as. Which put him several inches shorter than me!

"He was an OK-looking guy," adds Cathryn, but she admits feeling disappointed. "It's not that I was so bothered by his shorter, stockier build. It's more that I felt misled, which threw me off."

So, we get that he may have misrepresented himself a bit, but how about his character, we asked. Was he a warm, fun guy—the life and soul of the party—just like she thought from his pictures?

"I had to totally lead the conversation. He was not outgoing at all—way less social than his pictures suggested to me."

We asked if any of her predictions about him, based on his profile pictures, were correct.

"Well, yes! I called that he was 'into family' right, but I did not quite get how extreme this was. When I could get him to talk during our date—which was rarely—he only talked about his family. He brought them into just about everything! It seemed to be all he was ever thinking about. Slightly weird. And 'laid-back' I got right too. When he finally got comfortable, he was almost comatose! Toward the end of the date he was totally slumped, bringing his energy level, and his height, down even further, all of which made him seem in real life totally unconfident."

Of course, Cathryn realizes the irony of the situation: That despite the best of intentions, neither of them were really what they had advertised on their profiles, that they were both trying to put their best foot forward. However, Cathryn, as many of us would, took what he had chosen to include on his profile at face value. The picture of him at the wedding may perhaps have captured the one and only time he was the life and soul of the party. Given that she was not completely truthful either with the snapshots offered on her profile, she admitted that it would be no surprise if he also made incorrect assumptions about her, with nothing to base his expectations on other than that thin slice of life she posted online.

Both parties were left disappointed.

Misrepresentation is highly likely to happen in these types of situations, and the resulting disappointment, though tangible, is perhaps not such a surprise, given the conundrum of filling out the profile questionnaire. "What am I supposed to look like and say? 'I'm Cathryn, looking for the love of my life. Here I am eating pizza in bed—wanna date?'"

Just as in Cathryn's story, reading body language both in person and online involves making judgments based on a very thin slice of the data, and this data is often corrupted even before we get our chance to interpret, or misinterpret, it. It is no wonder, then, that when we don't take the opportunity to critically think in the moment, to observe all the details we can and to test our assumptions, it is easy and likely that we will make terrible errors of judgment based on gut feelings, biases and innate patterns of thinking about others—feelings that felt and seemed so right at the time that often end up proven incorrect.

READING ANOTHER'S BODY LANGUAGE and getting it right, and then acting on your interpretation, can surely bring positive consequences: in Paul's case, catching a killer; in Alyson's situation, helping someone precious to her. However, the negative consequences of getting it wrong can also have an impact on us, from disappointment that your date wasn't who you thought they'd be to long-term feelings of loss, sorrow and regret as a result of not seeing something for what it really was. "How did I not see that breakup/job loss/family feud coming?"

This book will enable you to experience the life-enhancing power that comes with improving your ability to get it right.

Whether you choose to jump around and read specific sections, enjoy only certain chapters of interest or rip through the entire book from cover to cover, you will learn about a methodology by which to observe and assign meaning when it comes to body language, to get you closer to knowing the truth of a situation. This book offers a clear process for you to follow, teaching skills that will help you address these main questions: How can I make more accurate judgments about what people really think, feel and intend toward me from their nonverbal communication? How can I test how right I am about my judgments? How can I best govern my actions with the power of this knowledge?

This book presents for most a whole new way of thinking about the meaning of body language. You will learn a powerful new process for making and testing assumptions about the meaning of the behavior of others, a process you can take into any and every situation. Use it and you will gain a powerful understanding around the truth and lies of what people are really thinking.

PART

ONE

GENUINE DECEPTIONS

I can read you like a book!
—All of us

Imagine a world where no one can pull the wool over *your* eyes. Think about the power you would have if you could detect someone's deepest, innermost thoughts regardless of what they were saying to you. Living your life where the truth of the matter would always be in plain sight for you. No secret subtext. No covert conversations. Nothing ever left unsaid to you. No mystery. No mistakes. No mess. What a wonderful possibility.

But isn't this just a fantasy? Every time you click on the link to yet another article that baits you with the promise of teaching you how to discern what is really going on in other people's heads, are you already being lied to?

In order to interpret what someone is really thinking by analyzing their body language, there are truths you need to know first.

1

BODY LANGUAGE LIES

LET'S GET STARTED by giving you the most all-encompassing and powerful truth about reading body language, while revealing its greatest lie: You cannot read body language.

Live nonverbal communication, or body language, is a human communication system, although it is not technically a language in the dictionary sense of the word, like English, Greek, Yoruba, Cree or Mandarin are. It lacks many of the most important factors common to spoken languages; for one, live nonverbal communication does not lend itself to displacement—language's ability to describe something that is either not here at all or not here right now. We cannot rely on nonverbal communication to clearly describe a concept such as democracy; nor can we expect nonverbal communication to tell us that the neighbor's cat has been missing since last Tuesday.

Additionally, live nonverbal communication does not allow reflexiveness, which is a language's ability to talk about itself; it would be an impossible undertaking to give a nod to your own future nod and for anyone to get that nod about the upcoming nodding.

Body language is the communication system that displays behaviors elicited in response to the environment, the experience and interpretation of which can differ from country to country and between cultures and people. These nonverbal behaviors can certainly communicate our feelings and intentions in the moment. And although body language is a physical response to our complex environment, it also has the capability of affecting it.

Hang on, you might say—what about all those books and articles and videos and documentaries about reading body language? There are certainly excellent books, experiments, research, scholarly articles, online talks and documentaries about this topic. However, whether online or off, we have taken to using the analogy that nonverbal communication is *like* a language in order to make it simpler and within our reach when making decisions about how to respond to others' behaviors.

This reductionist approach to the complexities and many nuances within body language can help us understand the motives underlying a vast and complicated array of nonverbal signals. With this approach, sometimes we get it right, and the motives informing some physical actions turn out to be what we deduced. So the simplicity works when we make the right decisions. But often this simplistic approach leads us to the wrong conclusions—when we judge another's body language within the framework of believing it really is a language, with consistent rules for translatability, we can really get ourselves into trouble.

Our trouble is not transcended in the online world but exacerbated. Online, where we increasingly spend our time, the multitude of ideas and advice have further chance to become confused. Our engagement in the Internet of ideas results in our online world mashing up the real-world intricacies of nonverbal meaning into a simple clickbait of instant help and quick fix.

In our online world, technology puts in our hands the power to play with the boundaries of what body language is ordinarily capable of. Through photos and video, a moment or sequence of body language signs can exist in myriad future contexts and so can appear to be capable of displacement. Social media platforms such as Facebook allow us to repost images of ourselves from years before and make new comments on them. Though it may seem that the body language moment is happening now, in fact it happened hours, days, weeks or decades previously. These images are always up for interpretation, and so perhaps not surprisingly, when we post an image of ourselves, we are overwhelmingly keen to control that interpretation, to guide the viewer to see us in the way we would like to be seen. This holds true whether it is our online profile picture, a Snapchat share, our YouTube channel or our personal or company branding.

As viewers, we strive to understand the meaning of the images we see of others, and as creators of our own images, we attempt to control how we are seen in the present and future by the online world at large. So it's no wonder we are attracted to the easy-to-understand, one-size-fits-all general ideas about the meanings of body language, as this makes it easier and quicker for us to fit ourselves and others into simple classifications and categories. In addition, we may not often distinguish between the meanings of body language we encounter in person versus online. We mix and confuse the two, which can lead us to make some poor judgments.

Much of the popular thinking on body language, in keeping with the simplistic concept of translatability, follows an "if this, then that" rationale. It creates a set of absolute rules around gestures, the like of which we've all heard time and time again. For example: "Their arms are crossed—they are closed to me." "He rubbed his nose—he is definitely lying." "She crossed her leg toward me—she is so into me."

While there are certainly times when those readings and interpretations prove to be true, what is generally overlooked is the impact of the essential factor of *context*—the actual situation in which the communication occurs. That is, how does context frame the particular nonverbal actions we witness and therefore influence our interpretation of what someone may be thinking?

Let's look more closely at the example of the body language gesture and its widely accepted popular translation: crossed arms = the person is closed to you. We hear this rule and we think it makes sense. Crossing arms creates a barrier, thereby closing off the body in a defensive posture, intentionally or unconsciously blocking us off and closing us out.

For the most part, we have been happy to run with the easy-to-understand assumption of crossed arms meaning a person is closed to us. It is easy to see how this simple "if this, then that" idea gained momentum and became mainstream folklore—and ultimately authoritative "fact" and tacit "truth." The jewel left in the dust is any mention of the context in which this line of interpretation may or may not be accurate.

Context is critical when interpreting body language. Going back to our example, people cross their arms for a multitude of context-specific reasons other than being closed to us personally or to our ideas. Perhaps they're in a cold environment and crossing their arms as a barrier to the cold, or it's midafternoon and they're tired, so they're holding their arms high and tense to keep themselves alert. Maybe they're on their own at a singles bar, feeling vulnerable and therefore giving themselves a self-soothing hug. Or they could be in an important work meeting, concentrating by closing down activity in the hands and arms to direct energy and attention to thinking. So while they may be trying to remain in control, and they may be blocking unwanted stimuli, and they may *look* closed, just maybe—our point here—they may not actually be closed or blocking us or our idea at that moment.

We all tend to interpret situations in terms of our own frame of reference, as an expression of our egocentric perspective. In the words of Aaron T. Beck, regarded as the founder of cognitive behavioral therapy, with added stress or when we perceive a threat in a situation, as happens constantly as we negotiate our day-to-day lives, our self-centered thinking goes into overdrive, and out of "the multiple patterns contributing to another person's behavior, we select a single strand that may affect us personally."[1] In other words, we tend to focus on and magnify just one aspect of what we observe from someone else and jump to a conclusion about what they intend toward us that is potentially incorrect. We take someone's behavior as being about us, regardless of whether it is or not.

We also need to remember that making simple transactional deductions cannot effectively manage the reality of our everyday communications in shifting contexts, where the outcome of the last interaction is never necessarily the outcome of the next selfsame one. Just because someone crosses their arms and you deduce that they are closed to you—and it turns out to be true on this particular occasion—that doesn't mean that the next time you see this sign, either from them or anyone else, they too are closed to you. What was right the last time may not be right the next.

This complexity in human behavior demands a more nuanced set of tools, to enable us to more accurately make the right calls when interpreting body language. We must adopt a more intelligent approach.

2

POWERFUL THINKING

WHEN THINGS GET COMPLEX, the last thing we should do is create a complicated system to deal with the situation. Nor is it entirely useful to produce a lexicon of overly simplified or generalized rules to help us form conclusions.

Instead, we have created a unique, easy-to-learn process for recognizing and interpreting body language that requires employing mindfulness as well as critical thinking. If you follow our approach, you will think smart and fast every time you assess another's body language, whatever the situation. You will come up with more accurate judgments, a more accurate theory of mind—the attribution of mental states (feelings, intentions, beliefs and so on) to others and to yourself, and recognize that these may differ—and so more often get a handle on the truth.

This process of more intelligently assessing nonverbal signs is ultimately based on two simple premises, one about body language and the other about our brains: (1) All body language is a display of power or a response to a display of power. And (2) your brain doesn't know anything for sure about someone else's true thoughts and intentions by reading body language; it just makes assumptions and delivers corresponding judgments.

BODY LANGUAGE AS A DISPLAY OF POWER

By power we mean any force, be it physical, psychological, environmental, sociological or otherwise.

Every gesture, movement, signal or sound we make is a response, conscious or unconscious, to our overall interior and exterior environments. These gestural responses, our "body language," cover everything from how we stand, sit, smile or frown to how we position our heads, hands, shoulders, torso, legs and feet. All our gestures and combinations of gestures can indicate our inner emotional, cognitive and physical responses to power as we experience it in our environments, be it the power of other individuals, of the community, of the physical environment or of our internal emotional or physical states. Our body language can instruct others, tell the tale or lay clues as to how we intersect on a moment-by-moment basis with that power—often a roller-coaster ride of feeling peaceful, resentful, fearful, happy, angry, sad and so on. Also, our body language can show what we want in relation to that power: whether we wish to control it or go along for the ride. We display our feelings and our desires consciously or unconsciously, and these displays in turn have an effect on the environment.

Therefore, our physical behavior displays the constant interplay of power, between us and everything around and within us. Our conscious and unconscious actions keep us in a balance of power within our world for our security, comfort, pleasure, hopes, dreams and beliefs.

Everything we do has a bearing on this power play.

Remember how in Paul's story the murderer initially reacted to the institutional power of the law? He showed his disdain and lack of submission to that power by giving body language signals that displayed contempt. And Paul, recognizing the truth informing those actions, won the man's trust by showing that he sided with him on that disdain of power, leaning in on their conversation together to close their proximity and build their "closeness."

Now think about Alyson's story. Zoe's shoelace tying reflects her power to control her environment by stopping, effectively avoiding the scene of the earlier crisis and minimizing the chances of a repeat event. Alyson reacted to her daughter's nonverbal displays by building rapport in the moment, displaying sympathetic movements that mirrored her daughter's feelings of anxiety, and also by telling her that the power of the unpleasant feelings could potentially be controlled.

In Cathryn's story, both parties attempt to show off their relationship to power, and each is judged by the other once the rose-colored lens of the dating site is removed. Cathryn's date is judged based on pictures taken in one context and then posted to the online dating site. He used images of himself as a best man to convey prestige, showing off his power and high status within his social group. Cathryn's photo displayed, along with her power of good health, her refusal to submit to the power of social conformity, showing off a devil-may-care attitude on the exercise bike with her cocktail. Neither Cathryn nor her date-to-be was able to mount a real-time analysis of the other's power displays—or in other words, to immediately test any truth behind the signals. Perhaps, then, it's not surprising that Cathryn felt let down upon seeing the inconsistency of her real-life date with the powerful persona he first projected virtually; he transmitted some less charismatic signals in real life. We are limited in what we can display when we are representationally stuck in the moment of a photo. We can only offer some of the static puzzle pieces.

How much power we have, how we display this in our body language, how others perceive our behavior—all of these affect the way we think, how we evaluate and perceive ourselves and our societies, how we are influenced, our motivation and performance, and even our simplest physical functioning. Both nature and nurture are at play here. Our sense of power is formed by our communities, culture, experiences, concepts and bodies, and all the differences around these that we navigate. And everything is moderated by our environments' stability or lack thereof, our own changing needs and expectations, and the other people and cultures we come across.

Our sense of power is essential to us. It literally and emotionally moves us.

OUR JUDGMENTAL BRAINS

We cannot know for certain what someone else is thinking. We can't read other people's minds. Nor can we with certainty translate the gestures of others to know how they are really feeling. But we can observe behaviors and get a theory of mind about them, and then make assumptions about meanings, and from these we form judgments.

This may seem contrary to our most common notions about the human process of thinking. Most of us regard the brain as the most brilliant natural machine, and so we reckon that if we just enter the right information, we will, in turn, get a correct answer. Quality input, quality output! What's wrong with that?

The idea that the brain functions just like a machine is not new. The ancient Greeks compared the mind to a hydraulic system. This idea manifested for several thousand years as the "humors," a system of bodily fluids that needed to be in the correct balance and pressure with each other for good thinking. During the Enlightenment, René Descartes popularized the notion that our thinking worked on a system similar to the complicated gears of the cleverly designed automatons of the period. In the 1800s, with the dawn of electricity, the thinkers of that era compared the brain to a simple electrical telegraph system. Next, twentieth-century psychologists theorized that the brain operated like the early electromechanical computers of the time, with the physical brain being the set "hardware" and our thoughts the manipulative punch-card "software." Keeping with this trend, as we advanced in our digital capability, so also advanced the digital metaphor of the brain. Today most would agree that much like handheld electronic devices, our brains have memory banks of knowledge we can access in order to react in the right way. Most believe our behaviors are the result of how data is processed by the hardware of the mind, which has an unchangeable hardwired system, along with a more plastic element that can be reprogrammed, erased or corrupted like a memory drive.

Here's where all of this goes wrong:

A = computers are capable of behaving with what looks like human-brain-like intelligence—correct!
B = computers are information processors—correct!

Therefore:

C = the intelligent human brain processes information just like a computer—incorrect!

A more modern theory is that the brain is not an "if this, then that" information processor that stores knowledge in memory and retrieves a selection of data, providing an appropriate response. We are not simple automatons. The intensity of a stimulus needed to cause a response can change day to day, moment to moment. One trigger yesterday may have no effect today, or a greater effect, or just the same effect. The brain is not full of billions of on/off electrical switches like a complicated computer chip is; instead, it has hundreds of trillions of chemical-sensitive modules that from moment to moment require differing levels of stimulation to output another potential stimulus.

The current theory is that the brain interprets the world through the senses and then behaves according to predictions constructed via some simple principles. It can then change future predictions based on the successes and failures of how the last worked out. In short, it learns. By the way, no one at present knows for sure how it does all of that. But certainly, no computer yet comes close to having the senses, reflexes and learning mechanisms of the human brain.

3

MIND YOUR JUDGMENTS

WHEN WE TRY TO TRANSLATE, or "read," body language, our understanding of others' behaviors, feelings and intentions is based on our best guesses about the meaning of that body language, assumptions we have consciously or unconsciously made from the biased position we occupy in the world at that moment. We form a theory of mind about other people and their relation to the powers at play. We then respond, consciously or unconsciously, with our own display of body language, which reveals or conceals our relation to the power. And all of this sometimes in the blink of an eye.

Our interpretations of these power signals are very personal, based on our unique physical and cultural position in the world when we experience events. It's not that your own brain will have a complete set of unique tools for interpreting information, as we all share some universal responses to patterns of behavior. The unique deciphering comes from your specific take on it—your view, angle or skew— along with your current state of mind.

Every time you think you know somebody else's inner thoughts, feelings and intentions from reading their body language, what is actually happening is that you are making a judgment about what power they may have in relation to you based on the signals they are displaying or concealing around their response to that power—power they do have or think they have, or power they speculate is present in the environment around them, including you. You and they are both predicting risks and rewards around that power, and you both are responding to suit your own best interests.

By becoming more mindful during these moments of judgment, by taking into account the implications of context and the principles by which you are judging others' behaviors, and by becoming more attuned to yourself as part of the entire body language analysis process, you will more accurately decipher the body language of others and use your own body language in the moment in more constructive ways. You will build your knowledge, skill, confidence and competency when assessing the body language signs and behaviors of those around you, even and perhaps especially when under pressure.

SCAN FOR TRUTH

SO, HERE IS OUR critical thinking process, which you are going to learn and master by applying it to the case studies you read in this book. It's a simple four-step process:

S: Suspend judgment and be more descriptive.
C: Take in the **Context**.
A: Ask "What else?"
N: Form a **New** judgment and test it.

You can easily remember our process with the acronym **SCAN**.

S: SUSPEND JUDGMENT AND BE MORE DESCRIPTIVE

You get an instinct about what is going on in a situation, and rather than running with it, you suspend that judgment by employing mindfulness in the moment, taking a step back to examine as fully as possible all the details you sense—what the other person is doing, the key body language signals they display, how they sound, how your initial response makes you feel. This detailed examination—your description—engages your critical thinking and moves you away from knee-jerk judgments and wrong assumptions.

C: TAKE IN THE CONTEXT

Where are you? When? Who else is there? What is the situation? What is the background? Think about the conditions around and within the description—physical, psychological, digital and social.

A: ASK "WHAT ELSE?"

Think wider and deeper about other contexts in which the behavior may be at play. Consider details and "what if?" possibilities by asking what else you know or can bring to bear on the situation.

N: FORM A NEW JUDGMENT AND TEST IT

Refine or replace entirely the initial judgment you made with a more informed theory of mind. Get feedback by testing the new idea you have about the situation, or the old one if that is what you have returned to.

WE WILL BE USING our **SCAN** process to explore body language within three of the most important relationship umbrellas under which we make judgments about other people's feelings and intentions toward us:

- Dating
- Friends and family
- Working life

These areas of our lives can easily define our most important, impactful and difficult-to-do-without relationships.

We begin each chapter by describing, within each of these three main categories, common and relatable scenarios as well as classic assumptions and judgments we make about what others are thinking when we "read" their body language.

We explore face-to-face situations and those within the digital world. We review a diverse human landscape, looking at what binds us as humans through our behavior. There is always more that links us nonverbally as human beings than differentiates us.

We uncover and delve into the powerful nonverbal signals that can trigger us to make assumptions, taking into account the truth of our own behavior in the moment and how that may affect the assumptions we make.

Each chapter includes a dose of scientific fact or theory to help explain why and how we make these assumptions; our responses; popular hearsay; wisdom and new contributions from other experts in the fields of body language, behavior and culture. From all of this, you'll gain a greater insight into why people may be giving off the impressions they do, and based on your own emotional state and the context, how accurately you are judging what thoughts inform their body language, giving you a fuller and more rounded way of thinking around this.

Finally, we offer strategies to test in real time your changed or refined judgments, and then give you tactics for how you might respond to situations, be it in the physical or digital world, to give you the advantage.

Ultimately, this powerful method will allow you to read and effectively use body language within the most modern framework of science and expert opinion, both face to face and in the digital world. You are about to become someone with the power to differentiate for themselves the truth and the lies.

PART

TWO

DATING

What are you thinking?

—Everyone on a third date

Human beings have some of the most unique and complex mating rituals and practices in all of the animal kingdom. As our ability to be present both live and across multiple mediums and platforms grows exponentially, so too do the possibilities for how we communicate within the different arenas, and sending and receiving signs and signals in search of a partner can become increasingly convoluted and messy. Navigating the nonverbal signals we encounter live or online to get a sense of the truth and lies in each situation, and what they mean for us, is far from straightforward. Perhaps it's no surprise that our attempts to negotiate the multitude of nonverbal behaviors that go hand in hand with these rituals can either win the day or really land us in trouble.

Many other species in the animal kingdom do what humans sometimes refer to as *hooking up* to procreate and nothing else. Few species have the social bonds that tie partners together as soulmates until death do us part or for some lengthy duration. So if we humans are sometimes actually playing the long game, thinking long term, we in turn need to get our communication right around these dating and mating rituals. After all, whether the decisions we make are right or wrong, we may feel the consequences over many years or even for generations to come. We're in a high-risk situation, emotionally, socially and genetically.

Let's take a moment to compare our mating rituals with those of other species. It turns out we share some similarities, which is worth noting, as many of our ideas and theories about the meaning of body language are based on where we've come from and how we've evolved. Let's look, for example, at what we share in terms of power display, as it plays an important role within mating rituals.

Many animals, humans included, use color, size, movement, sound and scent in attracting mates, and all these expenditures will be at an intensity or rhythm that marks them out from their environments. For example, many species flaunt colorful aspects of themselves to stand out, displaying their powerful bodies and even social standing. Because of the intensity of these signals and the physical abilities animals need for the display to happen, they show off their health as well. Because of the expense of the display in terms of time, effort, energy, calories—in short, resources—the display will show the power of their social rank. In response to this power, the rest of the group can show submission, in effect by allowing the displays to happen. For certain species and communities, displays of dominance now and then are helpful for everyone in the group to make clear where they currently stand in the pecking order, or hierarchy. However, these displays in the animal kingdom can be high risk, as they may attract challengers and predators.

Though our human rituals may appear very similar at times to those of other species, there are crucial differences resulting from our advanced brain function, differing social landscapes, different expenditures of resources, different risk levels and differing goals and objectives from the start. Whereas some animal mating rituals can take just a few moments at a very specific time of year, for humans marketing themselves to potential partners, it can take anywhere from moments to years, depending on how, where and when we do so, and also on our goal. In the body language of mating, dating and seduction, we add an extra layer of nuance depending on whether we are trying to attract a buddy just for the night or find a partner for life.

Some of the body language signals we use to show off our power and attract others in both kingdoms are also the signals used to scare others off. So while we might puff out our chest to display power, are we also doing it to attract a mate, to warn off our competitors or both? And if this body language is directed at you, how do you know which the other sees you as, mate or menace?

This part of the book takes you through a sampling of identifiable dating situations and the power play within them that is signaled through body language. We'll bust some of the myths about dating body language and get down to the power, truth and lies that our non-verbal signals can leak. And we'll help you think more clearly about the signals you are sending out, to give you a nonverbal advantage in the dating game both online and off.

5

THEY'RE TOTALLY CHECKING ME OUT!

You are in a bar with your friend. It's singles night. You're both looking for that someone right for you, or perhaps for you right now. Through the crowd, you catch someone's eye across the room. You notice them looking at you and spot that they are running a hand through their hair. They look away, then look back at you again, still with the hand tousling the hair. You've heard that if someone is looking at you with their hand in their hair it for sure means they think you are hot and are flirting with you. You turn to your friend and announce, "I am totally getting checked out!"

HAVE YOU BEEN THERE BEFORE? How right or wrong were you in that moment? How can you evaluate the truth and lies about whether you are being checked out? Before you make your move, take a moment to go through the easy-to-follow steps below, to critically think through what body language is telling you about the situation.

LET'S APPLY OUR CRITICAL THINKING SCAN MODEL TO THIS SCENARIO, FIRST WITH STEP ONE: S—suspending judgment. In other words, put aside the first opinion, that they are checking you out, for a moment. You can always come back to it. Suspending your judgment to think about the options does not mean the initial judgment is wrong. It also does not mean it is right. You are just stepping back briefly to treat it as one possibility.

Let's also **be more descriptive** of what is happening and take into account secondary signals.

First, let's look at the key body language signal in this situation and examine how it works to display power, so that you can figure out how it moved you to assume you are getting checked out.

Hair display: The person you think is checking you out is making you feel that they are sexually attracted to you, and showing their availability to you by playing with their hair. We've been told time and time again, so much so that it is seemingly common knowledge now, that if someone is playing with their hair around you, they are into you. But is this true?

Hair flicks and hair self-grooming are a universal, cross-gender and cross-cultural way of displaying good health by unconsciously showing off genetic power and/or a diet high in nutrition, also therefore showing others that we are powerful. Hair displays can be tribal, sometimes identifying a social group, sometimes showing social rank in the group either by the volume or the height of the hair (giving a height advantage). A socially understood cost of the hair display equally shows prestige through wealth, as with highlights, a trendy cut, weaves and extensions.

Hairstyle can show similarity of tribe and rank in that tribe from a distance. How often can you pick out a friend in the crowd by their hairstyle, cut or color, or suspect someone may be into the kinds of things you are into from their hair? Conversely, have you ever felt you would not hit it off with someone because of their hairstyle? This would fall under the banner of tribal signaling.

Hair displays are a huge trigger for human beings and one of the most recognizable signals when determining whether someone may be a good mate. Displaying hair is a powerful unconscious indicator that attracts others, like a broadcast for others to take notice of you. One study by online lingerie retailer Adore Me tested sales results using the same female fashion model wearing lingerie and adopting different poses. It found that when the model was photographed with her hand in her hair, sales of the product doubled. The hand-on-hip pose—a popular pose among some female Instagrammers trying to make their arms look more elongated and skinny—did not resonate in tests nearly as well as a hand touching the hair, not even if a discount was offered on the merchandise.[1]

Hair displays often take the form of preening or reflexive self-grooming behavior, a characteristic that occurs throughout the animal kingdom. When we view someone we are attracted to, we may automatically respond by sprucing up to compete with rivals. The gesture attracts attention and shows off the power of good health. If our hair appears to gain body, it effectively increases our size and so in some cases our perceived status. Some hair products will even create a spiky look, which warns competitors to stay away from the pseudopoisonous quills.

So at first glance, if they are touching their hair—it's looking pretty good for you!

But what more do we see in this scenario?

Targeting: Remember, you caught eye contact with this person. Humans use eye contact as a signal of targeting. As opposed to other mammals, we have highly visible whites of the eyes, which make it easier at a distance to see where another is looking. So it looks as if you may be the target of the hair signal. They look away, then look back at you again, repeating the targeting signal at you. Some tests show that human beings need at least eight of these eye signals to realize they are being targeted. Hey, maybe you missed the first seven or so. Things could definitely be looking up!

See the Whites of Their Eyes

There are over 600 species and subspecies of primates on the planet, and although humans share a sclera, or visible eye whites, with some of these species, the whites of our eyes offer us tremendous advantage. The human sclera is whiter and a more visible part of the eye than it is in other primates. Like everything else in evolution, it comes down to benefit within a niche. With an easily visible sclera, even subtle eye movements can be easily detected from some distance. This makes it easier to detect emotions and intentions, and to understand where another's gaze and attention are directed. All these elements increase our ability to cooperate and so to survive. As our ancestors developed these traits, those who could cooperate the best passed them

➡

---

on to their descendants. Because of this, it is intuitive for humans to follow each other's line of sight when simply indicated via the eyes. Most other primates need a full turn of the head to be stimulated into following a target.[2]

LET'S MOVE TO STEP TWO OF SCAN: C—take in the context. Here's where things start to get a little more complex. You are at a bar on singles night. It's crowded. Odds are high that people are hoping to hook up with others. Given this, the odds are now less that it is you who is being checked out. Who else is close by? Your friend? Anybody else? So was the flirt gesture actually directed toward you, or could it have been what we might call a "feint," a deceptive gesture directed toward you but designed to attract the attention of someone else? The question is, is this person flirting, unconsciously or not, *toward you*, in order to show off their power, demonstrating that they are getting noticed and so to capture the interest and desire of *someone else* by creating a sense of competition and high value around themselves?

NOW LET'S LOOK AT STEP THREE IN OUR SCAN THINKING PROCESS: A—ask "What else?" A great place to start is to be self-reflective, or mindful, of our own role in affecting the system. We can ask which of our own feelings and biases are contributing to the situation—that is, which of our desires we are projecting onto other people. For example, take a moment to think about your own feelings of confidence in this situation: If you believe you look great, are well dressed or have put some extra effort into how you look for this event, you could be more likely to believe you are going to get attention. Has that confidence caused you to feel you are of high value in the room? Did you walk in with that feeling of confidence? Are you perceiving the environment as low risk (because of potentially high testosterone levels—regardless of whether you're male or female)? Perhaps you had a super successful day at work and are riding high on that wave. Or you may be feeling less confident but really desperately want to find a mate and to be looked at and admired—in which case, your bias or hope is that they are signaling to you.

SO HOW DO YOU EXECUTE *N*, STEP FOUR OF OUR SCAN PROCESS—make a **new judgment** and get feedback on what the person is thinking about you with a **test**?

There are plenty of good signals that the environment is perfect for this flirt gesture to be targeted at you—or toward someone else in the room. But which is it?

They say opposites attract, but studies show that a person is more likely to be attracted to someone who is similar to them in a number of ways.[3] So the reality is that we often like those who are like us. Long-term compatibility is more probable with someone who is like ourselves.

Knowing that the chances of attraction may be higher the more you resemble each other, you can check if the person checking you out appears to look in any way like you. Or do they look more like someone else in the room, perhaps the friend you came in with? If the latter, it might be your friend they're attracted to.

Now look around the room to see who else may be similar to the person sending out the signals or who may appear to be of high value in the room—the male or female surrounded by other high-value dating and mating opportunities because of perceived status, height, looks, hair quality or clothing. If not you, maybe your friend is the target, or it could be someone else altogether.

Here is a great way to test your judgment and whether the odds are in your favor:

Try gently distancing yourself so you are physically farther away, perhaps even in a different part of the room, from your friend or from the person you have noted has high value, and see if the same signals are still being directed toward you. Are you still getting those eye targets and hair displays? If so, the next time you make eye contact, try gently holding a gaze with them. If they lock eyes with you, that is a good sign they may be interested in you; if you notice their eyes sliding down over your body, that may likely be the focus of their interest. But their holding a gaze, or looking at your mouth, may suggest your initial assumption was correct. If they do return your gaze, you could give them a smile to see if that is repeated back as well. Smiling is a great way to test if the signals are directed toward you and feel truthful.

Now, depending on how you want to classify a smile, you can come up with many different types: masking smiles that hide negative feelings such as fear, sadness, anger or contempt; smiles designed to soften a risky situation, such as the embarrassed smile, the placating smile and the "I told you that might happen" smile; smiles of acceptance, compliance or engagement; the smile of schadenfreude—malicious joy; smiles of the enjoyment of negative feelings such as enjoyable contempt, enjoyable fear and enjoyable sadness; anticipatory smiles for showing you expect something good to come; plain old fake smiles such as "the Pan Am Smile," so dubbed after the now defunct airline and alluding to seemingly fake polite smiles the airline staff would flash at passengers; and flirtatious or coy smiles such as the enigmatic Mona Lisa smile. All these smiles and many more can show up for different people and cultures in various contexts.

However, one smile, the Duchenne smile, is mentioned many times in this book. It's named after the nineteenth-century neurologist Guillaume Duchenne de Boulogne, who codified a number of smiles and many other facial expressions. The Duchenne smile is universal and connected to the feeling of pleasure or true happiness. It involves both voluntary and involuntary contraction of two muscles: the zygomatic major (raising the corners of the mouth by contracting the cheeks) and the orbicularis oculi (narrowing the eyes, which in combination with the cheeks produces wrinkles around the eyes). If the orbicularis oculi is not engaged, it's not a true smile of happiness.

In this context we suggest delivering a gentle Duchenne smile to signal your pleasure with the situation. If they return a similar smile, this could mean they are open to you too, given all the factors we have outlined.

The next test is to close the distance between you. It is time to approach. Remember, just as in the rest of the animal kingdom, mating among humans is not without some elements of risk, and so you may feel the anxiety associated with risk. Of course, you are in competition with others in that environment. By now you have tested holding a gaze and sending a smile, as well as taking the moment to research the overall scene, and so can act with more confidence that your initial assumption is correct.

Hey! But I've Got No Hair!
Given that by age thirty-five two-thirds of males in
the United States have lost their hair and by age fifty,
85 percent have, with all this sexual and status

➡

---

signaling with hair, many of you could be getting a little concerned. No worries. In a study conducted by Albert E. Mannes[4] at the University of Pennsylvania, men with shaved heads were seen by a group of average twenty-year-olds (60 percent of whom were females and 40 percent males) as 13 percent stronger and taller and with greater leadership potential than men with either a full head of hair or hair that is thinning. So if you are totally bald, though you may have lost some of those desirable hair signals around your genetic health, you may have gained others around your social prestige and general desirability in the right circumstances.

QUICK SCAN

S: **Suspending** judgment on your initial instinctual reaction to the powerful signal of attraction, the hair display, gives you space to be more descriptive and critically question how true what you see really may be.

C: By taking in the **context** of the busy singles bar where you catch the body language signals, you can better consider the likelihood that those signals mean what you first think they mean (i.e., flirting and if it is meant for you).

A: When you **ask** what else you can bring into your thinking, including your own state of mind, you can take into account how your own feelings influence how you believe others are feeling.

N: Your **new** judgment may not veer far from your initial instinct, but now you have a low-risk tactic (smile and close proximity) to test your more fully considered position that will influence the environment and may stimulate a response and shift of power.

6

PLAYING HARD-TO-GET

You are at a party with friends, one of whom has only lately been hanging out with your usual social group, and it dawns on you that you are quite attracted to that person and think there could be something romantic in the air. You notice that they keep glancing over at you, holding your gaze, and you can sense a little sizzle of some potentially powerful chemistry. Sometimes it even seems a bit hot between you. And yet, the next moment, you feel like they are ignoring you as they look away, focus their attention elsewhere and give you the cold shoulder, dismissing you and keeping you at a platonic arm's length. You can't quite figure out what is going on. It feels as if they

➡

are flirting with you one minute, and that the next
minute they're not. You are getting confused, feeling a little vulnerable, but are still quite optimistic.
Aha! you think. *They think they're a total catch.*
And they are! They must be playing hard-to-get.

BEFORE YOU PLOW ON with this person and invest more time into
what you hope could be a night to remember, or even a great long-
term relationship, you need to check out whether they are blowing
more hot than cold.

What are the key signals here that may have made you assume
they are playing hard-to-get? Another flirt signal: They look at you
and then look away.

They may be giving you a flirt signal, but this same set of movements
could just as easily be a dismissal signal. So what is the power being displayed or responded to here? Now is the time to start the **SCAN** process:
suspend judgment and explore whether your assumption of "hard-to-
get" is likely to be correct, or perhaps a lie you may be telling yourself.

Now **be more descriptive** of the key flirt signal you are picking up
on, the relationship to power it demonstrates and the value it creates
for both parties. The flirt signal in this case is a targeting look at you,
followed by a clear head turn away, showing interest toward you and
then interest seemingly elsewhere, or perhaps toying with that initial
interest. Again in this scenario, the targeting is clear and powerful.
The person shooting you the look is communicating that they have
targeted you and see you as potentially valuable. Both parties in this
case initially win the power play as both gain power.

However, the flip side of this—the head turn—feels dismissive, like they are taking your power away. Signals that can stimulate feelings of flirtation and attraction have some of the exact same elements as signals that can stimulate feelings of indifference or being rejected. The simultaneous approach/avoid power of these signals creates an opposing attraction/repulsion force that can be best described as allotropic—two different forms of the same property existing within the same physical environment. To you, it feels as if the person is blowing hot and cold; they are open and closed.

When they retract the targeting signal and turn their head away, the power play could be any of the following:

1. *I thought you had value, so I looked at you, and it turns out you don't, so I'm dismissing you* (and so looking away). In this case the person who gave the look keeps all the power and status, and the party is not looking so good for you after all.

2. *You caught me looking at you, and now you have power because you know that I think you have value; but to keep control of the power and to hold on to my high status, I'm taking away my look.* This is our hard-to-get scenario.

3. *I wanted to give you power by making sure you saw me looking at you, and now I'm looking away.* Additionally, they are displaying their neck, which shows vulnerability and awards you more power by creating for you a low-risk situation—an availability signal, low-risk atmosphere, inviting an approach.

Now let's take into account any other exposures you may also observe: Any hair displays? Are they touching their neck? If so, they may be exposing their armpit and also showing off their wrist. These displays allow pheromones to escape, signaling anything from dominance to availability. Exposing vulnerable points on the body may be a sign of submission. Women and men will often do this sub-consciously with people they want to attract. Are you noticing any kind of belly display? This exposes the center of gravity and delicate organs around the stomach area, which again could display vulner-ability or dominance.

The Power of Rejection

Psychologists from across the United States have demonstrated that rejection and physical pain are similar not only in that they are both distress-ing but also in how we feel them. These psy-chologists asked people to compare the pain of rejection to physical pain they have experienced, and often people rate their emotional pain as equal in severity to that associated with natural childbirth or even chemotherapy.[1] In both cases a doctor might easily administer opiate-based pain relief. How often have we self-medicated to get over rejection when left to our own devices? When asked to rank rejection alongside other emotionally painful experiences, such as dis-appointment, frustration or fear, those all paled in comparison to the pain experienced from rejection. No wonder we attach a high risk to those power plays that may end with us getting rejected. Having your heart torn out is not so

➡

---

much a metaphor as a literal experience of the pain.

But why is this? Humans are social animals. Being rejected by our social group in our pre-civilized past and even now can mean losing access to food, protection and mating partners, making it extremely difficult to survive. In our pre-civilized past, being ostracized would have been akin to receiving a death sentence. Because the consequences of ostracism were so extreme, our brains developed an early warning system to alert us when we were at risk by triggering sharp pain whenever we experienced even a hint of social rejection.

Brain scans show that the very same brain regions get activated when we experience rejection as when we experience physical pain. Some psychologists believe it is this power of rejection that can lead some to a dependence on opiate drugs, to manage the pain of their feelings of rejection from, or abandonment by, their social group.

SCAN some more and take into account the **context**: How seemingly comfortable is this new friend in this party environment? Do they know people, are they relaxed, is the atmosphere apparently fun? How do they appear—smiling and having a great time?

What about the social context? How do you fit into this group? Are you powerful and valuable in your social circle? If you are powerful and a leader in this social context, everyone may just be looking at you more, as people tend to do—to look more toward the leader for cues as to how to behave—and the person in question is simply falling into the same pattern.

Additionally, what can you deduce about their flirty behavior in the context of their general or normal body language? Let's find a baseline.

Baselining, a commonly used technique in deception detection, is simply collecting useful details about how a person normally reacts under normal conditions to fairly normal stuff—that is, the way a person behaves without any special or extraordinary reason to act otherwise. Detectives and body language experts alike are often tasked with watching others' body language to determine whether someone is lying, or perhaps if they're attracted to us or to others. However, not everyone behaves the same way under those circumstances. By establishing a baseline in someone's behavior, or determining their "regular" pattern of behavior, you can then observe when and how that behavior changes.

To quickly establish a baseline in this situation, look to see if this person is engaging in the same flirty behavior with others at the party, or perhaps with everyone at the party. If a person values you, then they may look at you more often than they do the others in the group, but if they are doing this with everybody, then this is their baseline, perhaps because they compulsively behave this way, or you are potentially one of many options for them that night. Determine what percentage of the other's gaze you are getting, to determine if you have any leading edge. The person who likes you will have more eye contact with you than with those around you.

If their behavior stands out as being just for you, **SCAN** further and **ask what else** is going on. Let's look at some behavioral and psychological theories in this area.

Ample studies and experiments show that, in certain circumstances, there can be an advantage to playing hard-to-get when trying to attract a mate;[2] and certainly, the Internet is rich with articles and how-to guides on successfully playing the hard-to-get game, both in person and via text. So hard-to-get fits with scholarly as well as popular and romantic narratives about the different stages of mating—the fun of the chase, and part of the excitement.

Part of the benefit attributed to this game is that it fits in with a mind-set that the person playing hard-to-get shows their power of choice. They are playing with their ability, or power, to choose you or someone else. This fits in with social exchange theory, which offers a perspective (in this case) that how we choose mates depends on a combination of factors, including youth, beauty, social rank, kindness, creativity, humor and financial status, in order to create a combined index when weighing up suitability at first glance. So while they are potentially weighing up how desirable you are to them, at the same time their game of hard-to-get increases their value for you as a potential mate, as they are showing off their power at that moment in the social context.

We can also factor in persona theory, Carl Jung's idea that our mates become a barrier or a mask between us and the rest of the world, and this factors heavily into how we select a mate, which in turn is based on how much the mate enhances our self-esteem and self-image.

So at the end of the **SCAN**, your **new judgment** is that at this moment anything is possible, and you cannot know for sure that they are playing hard-to-get. They could be considering getting together with you, or maybe considering something or someone else. Certainly they have gotten your attention and they know it, as they are not indicating any fear of rejection in directing their focus away from you periodically. Maybe they are doing their own testing to see if you are searching for their attention even when they are focusing else-where, to weigh how much power they may hold over you. Their behavior, though seemingly ambiguous, has the potential of increasing desire on both sides.

Now to get feedback with a **test** that might help you know what they are thinking: Our instinct when someone we are interested in plays hard-to-get with us may not always be to give up and find someone else who is throwing themselves at us. You can safely test your power and value within this flirtation exchange and how much power you can safely exercise in moving this flirtation to the next level.

To immediately move in before weighing up all the signals is risky, as it may well end in rejection, which as we've seen may be pretty much the end of it for you. But if the person shooting the look did indeed open up that vulnerable neck area, they are essentially signaling to you that your risk of rejection is low. And don't forget, looking away and exposing the vulnerability of the neck releases pheromones, chemicals that can communicate information about genetic compatibility, sexual orientation, gender and sexual readiness by affecting us unconsciously and physically. Pheromones can be a powerful contributor to why we eventually choose the mates we choose.

One way to tell if this person is interested in you is to maintain a slightly prolonged period of eye contact with them and see what happens to their pupils. The pupils of a person who values you may dilate in your presence. According to tests, pupils generally dilate when we look at anything we like, are stimulated by, or are aroused by and attracted to; furthermore, our brains are hardwired to recognize this dilation when we see it in the pupils of others and to be attracted to it.

So, assuming they have repeated the targeting gaze at you, followed by looking away, the next time they make eye contact with you, look more deeply into their eyes. Be observant: Are their pupils large? If their pupils are dilated, your risk of rejection in moving forward to your next steps is greatly diminished.

Cheap Signals
Have you ever received a powerful nonverbal message from someone who risked very little by sending that signal? We call that a cheap signal. Species other than humans also exhibit cheap signals. Quite

➡

often these signals lead to catastrophic effects for both the sender and receiver.

For example, a bee signals to its hive that there is food nearby. The bees respond to the location and find no food. The hive, after wasting considerable resources on a false alarm, will most likely kill the bee that sent the cheap signal; because it took so little effort for one bee to send many on a fruitless task, it is best to eliminate that bee for the sake of the hive. We should be wary of powerful signals that may have a similar impact on us. Especially when we suspect there is low risk and little cost for the person sending the signal.

In advertising, it is the perpetual "Liquidation Sale!" sign the expensive furniture shop uses to lure you in even though, mysteriously, the store never closes. It is the Internet clickbait that prom- ises an incredible story yet delivers just an ad for some strange, fat-busting fruit. Equally, it is the politician who promises a change during election debates and U-turns once they take office.

Cheap signals are easy both to send and to engage with, particularly online, and can lead us down the garden path. Just think how simple it is in virtual environments to send flirty messages, responses and emoticons when you are not face to face with your audience. Do you find that potential suitors flirt with you more online than in person? Online there is sometimes close to zero social risk, as almost no one is watching. The nonverbal signals used either online or live remain the same, but online those signals are not under live examination by the sender's social group, with all the opportunities for immediate scrutiny and feedback that this context offers: low risk = low cost. If you think you are on the receiving end of a cheap signal, you may indeed be the target for another's practice run at flirting, which can leave you feeling you've been carelessly toyed with. And of course we need to watch out for those cheap signals that are potentially bad for us—signals intentionally meant to con us.

QUICK SCAN

S: By **suspending** judgment on your initial instinctual reaction to the two different meanings within the same physical movement (target look and then look away), you can briefly counter the powerful effect of these conflicting approach/avoid signals.

C: Then, taking in the **context** of their baseline of behavior within the larger social context, you can more accurately reevaluate the signals. You are being more conscious of how context affects your evaluation of behavior.

A: When you **ask** what else can be brought into your thinking from the worlds of psychology and behavior, you are able to explore the meaning and possible benefits of playing hard-to-get, and so open yourself up to testing your ideas against other models. This again briefly takes you into a more conscious state of mind.

N: Your **new** judgment expands your initial assumption of hard-to-get to include other possibilities and illuminates for you that others are likely judging you and testing their assumptions as much as you are testing yours.

7

JUST FEELING SORRY FOR ME

You've recently met someone new—a friend of a friend—and you are completely blown away by them. This person is so great that you assume they must have a partner or at least plenty of dates with people who are like them—that is, super awesome but totally out of your league. This person is high status, a cool dresser, always making funny comments at just the right moment. Although you are attracted to this new acquaintance, you are not about to let them or any of your other friends know the truth of it. You risk looking like a fool if your feelings are discovered, as of course you would not expect they would like you in the same way.

➡

One night you host a small get-together. Your crush shows up and then pays lots of attention to you. You assume they are simply being super nice because they'll probably need to take off to another party any minute, and yet they spend the whole night supportively at your side, looking and smiling at you, laughing at your bad jokes, even physically reaching out and touching your arm a few times, right in front of your friends. You feel great. Then you wonder if this person is messing with you, until it dawns on you that they simply think you're an emotional charity case and must be feeling sorry for you.

LET'S **SCAN** THE WHOLE SCENARIO. First, **suspend judgment** and take stock of exactly what could be going on by being **more descriptive**.

Look at the key signal that led to your judgment—the public display of affection (PDA), the power of the person reaching out and touching your arm in a social setting. Now, while it could be true that they are feeling sorry for you, it could be that they like you.

Feeling the power of the PDA may briefly surprise and delight you; however, you ultimately default into feeling negative about it because you have deeply rooted feelings of unworthiness. You cannot believe this person would like you. You assume nothing will ever happen, and then when the other person reacts positively to you, this does not change your mind but instead catapults you into disappointment over your unworthiness. Instead of feeling they could be into you, you default to a place where you assume they feel sorry for you.

So why the assumption of pity?

Sad facial gestures are pretty clear and are universal. In this situation, body language signs that may indicate you are correct in your assumption are signs that could communicate sad feelings toward you and so may suggest pity. You would notice the corners of the lips and the upper eyelids drooping down; eyes in an extended gaze and that possibly are damp; eyebrows slightly pulled together in the middle or downward at the edges; a mouth that is turned down at the corners; or their head tilted to one side. If any of these signs were displayed you may indeed be onto something. However, there appear to be more indicators saying they may be attracted to you:

This friend of a friend has been hanging out lately with your regular gang.
☑ **Social alignment.** They already share many of the same values as you and your friends, so they are more likely to be into you than not.

This person is just so totally great and you are attracted to them.
☑ **Personal fit.** They must have some fundamental qualities that are driving your desire for them.

You host a small get-together. Your cool wish-they-were-more-than-a-friend shows up.
☑ **Proximity.** Again, you share social values and it is easy enough to get together.

This person was at your side, looking and smiling at you.
☑ **Targeting.** We have looked at this body language signal in the previous two chapters.

They laughed at your jokes.
- ☑ **Resonance.** Again, they are able to relate to your experience of the world.

They touched you by putting their hand on your arm . . . in front of your friends.
- ☑ **Ownership signals:** claiming ownership by touching who they want in front of the group.

All in all, this looks pretty positive for you and points toward your initial assumption being incorrect.

What is the **context** that may be making this feel negative to you? You are in a fun social atmosphere at your own place, after all, therefore having the advantage of being in familiar territory. Is there something else going on for you, a specific lens through which you are looking that is perhaps skewing your interpretation? Are you feeling down? In a bad mood? And what has gone on recently for you relationship-wise? Is your own context of negative past relationships winning out above any other framing of this moment? Did you just break up, go through a negative experience, get some bad news? Or is anything giving you a feeling of depression generally? Is there something else going on for you that could be clouding your perception?

What is most powerful here is the way we value the signals we see around us in relation to ourselves. We provide our own emotional context, which can completely override and often skew anything that, when we consider it objectively, tells a different story. A good way to try to see our way through our own clouded perception is by projecting interactions into a different context; in other words, pretend you are observing this same exchange between the person you like and someone else at the party. Would you still feel the same way—that the other person is being pitied?

And the social context: If you critically consider your value in this group, do you believe you are less valuable than others? If you have undervalued yourself, it is possible that no signal or group of signals will be powerful enough to convince you that someone is attracted to you. But if it is true that you are so value-less, why would anybody show up to your party at all? And clearly people did, and you have friends, and so you do have more value and power than you are giving yourself credit for. However, along the same lines, it may be possible that your friends sense your insecurities, and through empathy and kindness may wish to make you feel better about the power of your social position by giving you extra signals to prove your worth and value.

Ask what else you have seen that suggests they could be feeling sorry for you.

As well as facial displays of pity, we can look to pupil size, which may be an indicator of sadness. People judge a sad facial expression to be more intensely sad as the pupil size decreases.[1] We mirror each other's pupil size, and so our pupils may also become smaller when viewing sad faces with small pupils. No parallel effect exists when people look at neutral, happy or angry expressions. The greater the degree to which a person's pupils mirror another's, the more empathetic that person is.

Now let's look at how to **test** and get feedback on whether you should stick with your idea that they are feeling sorry for you, or move on to a different position and a **new judgment** about what they are thinking.

If you are at a bit of a low ebb, perhaps feeling a bit depressed and insecure, you need to be sure that what you are seeing from them is not mirroring, or them feeling sympathy for you. So here's the low-risk test: Take a breath, pick up your energy and put on a full Duchenne smile with your mouth and eyes, rather than trying to soften any sadness with a masking smile just in your mouth. Contrary to popular belief, studies show that most people, under ordinary conditions, can convincingly fake a true smile.[2] Show up at your most positive and upbeat and see if they are still giving you the same level of attention. And now look for any pupil dilation when they look at you. They probably aren't feeling sorry for you if you yourself are not demonstrating the behaviors of feeling sorry for yourself. And if they are feeling sorry for you, once you display more buoyancy in your attitude and overall demeanor, they will feel their mission is accomplished: They cheered you up, or if they really do like you, you will appear more open to their attention.

BODY LANGUAGE MYTHBUSTER
Dilated Pupils Signal Sex

How many times have you heard that if someone's pupils are big, it means they are attracted to you? How true is this? Our eyes naturally dilate to allow in more light, but dilation also occurs in response to what we are thinking and feeling. When we're interested in something, our pupils dilate. The iris muscles are under the control of the autonomic nervous system, which deals with involuntary reflex actions, and so pupil dilation is difficult for us to consciously control. So it is when we are around something we desire. And we tend to be attracted to people with larger pupils simply because they are displaying that they are interested in some way in us. It feels therefore less risky if we make a move.

➡

But over the centuries and across cultures, we have found ways to make the pupils dilate or look bigger, even when they are not being naturally stimulated. Today, people put on eyeliner and wear contact lenses to do this. In the past, people used belladonna plant extract to dilate their pupils, in an effort to appear more attractive. The atropine in belladonna, or deadly nightshade, is an anticholinergic that blocks the effects of acetylcholine, the neurotransmitter released by parasympathetic nerve cells. What this ultimately means is that the pupil cannot constrict and so only relaxes into dilation. People don't tend to use this method any more. However, caffeine and over-the-counter decongestants can produce the same effect. And of course, conversely some people will try to cover up if they are feeling an attraction. This could be the poker player who wears sunglasses, trying to conceal their attraction to a hand of cards they hold while lying to other players about its value or bluffing. Or it could be the legendary Chinese jade dealer behind tinted spectacles who hides their delight at a great deal being presented. So although it's no myth that dilated pupils can indicate desire, there are ways to create or counter the effect. Therefore, in the world of body language, dilated pupils should in no way be viewed as a certain signal for sex.

QUICK SCAN

S: Suspending judgment allows you to explore your feelings about the public display of affection and recognize how your reasoning caused your initial assumption that the person is just feeling sorry for you. You also allow yourself to consider more holistically the visual cues, as well as the other nonverbal stimuli you receive. Touch can have an incredibly powerful effect alongside or even without visual cues.

C: Examining the social and particularly emotional **context** here encourages you to take into account feelings and moods you have been going through lately that override and skew your interpretation of the body language, setting the stage for biased judgments. We may see through our clouded perception by projecting interactions into a different context.

A: Information can change when your eyes focus in or pull out. **Ask** yourself what other details you see by getting closer.

N: Purposely changing your demeanor or physical attitude for a moment is a great way to test whether others will change in response and whether a **new** judgment may be accurate.

8

I'M BEING GHOSTED

You are waiting for your new-ish significant other. They are late for the date you made a couple of days ago. You contacted them a number of times to confirm earlier in the day, but they have not gotten back to you. Given that you have been waiting for over an hour and there is still no reply through any of the various communication channels you both use, including ones where you can see they have read the message—"Where are you? Are we on for tonight?"—you are suddenly getting that horrible feeling: *What are they thinking? Am I being stood up? Or worse, am I being ghosted?*

SCAN THIS SCENARIO by **suspending judgment** and **being more descriptive** as to what is going on. The key signal is body language that seems so simple and obvious, but in discussions and studies around nonverbal communication the power it displays tends to get overlooked: the number one telltale sign that gives you the feeling someone has decided to call off the relationship abruptly and unkindly: they become completely absent.

Ghost in the Machine

The feeling that someone is indifferent to you can be more hurtful than if they hated you. *Ghosting* describes situations where someone you believe cares about you, whether it be a friend or someone you are dating, suddenly disappears from contact without any explanation at all. No phone call or e-mail, not even a text. This nonverbal maneuver isn't new—people have long done disappearing acts on each other. It's just that in today's digital world, ghosting is so much easier to do because of the ease of making contact in the first place. In online dating, there is no loyalty to any one date and no real sense of any social cost if you disrespect someone. Easy in, easy out. There are plenty more dates where that last one came from.

Regardless of the ease of opting in or out in this context, the emotional effects surrounding the human interaction remain the same: Even though the ➡

---

relationship may have sprung up quickly and haphazardly, if you are on the receiving end of the abrupt communication cutoff, the feelings are no less difficult to deal with. You don't know how to react because you don't really know the truth of what has happened, and you no longer have any guarantee of a responsive audience to your reaction. Your position in this case is ambiguous and can be painful.

Staying connected to others is so important to our survival that our brains have developed a social monitoring system that scours the environment for cues so we know how to respond in social situations. If you are ghosting someone, you are basically taking away cues from people in whom you have previously invested social capital. Being ghosted can leave a person feeling out of control and powerless. Ghosting can be viewed as careless behavior and in some extreme cases a form of emotional cruelty. It can be that the "ghoster" does not have the courage or maturity to deal with the discomfort of their emotions or yours, or they don't understand the impact of their behavior, or worse, they don't care. You may even be involved in a cruel power game.[1]

But before you assume you're embroiled in an abusive situation or you're being ditched, let's examine this event in a wider **context** of past encounters, both yours and those shared with this person, to figure out if there is any justification for giving them the benefit of the doubt and revising the assumption that they are ghosting you.

They are a no-show and you are getting a horrible feeling. Do you have a sense of déjà vu? Has anything like this happened to you before with other partners? If so, that once bitten, twice shy feeling may be moving you to assume that this person, too, has called it quits without so much as a text. There could be multiple reasons why they've not made contact: Their mobile device is lost or not working; they got stuck in a meeting; they were driving a long distance and couldn't use the phone; or some kind of emergency has come up. If you have experienced ghosting in the past with others, you may be bringing your own biases into play and making an incorrect assumption.

But if this situation has happened before in this relationship, was there a valid reason—such as their working in an environment in which contact is tricky (e.g., in a hospital or on a transportation system of some kind) or being subject to a work-related communications blackout—to make this par for the course?

Let's **ask what else** we can consider. When two people are attracted to each other, they can act in many different ways to hang onto power in the relationship (tease, ignore, be thoroughly annoying); at the end of the day, though, if they really are into each other, they'll always find a way to come together, to engage in whatever behaviors they are taking part in with respect to each other. In other words, if someone is into you, they'll find ways to show up to participate in the exchange, whatever that is. You'll notice them popping up in your vicinity regardless of whether it is physical or virtual. This is something we can all overlook initially, but once you realize it, you'll start to see how being present or not is taken for granted but is the most physically impactful aspect of a relationship.

Just how physically close we get to others is, in body language terms, called *proxemics*; it's the amount of space people feel necessary to set between themselves and others. This is one among several sub-categories in the study of nonverbal communication, including haptics (touch), kinesics (body movement), vocalics (paralanguage) and chronemics (structure of time).

Anthropologist Edward T. Hall developed the idea of proxemics by describing the interpersonal distances of human beings (the relative distances between people) in four zones: intimate space, personal space, social space and public space.

Intimate distance for embracing, touching or whispering:
Close phase: less than 6 inches (15 cm)
Far phase: 6 to 18 inches (15 to 46 cm)
Personal distance for interactions among good friends or family:
Close phase: 1.5 to 2.5 feet (46 to 76 cm)
Far phase: 2.5 to 4 feet (76 to 122 cm)
Social distance for interactions among acquaintances:
Close phase: 4 to 7 feet (1.2 to 2.1 m)
Far phase: 7 to 12 feet (2.1 to 3.7 m)
Public distance used for public speaking:
Close phase: 12 to 25 feet (3.7 to 7.6 m)
Far phase: 25 feet (7.6 m) or more

The first two zones, the intimate and the personal, describe the region surrounding a person that they strongly regard as theirs, often falling under the umbrella of the more general term *personal space*, made popular by anthropologist Robert Sommer in 1969. Hall's work was groundbreaking for its focus on how people of different cultures psychologically understand and use the space around them. He found that most people and cultures value this personal space and feel discomfort, violation, anger or anxiety when it is invaded. Permitting someone into your personal space or entering somebody else's personal space is a strong nonverbal sign of how we feel about the strength of the relationship; how much power we feel comfortable or compelled to take in that relationship, what boundaries are therefore appropriate and, on the flip side, how welcome or not we are when getting up close and personal with someone.

The intimate zone and personal zone are generally both reserved for close friends, lovers, children and close family members. The close social zone is used for conversations with friends, to chat with associates, and for group discussions, and the far social zone is reserved for strangers, newly formed groups and new acquaintances. The public zone is used for speeches, lectures and theater; essentially, the public distance is that range generally reserved for larger audiences.[2]

Here's what Hall doesn't consider, though, about being so far away that you are not within any detectable distance. If you use Hall's idea and his linear algorithm, the farther away we are from one another, the less heightened the emotional connection or reaction to others and the less power they have over us. However, we can also see that in some circumstances, the farther away they are, the *more* power they have over us. Distance does not necessarily decrease someone's intimate or social power just because they cannot be heard or seen. In some cases, distance may in fact increase someone's power over us. Absence can be more emotionally powerful than closeness and, as the old catchphrase goes, make the heart grow fonder. This is largely dependent on how we choose to respond: whether we continue to attempt to engage with the person in hope, attempt to engage simply to get some closure, or oblige their ghosting behavior and match it, thereby accepting the end. And if we are just not sure what is going on—being ghosted can be confusing—or what we want to happen next, we can still **test** our old and **new judgment** about the situation without risking too much.

It is possible you are being tested by this person: They may be knowingly (or not) testing how accepting or resilient you can be in the face of their erratic behavior, or how committed you are to the relationship. And even if you decide not to play into any sign of manipulation and to opt out and drop them, from their point of view you could still be in their sights. From a nonverbal perspective, you have none of the usual cues to respond to, as the ghoster has taken away all gesture, touch, posture, facial expression, eye contact, clothing, hair and voice quality, rhythm and intonation. However, what they cannot take away from you is *time, context* and *environment,* so you can still lay criteria around these factors.

For example, you can exercise power by requesting that the ghoster reply within a time restriction you set. For instance, five minutes.Alternatively, you can choose to tell them to take all the time they want or ask them how much time they need, thereby giving them your approval to control time. Similarly, you can take power by choosing to define the context of their ghosting by saying to them, "I take it you are very busy today." Finally, you can commandeer the communication outside of the environment of however you have been communicating with them up until then. For example, stop trying to reach them on your handheld device. Instead, give them the simple directive "I will see you at your place soon," thereby dictating both place and time, and then physically show up there and then. All these options of course have potential upsides and downsides. Indeed you may decide to lie about showing up on their doorstep in the next few minutes just to press time and bring about a response. But at least all this allows you to exercise powerful options rather than being left for dead by chance or design.

QUICK SCAN

S: Someone not being present can cause a powerful judgment about them and their intentions toward you that may need **suspending** in order to get to the truth.

C: Your past experiences, whether recent or farther in the past, create a powerful **context** in which you judge others.

A: Always **ask** yourself whether the expert ideas you have read when it comes to body language are still valid. What was best thinking yesterday is not necessarily the right thinking today.

N: If you suspend judgment, you can still get it back and hold it alongside your **new** judgment to test.

9

WHAT A COMPLETE PSYCHO!

For months it was going better than you could have hoped. Your new love interest had been totally charming, and you were head over heels for them. You were getting so much physical attention and affection that sometimes it was almost overwhelming. They simply never wanted to let go of you. They said you were everything to them. You thought you might be in love. You think they might have been too.

Then, out of the blue, they are nowhere to be found. Days pass before you see them again, before they reestablish contact with you. When you ask about their sudden disappearance, they tell you a wild and unbelievable story, but their

➡

accompanying body language makes them seem completely truthful. They look you in the eye and are calm and open. The contrast between how they look and what they say feels weird and makes you uncomfortable. When you dig further, their body language grows erratic and seems angry: their body suddenly looks bigger, as if it is taking up more space, and their eyes become intense and lock onto you. You assume they are lying and end it with them.

But they will not go gently, coming back to you expressing their strong belief that you are meant only for them. They have always been so charismatic and are again back to being tactile with you, sweet and charming, until you bring up the details around their disappearance. They won't give up their crazy stories, though, and now you feel they are actually pushing their weight around, looming over you, controlling, really being quite intimidating. The contrast in the extremes of their behavior is beyond off-putting and feels manipulative and scary. You feel a tightness in your gut and even a little powerlessness as you say to yourself *What a psycho!*

HAVE YOU GOT IT all wrong?

What's the difference between blowing a bit hot and cold, as you saw in chapter 6 on playing hard-to-get, and dangerous swings in behavior that make you feel head over heels one moment and intimidated the next? When can we safely and fairly judge someone else's behavior as manipulative and full-on scary?

Normally at this point we would follow our process and **suspend judgment**. Well, in this situation, given that you feel it is scary, we do not!

BODY LANGUAGE MYTHBUSTER
False Evidence Appearing Real
Have you come across the idea that fear is just an illusion? Gut feelings like fear exist to save our lives. We all know that in some cases fears are unfounded; however, when it comes to human relationships and a strong gut instinct of being unsafe, buying into popular catchy acronyms such as FEAR (false evidence appearing real) can have extreme and even deadly consequences. You don't want to gamble your life on such acronyms just because they have done the rounds on Facebook and Instagram. Pressing "like" doesn't mean you will then be immune from any situations with a potential to cause you harm.

It is very easy to label someone "psychotic." It has become a very popular blanket term to cover anything from moments of simple and harmless human behavior to out-and-out criminal insanity.

But given that in this case you feel unsafe, let's stick with your assumption. In fact, in any situation where you ever feel unsafe, you should always pay attention to your instinct, keeping it front of mind.

There is a generally accepted checklist for clinically diagnosing psychopathy, called the Hare PCL-R (Psychopathy Checklist—Revised), originally developed in the 1970s by Canadian psychologist Robert D. Hare. The checklist focuses on whether a potentially psychopathic individual shows selfish, callous and remorseless use of others and partakes in chronically unstable, antisocial and socially deviant lifestyles.[1] Based on the parameters of this checklist, if you are getting a gut feeling that someone appears to be a psychopath, they could indeed turn out to be a callous, deviant person who acts with no remorse, and so you and those around you are potentially in big trouble. If, however, you discover they are just consistently very selfish, though at the lower end of the psychopathic spectrum, and you aren't actually in physical danger, it's still not so much fun being around them.

Clearly, a psychiatric test of this nature is best administered by suitably qualified and experienced clinicians under scientifically controlled conditions. However, there are some very good tests you can use to gauge the validity of your feelings about someone that may further justify sticking with your judgment.

A great friend of ours and also one of the greatest body language experts we know, Joe Navarro, is a twenty-five-year veteran of the FBI, where he served in the National Security Division's Behavioral Analysis Program. In his book *Dangerous Personalities: An FBI Profiler Shows You How to Identify and Protect Yourself from Harmful People* (coauthored by Toni Sciarra Poynter),[2] Navarro offers some very useful advice for determining whether you may be involved with what he calls a "dangerous personality." He talked to hundreds of individuals who had been victimized by social predators. These victims gave descriptive accounts of their abusers' qualities and actions, in their own words (nonclinical, largely unedited). If several of the following words resonate with you, because of how someone acts or makes you feel, Navarro recommends that you seek help or distance yourself:

abusive, aggressive, aimless, amoral, antisocial, arrogant, bad, bad boy, belligerent, bully, calculating, callous, charismatic, charming, cheat, cheater, clever, cold, cold blooded, con, con artist, con man, conniving, contemptuous, controlling, corrupt, creep, creepy, criminal, crude, cruel, cunning, dangerous, deceitful, deceptive, degenerate, delinquent, demeaning, depraved, destructive, discomforting, dishonest, disingenuous, evil, exploitive, fraud, guiltless, immoral, imposter, impulsive, inconsiderate, incorrigible, indecent, indifferent, insensitive, intimidating, irresponsible, leech, liar, manipulative, mean, parasite, possessive, risk taker, sadistic, self-centered, selfish, shallow, sleazy, swindler, temperamental, thug, toxic, twisted, undependable, unfeeling, uncaring, violent.

So, yes—some of those words could apply to any one of us some of the time, and in fact, a few of them, such as *charismatic, charming, clever*, describe characteristics that are also attractive to us. And obviously, just one or two of these behaviors does not make for a "toxic personality." But as Joe says, "Where a person consistently demonstrates a large cluster of behaviors as cited in this list, we are most likely looking at someone who is a social predator."

Let's put our story in the **context** of this list by picking out a few of the words associated with your being around this person: *charming, overwhelming, uncomfortable, absent, head over heels, intimidating*. Notice anything interesting? When we are thinking about behavior and meaning, whether nonverbal or verbal, one of the areas that stands out is contrast. It is often the contrast—stark differences in signals that occur in the same time frame—that confuses us and alerts us, much more than any single sign. For example, in our story, if the person was always charming, you would not necessarily be alarmed; however, what you see is a change from charming to intimidating, from overwhelming to absent, and from head over heels to uncomfortable.

Our primitive brains are alerted by high contrasts of all kinds. Contrasts signal a potentially unstable and therefore inhospitable environment. Also, we can note the stand-alone extremes: *weird, long absence, wild stories, charismatic, only for them, won't give up, really quite scary.*

To decide whether we should approach or avoid a situation, our primitive brains look out for extremes in any environment, as extremes have the potential to work against us and could prove detrimental to our survival. So of course all of this is scary.

If you know or are in a relationship with someone like this, you need to seek help in order to protect yourself from becoming traumatized mentally or psychologically; and obviously if there is violence, and often there is, you need to seek help or even shelter. **What else** do you need to know here? Nothing. You don't need to **ask** anything. You don't need to make a **new judgment** about this situation. With the extremes in the behavior, the situation feels quite unsafe for you, and that is enough.

But what is the next step? *Get help*—from someone you trust. This could be a friend, family member, colleague or someone in your community who you always feel very safe with. It is important to avoid the temptation to give feedback to or test the person with whom you feel unsafe and look in turn for their feedback to you. Remember: You already called off the relationship. It's now time to get feedback from others on how to maintain that distance.

SHOULD YOU GIVE THEM
THE BENEFIT OF THE DOUBT?

Here's something more from our dear and trusted friend **JOE NAVARRO** that we hope you will keep in mind for yourself and everyone you care about. If you read any part of this book twice, make it this part, as it could save your life or the life of someone precious to you.

People tell you all the time "Don't be judgmental," and for the most part they are correct; nevertheless, we should try to be aware and attuned to others' behavior to gain insight into what they are transmitting (communicating). After all, our bodies communicate effectively what we feel, think, desire, intend and fear. There are times when we should not suspend judgment, and that is when our bodies speak to us with unease, uncertainty, apprehension, anxiety, caution or fear. It is at those times that we must listen carefully to what we sense.

Our brains process the world around us mostly subconsciously; in doing so, the brain senses things we don't have the cognitive attention span to notice (a person following us, a door unlocked that shouldn't be, etc.). There will be times when your stomach will tighten, your hairs will stand up or something inside you says be careful, something is wrong, don't go near this person, stay away, you are in danger. It is this warning system Gavin de Becker spoke of in *The Gift of Fear*. My years as an FBI agent talking to victims and being a witness to crime have taught me to never stop listening to those messages from your body—they are there to save your life.

QUICK SCAN

S: Suspending judgment is not always the best course. When in any potentially dangerous situation, go with your gut instinct.

C: Fear is designed to save your life when in the **context** of danger.

A: When feeling fear in a potentially dangerous situation, **ask** nothing more of it.

N: Don't wait to form a **new** judgment when your safety may be at risk. Instead respond in a way that moves you away from the potential danger. Seek further help from anyone you feel you can trust, and as soon as possible.

10

THEY ARE RUNNING THE SHOW

Your friend has been in a monogamous relationship for a year. You don't know their partner very
well—no one has really seen them much since they
got together—but the consensus among your social
group is that it's all good. A few of you arrange for
a long overdue lunch at a cool new restaurant with
the happy couple. You are surprised when your
friend and their partner show up looking, well, like
the same person, dressed in very similar clothes,
even sporting similar haircuts. You go to sit beside
your friend, but there is some hubbub and their
partner ends up sitting in between you, physically
blocking the two of you off. The waiter comes,

➡

your friend orders, the partner clears their throat
and your friend suddenly changes the order. Coincidence? Toward the end of lunch, you lean in toward
your friend so you can make plans to get together
one on one, when the partner abruptly stands up to
leave and your friend equally abruptly jumps up to
join the partner. *Wow!* you think as you look at the
partner. *My friend's partner sure is running the show!*

YOUR ASSUMPTION IS THAT your friend is in a relationship with someone who is running the show, or in other words, they are in the physical and mental clutches of a control freak. Do you need to arrange an
intervention with your friend about their controlling, domineering
partner? Hang on. Let's **SCAN** this situation and so **suspend judgment**
and **be more descriptive**.

Let's look at a key nonverbal signal in the scenario that helped you
jump to your conclusion: The partner abruptly stood up to leave.

Standing up at full height is a very powerful nonverbal signal. The
person standing towers over the others and in particular their partner seated right next to them, effectively showing off their size—a
classic body language signal of dominance or territorial aggression.
We share these dominance signals with other species in the animal
kingdom. Charles Darwin was among the first to suggest that males
might be larger than females in many species of mammals because
the large size was advantageous in contests over mates.[1] So far, your
assumption of your friend's partner being domineering seems like it
could be on the money.

What other body language do you see in this situation? When you try to sit beside your friend, the partner physically intervenes by sitting between the two of you, blocking your way, cutting off your visual and physical access. And what about the throat clearing by the partner during the food ordering and the apparent coincidence of your friend changing the order? Throat clearing is often a dominance display in other primates, including chimpanzees;[2] it may be part of an attempt to interrupt, overrule, challenge or make one's presence more keenly felt by others, as seems to be the case here. Now we have more proof that there is indeed a control freak running the show.

Controlling food, drink, personal space, way of dress and movement—all these signals could easily point to a narcissistic controlling element to the relationship where your friend is being suppressed by a person who is generally overtly selfish and craving attention and status.

More specifically, the grandiose narcissist often displays high levels of aggression and dominance, consistent with the body language signals in our story. They tend to come across as more physically confident and less sensitive to others' physical needs. Focusing heavily on their own territorial needs, they cannot really see a partner as an entirely separate person. This is seen in their attempts to control what they wear, how they move and where exactly they show up. They need to take care of everything, because in their eyes their partner is undependable, uncooperative or unfit.

High and Mighty

In popular usage, the terms *narcissism*, *narcissist*, and *narcissistic* denote absurd vanity and are applied

➡

---

to people whose ambitions and aspirations are much grander than their evident talents. Increasingly, we use these terms to describe people who are simply full of themselves, regardless of whether their real achievements are spectacular. Outstanding performers are not always modest, but nor are they necessarily grandiose. Muhammad Ali boasted, "I am the greatest!" but that was no lie. He was!

The primary requirement for narcissism in a clinical sense is self-absorption, a grandiose sense of self but a serious miscalculation of one's abilities and potential greatness. It's perhaps the difference between being optimistic and totally unrealistic. Additionally, the narcissist is so convinced of their high station that they expect others to recognize their superior qualities immediately. They will be comfortable and buoyant in environments in which the fantasy will not be questioned.[3]

Finally, the narcissist fails to recognize when their aggrandizement affects the comfort of others. Muhammad Ali was never unaware of the fact that his boasting really annoyed his opponents.

Let's now consider the **context** in which these signals occur.

The situation we are examining takes place in a trendy new restaurant, with staff trying to fit many people around a table. In this case, being somewhat cut off from your friend may be more about spatial constraints and less of a power play by the partner than you assume.

What about the social context? Your friend has been largely absent from the group since getting together with their partner, who is not a part of your close group—your tribe—and, as yet, an unknown quantity. The real social power is with the tribe. What you and your closest friends see in the couple's behavior could well be their response to your collective power. The partner is getting to know, or possibly looking to be accepted by, the significant other's oldest and dearest friends. And there could be a mix of anxiety and uncertainty underlying the entire experience, not just for the couple but also for everyone there, as everyone unconsciously assesses where they might now fit in the social order. Examined within this context, the strong body language signals for control can be interpreted differently; for example, throat clears can also indicate anxiety, uncertainty, deception or simply that someone has something caught in their throat. Their standing up to leave may equally be a reaction to social anxiety, and the partner sitting between you and your friend, a protective gesture to control the impact of the group's social power.

Chimpan-A-to-Z

The chimpanzee's cough-threat, or what renowned primatologist Jane Goodall called "the soft bark," is a grunt-like sound uttered through a slightly open mouth. It is a spontaneous sound produced only under the correct emotional conditions; that is,

➡

---

primates cannot fake it. It is directed down the hierarchy, by higher-ranked to lower-ranked individuals. This call indicates slight annoyance and functions as a mild warning to prevent a subordinate from moving too close to a higher-ranking chimp or from doing something the caller clearly disapproves of, such as reaching for a piece of their food.

Ask what else you see. What about the similar clothing and hairstyle? The couple shows up looking more or less like twins. Is this the clincher, the evidence that your friend is indeed with an all-controlling narcissist? Or is this a case of mirroring, a common trait of couples in relationships that can go on for some time?

Mirroring, a staple of body language, is a symptom of limbic resonance. Limbic resonance happens when the neural connections in our limbic systems—the part of the primitive brain specific to social mammals that governs some of our emotions and relationships—align with someone else's. Cats, dogs, horses, elephants and humans, among many other mammals, have limbic systems of varying capacities. Some species, however, such as most snakes and lizards, do not. Animals with limbic systems live in groups and raise their young. Those without them live more solitary lives and in some cases abandon or even eat their young. The only reason you will likely find a random bunch of snakes hanging out together is because that's where the food is, or the sex.

Mothers and infants have limbic resonance, as do lovers and best friends. These relationships compel us, both unconsciously and consciously, to give up more of our desire for autonomy and differentiation and readily enter into a profound neurochemical connection between limbic systems. So as limbic resonance softens the boundaries of who you think you are and who you think others are, we start to act more alike, mirroring each other's actions, behaviors, viewpoints, emotions, breathing patterns, facial expressions and signals. Mirroring can last for a second or a lifetime. In fact, perhaps your feeling of unease could also be your picking up on and mirroring the feelings of unease and anxiety that are being communicated through the key signals witnessed in this scenario.

So, after considering all this information, how can you safely **test** out any **new judgments** as to what is going on and get further feedback on the thinking behind it? Once the friend left, you have the benefit of time and space, and so the simplest test is to try to arrange a time to see your friend alone and see if the partner interferes or intervenes. Ask the other friends who were at lunch. They might have some intel that you are not aware of and can either put your mind at rest or convince you that you need to intervene. Another strategy you can employ if you are still not sure: The next time you meet with your friend and their significant other, use body language that will put the partner at ease. Employ gestures that are open around the torso and the hands. Smile and gently nod your head as the partner is speaking. Speak in an open and friendly tone. Then not only will you feel calmer and more open, but if this is a case of anxiety getting in the way, you will help them to feel calmer and more open as well. If that doesn't open the partner up to you and release their hold on your friend, it may be time for intervention.

BODY LANGUAGE MYTHBUSTER
Selfies Are Narcissistic

Aren't all those celebs who constantly post selfies simply displaying their narcissism? Does narcissism play a part in the modern-day trend of selfies rampant on social media that we use to show the biggest and best sides of our lives to others? Well, it is possible that any personality disorder—like narcissism—has to be on the outer fringes of socially acceptable behavior in order to be classed as unhealthy. And so if we are all taking selfies, then this is now socially acceptable and not socially deviant. So an argument could be made that we can't call our friends out as narcissists just because they post an occasional selfie of themselves. And it becomes even more difficult to call celebrities—whose jobs may rely partly on posting grandiose selfies daily—narcissists rather than entertainers. When deciphering if a behavior is out of the ordinary, context is everything. Just because someone looks like they have a selfie obsession does not necessarily mean they are self-obsessed.

QUICK SCAN

S: Suspend judgments that are based on overriding physical movements that powerfully affect your view of others or your feelings about how they view you—in this case, height dominance.

C: Understand that those who are not a part of your tight social group will be managing its power and may react to it in uncomfortable or unusual ways for you. Sometimes your group is the powerfully charged **context** in which others' behavior can be set off balance.

A: Always **ask** what else is happening that can be put down to unconscious mirroring. Some social behaviors are simply a copying process, nothing to do with individuals and everything to do with social groups.

N: New judgments can easily be tested by consulting others who are familiar with the situation to find out if they have made similar or vastly different judgments.

11

I'M GOING TO PAY FOR THAT!

You've been dating the same person for a little while now and things so far couldn't be better. You are in the honeymoon phase. Every day you grow more comfortable together, learning each other's lovable habits, idiosyncrasies, likes and dislikes, what makes you both happy or sad. It's all good.

You have a date planned and you show up late: not just a few minutes but almost an hour. Your excuses: Your phone battery died, you couldn't call, you were stuck on the subway—all of which is true. You have a good reason for being late. You arrive full of apologies. Surprisingly, your date smiles and seems totally fine—cool, still and calm. They even

➡

look a little *too* calm, almost serene. You ask if they
are OK and they say they are. You assume this is
potentially a time bomb that will explode when you
least expect it. Regardless of their outward body
language of tranquility, you think, *I am going to
have to pay for that.*

WHAT IS IT ABOUT THE BEHAVIOR in this situation that makes you
jump to the conclusion that it's only a matter of time before you will
face the full force of your date's wrath? Let's **suspend judgment** here
and **be more descriptive** of what you are seeing and the circumstances.

The key signal that is setting off alarm bells for you is their body
language of tranquility, which directly contrasts with your expectation of anger—how you think they should react. You don't trust the
calm reaction, and so the conclusion for you is that they are suppressing their anger. But how can you prove this? How do you detect suppressed anger? Suppressed anger by its very nature does not show up
in body language terms as obvious, energetic or overt signs of anger,
or as aggressive behaviors such as clenched fists pounding on the
table, raised voice, downward vocal inflection and stamping of feet.

However, you would perhaps be able to detect some micro-
expressions—brief, involuntary facial expressions that show what
they are really feeling. Anger micro-expressions that might leak out
are generally understood to include vertical lines between the brows,
brows drawn together, tense lower lids, tight and narrow lips, glaring
eyes, dilated nostrils and a jutting lower jaw, with all three facial areas
involved in the gesture.[1]

Even with the best of intentions, not many people are trained or practiced enough to be able to consciously detect these subtle moments of telltale body language in the moment. Even so, you may have picked up on them unconsciously, and this is causing you to distrust your date's overt outward appearance and words of calm. Instead you suspect they may unleash a powerful rage on you.

If you are expecting to see anger, then signals that are similar to anger but not indicative of it—for example, facial signals that could potentially indicate worry or concern, such as squinting eyes, a furrowed forehead and tight lips[2]—could make you think the volcano is gearing up to blow. But is it really?

Let's look at the **context**. You've been dating for a little while, but the relationship is still relatively new. You do not have a baseline as of yet for how this person reacts to a situation like this . However, you are bringing with you a cloud of expectation of an angry response. You have therefore provided a context that demands anger from your date.

BODY LANGUAGE MYTHBUSTER
Body Language Says It All

Ninety-three percent of all communication is nonverbal. *Excellent*, you might be thinking. This means you can say any old words you like to anybody and your body language will do the heavy lifting of getting your meaning across. Well, not exactly. The classic study by Dr. Albert Mehrabian concludes that "the total impact of a message is based on: 7% words used; 38% tone of voice, volume, rate of speech,

➡

---

vocal pitch; 55% facial expressions, hand gestures, postures and other forms of body language."[3]

Mehrabian never claimed you could view a movie in a foreign language and accurately guess 93 percent of the content by watching body language, nor is he implying that words are unimportant for getting across meaning. His research was focused on the communication of emotions, specifically liking and disliking. The nonverbal aspect of communication won't deliver 93 percent of your entire message, but it will stimulate theories in the viewer as to the underlying feelings and intentions that inform the meaning of the spoken content. People will evaluate most of the emotional content of your message not by what you say but by your nonverbal signals.

Ask what else could be forming these expectations. What is your history with others in terms of how they have reacted to your lateness? Did you have a past partner who was angry if you were late? Past experiences may have shaped how you now expect all others to behave in this circumstance. This is leading you to have a strong pattern of expectation and then mistrust should the other person not fulfill that expectation.

However, they could just be feeling happy and contented you are there now and you had a credible reason for being so late. You just can't believe that, unlike others in your past, they would be so forgiving. It's all too different to feel true.

There are **new** assumptions you might make from all this. If you indeed are picking up on micro-gestures of anger, it could be that you are repeatedly making promises to your partner that you don't or can't keep, and over time they may grow angry and eventually blow up at you.

Alternatively, as you are most moved by the sense of serenity they are displaying through their stillness and smile, it is entirely possible they are so into you that they are just content with your presence regardless of your being late.

How can you **test** any of these new assumptions and **new judgments** to get more feedback on what they are thinking? Maybe this relationship is far enough along that it can tolerate the test of letting your date know your worry and asking for honest feedback on it. It's time to talk about the feelings you are getting from the body language you see—and don't see. Tell them they look really happy and calm, even though you're so late. Tell them you're worried they might actually be upset with you but are not letting you know. Let them know you'd like them to be honest with you if they are upset and that the two of you can work it out together.

Aggression in the Walk

This research is in its early days, but all the same, it's something to keep in mind when deciding whether someone is aggressive or not.

Exploratory research from the departments of sport and psychology at the University of Portsmouth suggests you can predict certain personality traits from the way people move their upper and lower bodies while walking. "We find that increased upper body movement (relative to lower body movement) can indicate latent aggression," lead researcher Liam Satchell told MedicalResearch.com.[4]

QUICK SCAN

S: Your judgments can sometimes come from not seeing something you expect to see. Powerful initial, kneejerk reactions that may need **suspending** are as much about the expected as the unexpected.

C: In the **context** of new relationships, you can be surprised and wary of others' reactions when you don't get the reaction you would have in the previous similar relationship.

A: Always **ask** what else you are layering into the interpretation of a situation, what past experiences may be influencing your judgment.

N: **New** judgments can give you the opportunity to check your habitual behaviors, be transparent about old concerns and turn over a new leaf.

12

THEY ARE *SO* MAD AT ME

It's your third date and you've decided it's time to take things to the next level and cook dinner in your home for your new romantic interest. You've cleaned up your place, been to the market, made a go-to favorite dish—in short, you've made an effort as you're starting to have high hopes for this one.

Your date arrives at your place, and something is feeling a bit off to you. You think it's nothing, probably just your own nerves. You want the evening to go really well, after all. You get drinks rolling, thinking that will loosen things up. But your date is frowning more and more heavily, and you begin to feel they may be angry or annoyed. You ask them how they

➡

are doing and if they're OK, and they say they're
fine. But then they sink down onto your sofa looking
increasingly upset. Your insides start to churn as you
think, *What is wrong here? Is it me? Is it my place?
Did they tell me they were vegan and I've forgotten?
Should I throw out the steak? They are so mad at me!*

LET'S LOOK AT a key body language signal that would give you the impression they are mad at you: They are frowning and looking more annoyed by the minute. Let's **SCAN** the situation, **suspend judgment** for a minute and **be more descriptive**.

Frowning closes the eyes, so the frowner does not get overwhelmed with visual data or stimuli; and frowning also protects the eyes and the face. While frowns vary somewhat from culture to culture, most people recognize the frown as a negative facial expression, which is likely why it is making you believe that your romantic interest is feeling negative toward you. However, although it can be one sign of anger, a frown on its own is not enough to let us know someone really is angry.

BODY LANGUAGE MYTHBUSTER
Frown Lines Are an Angry Look

Take an Internet tour of the world of cosmetic surgery
and you will find plenty of ways to take away your

➡

angry frown lines, for instance, with products like Botox. While that may do the trick, knitted eyebrows alone do not equate to anger. The signal for anger is more complex. In addition to knitted or lowered eyebrows, anger also features a tight top lip, a raised upper eyelid and tightened eyelids. The head may be tipped down to protect the neck with the chin, and the nostrils may be flared. So although softening the lines on the forehead with a neurotoxin that blocks the signals to those muscles can reduce one of the indicators of anger, if someone is truly angry, most of the time that won't be enough to hide it.

When someone is angry, their eyebrows will tilt in toward the center of the face or both will be flat and lowered. The eyes will have a glare to them. In some instances, the eyes will narrow, but in others, even with the eyebrows down or flat, the eyes will be wide open. The microexpressions of anger we see around the mouth include narrowing of the lips as if the angry person is trying to hold their mouth shut, perhaps so as not to let a word out, or perhaps in frustration or disapproval.

But in our story, you are focusing only on the frown. And because a frown on its own does not necessarily mean anger, let's look at alternative interpretations. A frown can also signal disgust, sadness, nervousness, tension, confusion, deep thinking or concentration. Needless to say, however, it does loom large as a sign, as at first blush, it can have the effect of eclipsing all other signals on the face that may tell you more about what is actually going on.

This is good news, in that your assumption that your date is mad at you is looking a little less likely at this point. There just is not enough data to say they are angry, and if by chance they are angry, there is no reason at this point to truly think they are angry at *you*.

So let's look at the other body language signals for more clues. They sink down onto your sofa. This shows a feeling of powerlessness. Giving in to the power of gravity can make someone look like they have the weight of the world on their shoulders. We are all working against gravitational force when we are upright and standing tall. To sink or slump down shows we're passive in our response to the force of gravity, and by giving in to it, we have lost the power of even standing upright. It could indicate defeat, exhaustion, depression or simply relaxation.

Time to take in the **context**. It's your third date with this person but the first time they have been to your home. Is there something about your place that is troubling them? Perhaps they had made some assumptions about you and your lifestyle, based on their impressions of you on your first two dates and on what information you shared with them. Upon closer inspection, it could be that your lifestyle, what you represented of it, is not what they thought or envisioned, and their body language is showing their confusion around this. As we pointed out, frowning can signal confusion.

PROFILE PICS

We asked **SASKIA NELSON**, the talent behind the multi-award-winning and internationally acclaimed Hey Saturday, the UK's first and coolest dating photography business, her best advice for posting online dating profile pictures—how to show something true about yourself through your photo (like your interests) while not misleading viewers.

It's challenging to tell your story via photos without misleading people. If you like sports cars, Ferraris for example, it would definitely be very misleading to show a photo of yourself standing next to a Ferrari if it isn't yours. However, you could have a photo of yourself at a car show or rally to show that cars are an interest of yours. Or you could be photographed with a book about cars. If you think creatively, you can find clever ways to hint at your interests, without making the photos look too planned and posed, which isn't good for dating photos. Dating photos should be natural, relaxed, happy shots—as though you've been caught out and about by friends.

I think people will look at someone's photo and often make snap judgments (probably subconsciously some of the time) about a person and their lifestyle based on what's in the photo. Every photo gives away clues about the person's character. If it's taken inside their house, for example, then they'll be looking at the furniture, checking out how tidy it is and so on, and for dating we always try to be aspirational at the beginning. We make the effort for the first few months of dating someone, showcasing only the good things about us (e.g., we wear makeup and our best clothes, are always in a good mood and have a tidy house). So with dating photos, people should be aspirational but authentic in this way.

Alternatively, the behavior of your new companion—sinking down into your couch—could indicate that your home is a welcome refuge or comfortable space for them. They feel instantly at ease and relaxed, and they can really be themselves. Perhaps your love interest needs a calm and safe space to weigh up something else that is troubling them. So sinking down into your couch could actually be a positive signal, showing you their high comfort level being with you in your home.

Ask what else you should consider. There is a definite conflict in their behavior. You were hoping for a fun and happy date that might take the relationship up a notch, and instead you experience signs of anger, sadness, confusion and powerlessness, leaving you wondering where you stand. Their body language is even in conflict, showing losing power by sinking down in the sofa while also actively displaying a frown. Also especially notable here is the contrast between words and actions. Remember, they said they were fine. As we saw in chapter 9, "What a Complete Psycho!," often the contrast between verbal and nonverbal action alerts and confuses us. It is the actions others show, that spill out, that tend to speak to us louder than their words. Classic nonverbal communication studies by Mehrabian concluded, "When there are inconsistencies between attitudes communicated verbally and posturally, the postural component should dominate in determining the total attitude that is inferred."[1] In other words, most of the clues we get about the emotional intent behind people's words actually come from the nonverbal cues we are getting, and when there is contrast or conflict, we tend to believe the nonverbal.

So trying to form a **new judgment** about what is going on inside their head is not that straightforward, even if you feel you can dismiss the assumption that they are angry at you. Upon reflection, anger does not now seem likely, particularly if you also consider that anger, like happiness, is an energetic state. When we are angry, our heart rate increases, and we may have a difficult time relaxing or staying still. Anger is a state that accompanies us into postures of aggression or fight, and so the opposite "sinking" feeling is inconsistent with this and would seem to tell a different story. They could be confused by us, or anxious or upset about something else that happened before they showed up for the date, and they just can't let it go.

With so much ambiguity, rather than making any new judgment or assumption, perhaps the more useful and less risky tactic is to simply wait ten minutes or so, just long enough so that if they are experiencing some intense emotion brought on by other stimuli, like something emotionally heavy or disruptive that happened earlier, perhaps a news item or a YouTube clip or TV show they can't let go of, this gives them some time and space for the heavy feelings to dissipate. Go and check on your dinner, set the table, take a minute to finish off that work e-mail; in other words, gently put the brakes on any intense interaction for this first part of your evening to see if your date's demeanor shifts. If it continues, it could be that the emotion is turning into a mood, which is a lower level of emotional intensity sustained over a longer period, anywhere from a number of hours to a day. A heightened emotion sustained for hours may indicate an affective disorder, or the reaction to an extraordinary situation or stimulus.

Here's what you can do nonverbally to even out the atmosphere, to try drawing them out of their emotion or any mood, without risking looking like you have no empathy. Use relaxed body language, meaning calm and steady movement, steady breathing, light eyebrows and eyes. Sit and breathe in through your nose and then gently out through your mouth. Try to count each breath, in and out, for a count of four or five seconds. You want to assert steady, light and calm actions to attempt to draw their state away from a downward spiral. Avoid body language that is diametrically opposed to what they are doing, which may make you look as if you lack empathy and understanding. But if you mirror their behavior too much, you both risk spiraling down together.

And if nothing changes after a little while, you could safely investigate further by asking questions that allow them space to respond mindfully, as opposed to asking if everything is OK and pushing them toward a binary yes or no answer. If you frame your concern within a casual approach, this may allow them to explore what is going on and answer you more truthfully and in greater detail. You might ask, "What are you thinking about right now?" It could be that they experience some heavy emotions periodically and are feeling relaxed and viewing the relationship as already strong enough to test whether you will be able to handle them. Gently **test** the water.

RESTING FACE

Our friend and colleague **SCOTT ROUSE** is a body language expert and analyst, as well as an interrogator and interviewer. Here is what he has to say about the face we can make without intending to.

It's the face we all make when we're not talking to anyone and we're just sitting there, anywhere, by ourselves . . . waiting, drinking coffee, reading, whatever it is we're doing where no one else is involved and we think no one else is looking at us. Let's say you're at a coffee shop, having a latte. Unbeknownst to you, in walk the people you're going to have a job interview with later that morning. You're frustrated by how slow the Wi-Fi connection is that day. One of the key decision makers on hiring recognizes you from your online professional profile. In a flash, here's what runs through their mind: *Hey, that's who we're going to meet with later. Looks angry! Be sure to keep my guard up.* You haven't even met them yet, and you're already scoring very low on likability due to the thin slice of your body language they responded to.

When you're in public, always try to have a relaxed, pleasant look on your face—a resting face. And don't be too quick to judge others based on theirs.

QUICK SCAN

S: Suspending judgment on your initial reaction to just one body language feature, in this case a facial gesture related to an emotion but not wholly representing it, can help you realize you need to look for further indicators.

C: You are judged not only on nonverbal communication that is linked directly to your body but also by the environments you are seen to live in and that become symbolic of you, your attitudes and your personality. Your living **context** can be key to how others perceive you and you perceive them.

A: Ask what conflicts you see between what people say and how they behave. Be aware that most of our clues about the emotional intent behind people's words come from the nonverbal cues we are getting, and when there is conflict with the verbal cues, we tend to believe the nonverbal.

N: A simple way to test a **new** judgment is to wait a few minutes and see what, if anything, changes. These changes or the sustainment over time of any signals of emotional state may help your judgments get you closer to the truth.

13

A LYING CHEAT?

Your partner comes home a little later than
expected, and it seems to you that something is
up. It's hard to explain. There's a different rhythm
to their behavior. They are inconsistent in the way
they act, seeming happy and then stressed. In fact,
they've been a bit uneven for the last few days. They
even seem to smell different. You ask about this
and they dismiss your question by looking away and
saying they passed through the perfume section
of a store on their way home. They smell their own
wrist, and they rub their nose and then crinkle it
up as if they didn't like the smell. They avoid facing
you directly, turning their face and body away,

➡

their head hanging down and away from you. You assume they must be concealing something or feeling guilty. Your gut tells you they are lying. When you ask about their day, where they were and who they were with, they seem to get a bit shifty in the eyes, saying they had lots and lots of meetings with lots of people, and then they look down at the ground. You are sure of it: They are cheating on you! And they think they can hide it.

ARE THEY CHEATING ON YOU? Being cheated on is a common and powerful fear for many. Though there may seem to be plenty of telltale signs, let's follow the **SCAN** procedure and **suspend judgment** at this point to **be more descriptive** of the situation.

You may have read about some of the most common body language signals of lying. For example, liars often break eye contact and look away. They blink more often and have shifty eyes. Another sign is covering the mouth area, thereby communicating the brain's unconscious effort to close off communication; putting their hands around their mouth suggests the person does not want to talk about the subject in question. Also rubbing the nose may suggest lying.

In our scenario above, you focus on the key signal that leads you to believe your partner is cheating: They are blocking you out, looking away from you and down at the ground, pointing their body away from you. Studies show that a liar may physically show discomfort by avoiding directly facing the accuser or suspicious questioner, blocking them by turning their head or body, and avoiding making eye contact. You believe that further proof of infidelity is that your partner unsatisfactorily answers your question about their day and repeats words, for instance, *lots*. Verbal repetition can be a sign of lying; repetition distances the listener and helps buy the liar time to gather their thoughts so they can make up a story.

Let's look a little more closely at blocking. In the introduction we looked at how crossed arms can be a sign of blocking but that what exactly the person is blocking is open to many interpretations. In this scenario, they are turning away their body, face and eyes. Blocking is a protective behavior we engage in when we feel uncomfortable to some degree, or potentially threatened by some aspect of our environment, the person we are talking to or the subject of conversation. Aside from crossed arms, signs of blocking can also include eye blocking (as in shading the eyes); pinching the bridge of the nose; clutching a prop in front of the body such as a purse, book or drink; or placing a laptop in front of the body. Blocking can indicate various things, depending on the context, including lying, nervousness or shame. Feelings of shame may be indicated by the tips of the fingers resting on the side of the forehead, perhaps as a result of guilt or embarrassment, and also a head hanging.

This is normally where you would look at **context**; however, what you have so far is a collection of body language signals to which you have already assigned a context, with the assumption that your partner is cheating on you. But there are many alternative contexts that could also explain the behavior. Your partner could be coming home late from work for reasons other than infidelity. Something could have happened at work to make them not only late but also preoccupied, upset, nervous or shameful. Indeed, any number of things could have happened that they would rather not be truthful about. In other words, the possibility that they are cheating on you is just one context among untold others that would explain their timing and emotional behavior.

BODY LANGUAGE MYTHBUSTER
As Plain as the Nose on Your Face

Remember Pinocchio? Wouldn't it be great if there were a single physical sign that exposed a deceitful person as plain as the nose on their face? Well, there's a good reason the story of Pinocchio is a fairy tale. You cannot actually tell someone is lying based on just one body language sign. And to this end, the idea that people touch their noses when they are telling a lie is largely folklore. In fact, the idea that the nose alone can display subtle telltale signs of lying is pure fantasy. However, wrinkling the nose in disgust, if detected alongside other signals, could certainly indicate a deceitful person smelling their own rat of a lie, such as flaring the nostrils as part of the micro-gesture of disgust.

What else can you **ask** and consider to help you either confirm your first assumption or make a powerful new one? No one body language signal indisputably proves that information being given to us is a lie, that we are being deceived. In fact, as noted earlier, some signals can mean two opposite things, and in this scenario, the signals for lying may also be the signals for *not* lying, as you will soon discover. The judgment that someone is lying based on reading signals that have a dual and opposite meaning is referred to as the Othello error, a term coined by body language scientist and micro-expression expert Paul Ekman after the tragic Shakespearean character who kills his wife in a fit of jealousy because he mistakes her anxiety over being questioned about an affair as actual proof she is having one.

According to Ekman in his book *Telling Lies*, when we are trying to catch someone in a lie, we often fail to take into account that a truthful person may appear to be lying because they are under stress.[1] Their nonverbal signals may be revealing their worry of being disbelieved. A lie detector may be deceived in the same way, by misinterpreting nervous signals from a truthful person.

So here is the conundrum: The signals for lying may also indicate that the person is not lying, but just nervous. Shifty eyes, as in our scenario, have traditionally meant that the person is lying; this is why many liars make a concerted effort not to move their eyes or blink excessively. So a blank, fixed stare—the opposite of darting, blinking eyes—can indicate a dishonest response just as much as can the classic shifty-eyed look. Also, instead of fidgeting, the liar may stiffen and be very still, in preparation for confrontation. Further, you need to make some space for the possibility that you are being lied to for a different reason than infidelity, or perhaps you are not being lied to at all but are witnessing your partner in a state of nervousness around something that may be difficult for them to share.

If they really are lying, however, there should be other subtle signals of deceit that could be concealed individually yet add up to a lie. Changes in behavior may alert you that something is up, and if you've been with your significant other for a while, you know how they normally act, how they react to challenges or surprises, how well they listen and so on. Sudden unusual changes in their body language, from facial expressions to patterns of speech, can be an indicator that something significant has changed in their lives. The face of a person telling a lie or concealing the truth can appear less animated than it would if they were being honest. There may be little movement around the mouth as they suppress other facial movement in order to conceal the truth. A liar might be tight-lipped, again showing suppression. However, this could also demonstrate anger, or maybe even the anger at being caught in a lie.

The face could look drained and pale as a result of the anxiety brought on by lying. Blushing and sweating, classic signs of stress, are both physical reactions to the emotional strain that lying places on the psyche, but not always. A habitual liar may feel no stress in hiding the truth, and so the classic sweaty palms could be as much an indicator of other stresses as anything else. Heart rate and breathing may change as a result of feelings of anxiety around lying. The breathing may become heavy, or the person lying may experience breathlessness.

Nervousness may also show up through shuffling or shaking feet and legs, or other fidgeting. Hands may come into play: covering or rubbing areas around the eyes, the ears and the mouth, effectively hiding these areas from sight. Of course, this is not a surefire sign of lying, but again, if it is a change in behavior from the norm, it can mean something is significantly different.

Looking back at our scenario, we do see some of these clues: the change in behavior, unevenness in mood, the switch from happy to stressed. However, when we drum up negative ideas about someone, it is very often the lack of data we have about the situation that makes us default to negative assumptions and leads us to catastrophize. For instance, note how easy it was to come to the conclusion of infidelity based on a lack of information from the partner coming home late and their giving unsatisfactory answers to questions and suspicions. Having a lack of data makes us feel that the other person is purposely hiding information from us, making it easy for us to quickly riff on worst-case scenarios.

So while some of the physical characteristics of lying definitely feature in the scenario and feed into your first best guess, to think more critically about what is going on, you should consider that the signs could also be representing nervousness or shame about something other than cheating. Also, and importantly in cases of lying, you always need to consider body language in the context of the verbal cues. In this case, a better assumption is that something is definitely up with your partner, and you need to directly address what you perceive as a change in their behavior.

So how do you **test** these **new judgments** and assumptions to address your concerns constructively while avoiding being compromised, lied to or hoodwinked? You need to watch your partner's body language while listening to their story:

- ☑ Listen to see if their story keeps changing, at the same time watching out for a handful of potentially deceitful gestures.
- ☑ Listen for whether they are cutting out self-references in the story—someone not wishing to be implicated may take themselves out of the story as much as possible. This can also take the form of what some interrogators call *pronoun shift*, where the teller of the story starts as "I," shifts to "we," and may even attempt to disappear from being implicated by using the third-person "they."
- ☑ Listen for any changes of past tense to present tense—events in the past don't change, so if someone is changing the description of events, that may indicate stress around telling the details of the event.
- ☑ Listen for whether they use oaths, euphemisms or allusions; those are also potential verbal cues.
- ☑ Note any repetition of your questions before they answer; this can be a stalling tactic to give them time to invent a story. While

they answer, watch for their overall body language veering into aggressive behaviors.

When you are listening and want to put the other person at ease, use open body language. What might this look like? Sit or stand with your fingers of both hands interlaced across your navel. Tilt your head slightly to one side. Although these two gestures are not necessarily an indicator that someone is actually listening, they give that impression and can also trigger you into listening better.

LISTEN FOR THE LIE

DR. LILLIAN GLASS is a body language expert and one of the most prolific writers in the field; her books include *The Body Language of Liars*. We asked her to talk to us specifically about the voice and lying.

It is essential to always consider context when you examine deception in a person's speaking pattern. When a person trails off at the end of a sentence, it may indicate that they are not telling you the truth. If they have previously been speaking and didn't trail off at the end of a sentence and suddenly trail off when you ask them a poignant question or they share something with you, this is an indicator that they may be lying.

Besides petering off at the end of sentences, they may suddenly speak softly or clear their throat a lot, which reflects a vocal indication of deception. This is because their autonomic nervous system is taking over. It is something they cannot control as the tiny vocal cord muscles suddenly tense up, making it difficult to speak. In addition, the mucous membranes dry up, making it uncomfortable to speak. Hence the throat clearing and breaks in the pitch of the voice.

The voice may skip out for a moment so there is no audible tone, or the pitch may suddenly rise due to the automatic tightening of the vocal muscles. The voice may also suddenly sound hoarse or raspy because the saliva has suddenly dried up. You may also notice that they have more difficulty articulating certain sounds due to their dry lips and mucous membranes in the inner cheeks and tongue. Hence you may witness a lot of lip licking as they speak.

QUICK SCAN

S: The most powerful signals in this scenario, the blocking body language and looking away, indicate the need to **suspend** judgment to more carefully consider other signals, both nonverbal and verbal.

C: Can you bring any further **context** to bear on this scenario (e.g., Where are they likely to have been)?

A: Ask yourself if there have been times in the past when you may have committed the Othello error.

N: A **new** judgment will depend on other observations you make of subtle signals of deceit that together could add up to a lie. Consider, also, any major changes in behavior that may alert you that something is up.

14

DEFINITELY INTO MY FRIEND

You met someone at a party a few weeks ago and haven't been able to think about anyone else since, and you thought they were into you as well. And now you are together with them and a few friends, and they appear to be moving in . . . on your friend! Wow, they keep getting so close to each other. They even keep finding reasons to touch each other's faces. And you often catch them gazing at each other. You have told your friend how you feel about this person. You thought you had staked your claim. It would seem to you, though, that your friend shares an equally powerful attraction. And why wouldn't they? The person you're into is amazing, but sadly for you is definitely into your friend.

THIS COULD BE AWKWARD and upsetting, but is it true? Let's **SCAN** this situation by first **suspending judgment** and **being more descriptive** of what is going on.

What is the key body language signal leading you to the assumption that there is an undeniable and powerful attraction between your crush and your friend? They are gazing at each other, but the ownership signals you see are mainly in their proximity and—the icing on the cake—the face touching.

While gazing may sometimes indicate romantic intention, the ownership signals clearly show intention. Ownership signals involve closing the proximity between yourself and the thing or person you want to have power over by either leaning in toward them close enough to touch or by touching them and physically bringing them into your own territory. Touching with the hands can show care and can look sensual; this touching involves feeling with the palm of the hand things or people you would like to bring into your personal space and be close to and care for. Witnessing these ownership signals in this scenario would seem to confirm an initial assumption that your crush is into your friend.

Now, still with suspended judgment, let's look at the signals within **context**. You think this person is amazing. In the context of the values and beliefs of your social group, it stands to reason that if you are seeing something of real value in this potential partner, it is very likely that you aren't the only one. It is entirely likely that others at the party will also be attracted to your crush.

And, if you think there is no competition between friends, think again. All social groups have hierarchies. Regardless of what country, culture, community or socioeconomic circumstance you are in, your social group will have a pecking order, and as the members share the same values, they will all value certain resources being displayed by someone.

First, though, you need to recognize that the stakes are naturally high for you because your friend is involved. Your observations of body language are likely to be biased because you are already invested. So taking a step back and allowing space to be more mindful of what you are seeing is essential.

BODY LANGUAGE MYTHBUSTER
How Long Is Too Long?

Don't stare! For how long do you think it is appropriate to look at someone? For how long would you like to be looked at? Research from the United Kingdom shows that we may like to hang on to eye contact longer if we like the person we're having it with. Visitors to the London Science Museum judged whether videos of an actor looking at them for different lengths of time felt too long or too short in terms of what they deemed to be comfortable. On average, participants were happy with a prolonged gaze of 3.3 seconds. Change in pupil size was the telltale sign of how long was long enough for eye contact. Pupil dilation increased at a faster rate in participants who preferred longer periods of direct gaze.[1] Meaning, if I like the look of you, it's OK for you to stare at me.

What else is there to **ask**? In the story, you told your friend that you "claimed" the other person, but as we've already seen, the unconscious mind does not pay as much attention to what is said as it attends to the physical signals being displayed. So if you are not showing some clear signals of ownership, metaphorically speaking you have likely not adequately staked your claim in a way that others can really understand and get behind.

Historically, many countries held land rushes, where people could stake a claim for land ownership. Prospective owners would drive wooden and iron stakes into the ground to mark off their territory. They then armed themselves, ready to fight anyone who trespassed onto their claim. (Important to note: We are not suggesting this as the way forward in this scenario!)

However, like our situation here, this was a physical display of ownership, dominance over the space—clear nonverbal messaging showing that if you were on property that someone else had staked, and they were standing with their gun guarding it, it likely did not belong to you.

If you have not yet displayed to the person you are interested in some signals that you care, or have not nonverbally intimated in some way that you would like to bring them close into your territory—basically, not displayed signs of "ownership" toward them—they may very likely have no idea how you feel about them. After all, although they may be amazing, they probably don't possess the talents of a mind reader.

Is there truly any good reason for your crush and your friend to be touching each other's faces and gazing at each other? Unless they are both in training as cosmetic surgeons, not really. Sometimes your initial judgments will be correct. And this may be one of those times when you read the signs correctly, given the cluster of signals looking very much in favor of an amorous relationship between the two. However, you've assumed your crush is the guilty party by making a judgment that they are into your friend. Upon further reflection, however, it would appear that although it could be two-sided, an equally likely **new judgment** is that your friend is moving in on your crush.

You could **test** the integrity of your friend's commitment to pursuing someone they know you had an interest in by closing the proximity between you and your crush. This action may quickly see your friend off, reminding them of your earlier stated intentions. By leaning in or closing the space between you, you are clearly showing you believe you have some power, some "ownership," and have no intention of leaving the space open for someone else to move into. If neither your friend nor your crush shows they want to back away from each other and you are clearly the third wheel, you will have your answer: You are not welcome, you are the one needing to clear off and you don't have the power of ownership you thought you did.

QUICK SCAN

S: Suspending judgment is easier if you know the signals that trigger you into making that judgment. In this scenario it is the ownership signals setting off your alarm bells. Notice today how many ownership signals you think you see between people you believe to be in an intimate relationship. Which ones do you find most powerful?

C: Social groups like your group of friends share values, beliefs, likes and dislikes, and so there may be competition in this **context** where you think there is none. All social groups have a social hierarchy.

A: Ask whether you have adequately displayed nonverbal ownership signals to your crush to make your feelings and intentions clear. In addition, have you "staked your claim" in front of your friends to give a clear enough message unconsciously that they will understand and get behind?

N: A **new** judgment shifts the responsibility away from your crush and directs it toward your friend and, moreover, toward yourself, showing the need for immediate action. By leaning in or closing the space between you and your crush, you clearly show your intentions to them as well as your power within the group, at the same time closing the gap so someone else cannot move in.

15

A MATCH MADE IN HEAVEN?

You met online. The dating site's computer algorithm made the perfect match. After a suitable time of successful e-mailing and friendly phone calls, you met in person, and just as the computer predicted, everything seemed to click. You went on excellent dates, and now you are seeing more and more of each other. When you are together, it feels so right. When you laugh, they laugh. When you yawn, they yawn. You even seem to think the same thoughts at the same time. You are so in tune with each other, it has to be true love. Doesn't it? Is this your match made in heaven?

WHAT IS THE KEY SIGNAL in this story that has led to your judgment that this is a match made in heaven? It is being in tune with each other's actions—in effect, mirroring each other—that is so powerful.

Using the **SCAN** process, let's **suspend judgment** and **be more descriptive** of what is going on. Mirroring, as we've previously mentioned, is a major theme when considering body language. In romantic relationships, mirroring marks one of the early stages of infatuation, and it can be a telltale sign that couples are in tune with each other and mutually engaged.

As social, tribal beings, we tend to relax when we feel we are among those who like us and feel that they are like us. When mirroring a person's body language, which we often do unconsciously, we are acting instinctively and naturally to build rapport with people we like. By mirroring—essentially reflecting—postures, gestures, sitting positions, tone of voice and talking pace, we quickly build trust, connection and intimacy, letting us feel more at ease, comfortable and understood.

Infatuation is largely the product of potent and powerful brain chemistry. And the primary ingredient in that neurochemical brew is dopamine, a neurotransmitter best known for its ability to initiate muscle movement and pleasure seeking, and for its addictive hold over our personalities. It triggers that joyously obsessive feeling of new love.

When we are infatuated with someone, we generally feel positive about the new love in our lives. We think it will all work out perfectly and often tend to overlook or even be blind to their faults. We love the feeling we get when we are around the other person. It can even feel addictive, in that we can't stand being apart from them.

We mirror each other spontaneously. The other person shows up on time, anticipates our moods and desires, and unconsciously adjusts their pace to match ours. And we do the same. As University of California at San Francisco psychiatry professors Thomas Lewis,

Fari Amini and Richard Lannon explain in their work A *General Theory of Love*, our nervous systems are not self-contained: "Mammals developed a capacity we call 'limbic resonance'—a symphony of mutual exchange and internal adaptation whereby two mammals become attuned to each other's inner states." We looked at limbic resonance elsewhere as well, and it is particularly pertinent to infatuation.[1] When we're feeling infatuated with someone, we tend to see what we like, what is like us or resonates for us, and deny or downplay any niggling feelings of doubt. We can easily lie to ourselves.

In our scenario, there is still a question of whether or not it is love, truly a match made in heaven. For now, though, everything seems to be going your way, and indeed this could be *it* for you with this person, so your initial judgment may well be correct and you can look forward to good times ahead.

Let's now look at the **context**. Without a doubt, meeting your potential partner online changes the landscape within which body language cues happen, at least for the early part of an online relationship. First impressions and the key body language signals that help form those impressions are communicated through still photos that we choose for our profile pages. So how you show up in this context, what you choose to display about yourself—your pose, hair, clothes, props and environment—can be carefully arranged, considered and altered, often engineered not only to fit in with criteria of the dating site but also to support how you would like to be seen by others and to broadcast what qualities you are looking for in a mate. Interestingly but perhaps not surprisingly, studies show that 81 percent of online dating users embellish and lie in their profiles, mainly about their weight, height and age. However, except for a very few extreme examples of this, such as the odd claim to be a decade younger or six inches taller, the lies are minimal and do not indicate this pattern in the rest of the profile.[2]

PICTURE PERFECT

Our online dating profile picture expert, **SASKIA NELSON**, credited by *Time* magazine's photo blog for creating and kickstarting the new genre of dating photography, shares here her top three tips for creating the most effective profile photos.

1. **Look good:** Be confident and happy, and make sure you look like you would on a first date. Be the main focus of the shot. The main dating profile picture should be a close-up of a happy, smiling, relaxed person looking and feeling good about themselves.

2. **Stand out:** Use bold color to make the photos stand out in the sea of other dating photos. Be the only person in the shot (other people distract from you). Make sure the photo is bright in focus and good quality (good-quality photos attract good-quality dates). Make sure the background adds value to your photo and doesn't distract people from you.

3. **Tell your story:** Choose clothes that you love and that showcase you feeling at your best. Choose a background/location that fits who you are—somewhere you feel comfortable (coffee shop, street art, river, park, market, shops, pretty street). Do something you love if possible (in-line skating, reading, cycling, listening to music, browsing a market stall). Use props if you can without making the photos look fake. For example, wearing big headphones, reading the paper, holding a coffee cup, having a laptop nearby, even wearing a hat are all good for telling people a little bit about yourself.

Sunglasses aren't recommended for dating photos because the eyes are so important. People want to look into your eyes to gauge whether you are trustworthy or not, and so if you are hiding your eyes, it can suggest you're untrustworthy.

Everything in your photo gives people clues about who you are and tells them about your lifestyle, so make sure it's as representative of you as possible by taking time to think about your shots.

Back to our scenario. For you to get to a positive face-to-face meeting with a date with whom you seem well suited, how you construct your profile page and all the signals you choose to display must communicate essentially what you want to show about who you are and what you want. And it's not just yourself you are bringing to the table, but your overall context. That is, when you use online dating sites, you are giving visual cues for how you live, what you like, what you surround yourself with in the outside world and what you wish to be associated with. You in effect broadcast your tribalism through the signs you display in these photos, what you align yourself with, what is important to you and what you value, all in the hopes of finding someone who shares these same values, customs and beliefs. Displaying yourself in this way online, you can fully embed yourself within the context of your choosing, and hopefully you have managed, to quote the advice of Polonius in *Hamlet*, "to thine own self be true"; true enough, at least, that further down the road you are not shown up as having been false.

BODY LANGUAGE MYTHBUSTER
Using Your Body Language Is Inauthentic
Purposefully using body language to give a good impression is inauthentic, some say. Is this really

true? You write the best description of yourself for dating sites. You put the best photos of yourself online. You choose great clothes that best suit the style of the day, type of event and person you want to be seen as. And you rehearse over and over in your head how a conversation might go and the questions you wish to ask and answers you wish to give. So why would you not feel satisfied with doing the same with your nonverbal communication? There is a big difference between putting on the behaviors of something you are not and showing the very best of what you are. You would not show up to a date in a police uniform and tell your date you are an officer if you were not and the uniform was not yours. That would be lying. But why would it be so bad to display your most confident body language even if you are feeling a little unconfident? Of course, it's not bad at all. It's positive. Get out there and show the best of yourself!

What else should you **ask** and consider? There are a multitude of online dating sites in what quickly became a thriving industry. Sites vary in the services they offer. For example, there are dating sites reserved for people with particular religious beliefs, or of certain ages, cultures and special interests. The process of how each site matches you up varies. Generally, each profile questionnaire has a list of attributes or interests you can check off, and the technology of the site will match these attributes with other profiles on the site to get the highest match percentage. On some sites you can indicate how important an attribute is to you relative to others; the system is able to handle some nuance in the matching process. Some of the online dating systems can process complex personality surveys to find suitable matches and can even predict compatibility based on a history of the compatibility of others who have gone through the same process.

But does it work? Compelling statistics prove the efficacy and overall favorable user experience of online dating sites.[3] One study finds that "no compelling evidence supports matching sites' claims that mathematical algorithms work—that they foster romantic outcomes that are superior to those fostered by other means of pairing partners."[4]

In our scenario, how can you **test** if it is likely to be great for you, that you posted on an appropriate dating site, and the match you make will not crumble unceremoniously in a few months once the infatuation starts to fade? Perhaps your quiet questioning could be your defense kicking in against the fear of what could happen if and when that lovely infatuation wears off. There is always the risk that you may find someone is completely unsuitable after all.

STRIKE THE RIGHT POSE

Our friend **DANIELLE LIBINE** is a photographer who uses her expertise in body language to create pictures that send the right messages from a pose perspective. Her book *A Photographer's Guide to Body Language* is a great resource for not only professional photographers but also anyone who needs to put together a great photographed image. We asked for her advice specifically on how to pose your body language for the optimum online dating photograph.

Both men and women are more likely to contact people they find attractive, so we will want to use our best, yet honest, profile picture. What is considered attractive in photos is quite different depending on whether you are a woman or a man. Men are more attracted to women who are smiling, while women are more attracted to images of men showing strength rather than those with a smile. However, further research also shows that an aggressive expression creates feelings of mistrust, so while men want to avoid a big open smile, they don't want to have an aggressive closed expression either. Flirty body language in profile photos can be very attractive to men: a head tilt and body turned slightly away from the camera will often increase a woman's attractiveness score. When it comes to eye contact, men prefer images of women making eye contact. To summarize, women will have the most chances of connection with an image showing them smiling, making direct eye contact with the camera and using flirty body language, while men will want to use an image with strong body language and a relaxed, nonaggressive expression.

In this situation you will not form a **new judgment**, instead sticking with your initial judgment that this is a perfect match, and hopefully the infatuation and great things you see, the positive experience of the mirroring and the limbic resonance, will carry you through for some time. As and when they wear off, you still have the evidence that as long as both you and your partner were pretty good at representing yourselves relatively accurately in the first place, the site managed to make a highly suitable match. As time passes, with any luck you will grow together, and the odds of the match working out well continue to be in your favor. There is still no early test of how long a relationship will last other than asking yourself if you are willing to put in the work along the way and if you feel you can trust another to do the same. Maybe predictive analytics and artificial intelligence will become 100 percent accurate in the future. But right now it is safe to say you should go with your instincts on this. The **test**? The only way to win is to keep on playing.

SCORE ONLINE ATTRACTION

Our colleague from the world of behavioral research and investigation, **VANESSA VAN EDWARDS**, does an amazing job with her team at ScienceofPeople.com in bringing new insights on body language to help people succeed. She gave us her unique perspective about how to improve "hotness" in profile pics.

In our human behavior research lab, we analyzed hundreds of profile pictures from HotorNot.com, looking for body language patterns. We wanted to know if nonverbal cues can affect someone's perceived "hotness score." Princeton University researcher Dr. Alexander Todorov found that different images of the same person can create drastically different first impressions—and attractiveness scores.

So how do you make your dating profile picture more attractive? Here are the top three patterns we found:

We prefer full frontal—the PG kind. The photos with the highest scores tended to show individuals who "fronted" with the camera. They angled their torso and head toward the camera. Don't look off into the distance or look back over your shoulder—just give the camera and your future viewer your full attention.

Don't block with props. There was one big attractiveness buzz-kill: sunglasses. When we can't see someone's eyes, we are less likely to trust them. Even if you are in the coolest sunny location, take off those glasses so people can really see you.

The best color is confidence. Nonverbal cues are also sent with our ornaments—clothes, jewelry and colors. What's the best color to wear in your profile picture? Confidence is the best color in your closet. We looked at colors in both male and female shots and found no significant difference between high- and low-ranking women and men. However, confident poses were markedly different for both high- and low-ranking women. Attractiveness is as much about attitude as appearance.

Being attractive is not just about looks; it's largely about how you carry yourself.

QUICK SCAN

S: Limbic resonance and the mirroring that accompanies it is powerful in this scenario and prompts you to make a knee-jerk, highly optimistic judgment that you need to **suspend** to take a more measured look.

C: Online dating sites provide a **context** where you can carefully engineer what you display about yourself to support how you would like to be seen by others.

A: Ask yourself what the most important signals are for you to send online and why you rank them in that way. Did you choose the right online dating site to suit your needs?

N: Stick with your first judgment to ride the wave of a new relationship. However, if you find yourself back in the online dating game any time soon, how can you create **new** images of yourself that best show what you wish to communicate online? How might this help others judge you as a good fit for them?

16

THEY ARE *SO* BREAKING UP!

You were watching your favorite celebrity couple
on the red carpet last night. They have always been
so perfect for each other, and in many ways you've
fantasized that your own relationships would model
theirs. But now you are tuned in to the gossip from
the event and some body language expert is talking about your fave couple, saying, "Those two are
so breaking up." But how would this person know
what they are thinking of doing? This just can't
be true. What are they seeing that you can't see?
The two of them look so perfect together, holding
hands and kissing in front of the paparazzi. But the
expert shows a freeze-frame of one of their

➡

faces close up and points to a snarl of contempt
that to the expert signals the end of their romance.
Is that true?

ONE OF THE BENEFITS of modern digital media is that we can freeze the frame and pick out a single moment from a variety of events and places, zoom in on it and let our opinions fly. This exemplifies the epitome of getting a thin slice of data and extrapolating an overgeneralized prediction from it. But what is this momentary key signal showing you, and is there really any value in using one-thirtieth of a second to make a decisive comment on the future of a relationship? Is the expert giving too much power to one picture? Whether you are discussing the fate of your role model celebrity relationship as in this scenario, or that of a friend, or your own relationship, it is in your best interests to **suspend judgment, be more descriptive,** and critically think about what is really going on.

Let's look at this micro-expression of contempt in the wider context of the history of the science of micro-expressions. In their 1966 study, Haggard and Isaacs first outlined how they discovered micro-expressions, or "micromomentary" expressions while "scanning motion picture films of psychotherapy hours, searching for indications of non-verbal communication between therapist and patient."[1] They recognized and described those moments where an underlying emotion slips out in an almost imperceptibly quick facial expression.

Further to this in a series of studies, Paul Ekman's research found notable similarities between people from diverse Western and Eastern cultures in the way their emotional labels fit facial expressions.

Ekman was the first to document some universal expressions: anger, disgust, fear, happiness, sadness and surprise. Ekman and colleague Wallace Friesen later added contempt to the list of universal facial expressions.[2] The micro-expression for contempt is the action of the face pulling up a trace on just one side at the corner of the lip, with a slight dimple in the cheek.

Following from this, American psychologist John Gottman began video-recording living relationships, specifically looking at participants' facial expressions. Gottman was able to correlate these expressions with relationships that would last and those that would not. Malcolm Gladwell reports in his best-selling book *Blink* Gottman's theory that there are four major emotional reactions destructive to a marriage: defensiveness, which is described as a reaction toward a stimulus as if you were being attacked; stonewalling, which is when a person refuses to communicate or cooperate with another; criticism, which is the practice of judging the merits and faults of a person; and the worst of all, contempt, which is a general attitude that is a mixture of the primary emotions disgust and anger.[3]

BODY LANGUAGE MYTHBUSTER
Contempt Signals a Breakup
So there you have it. Contempt—an emotion people can express in the blink of an eye, signaled with an asymmetrical gesture where one side of the mouth rises in a kind of half-smile, is the strongest indicator that the relationship is doomed.

　　Well, hang on, though.

➡

It turns out that although Gottman saw the biggest correlation between contempt and a couple's not getting along, his study was a regression analysis. He took couples who had broken up and then looked at film of them in therapy and noticed there were feelings of contempt (i.e., a sense of not valuing the other). Given this, it would be generalization and even overstatement to create a causal, predictive analytic model that says if you see contempt, then there will always be a breakup. The look of contempt is not the cause but a symptom or response.

Furthermore, though many people enjoy the benefit of being able to recognize micro-expressions, usually through training, facial expression is only one aspect of body language; that is, the rest of the body and what it may be communicating is ignored.

And certainly it would be almost a blind gamble for anyone, even the experts, to predict an outcome from just a few frames of video. Like some gambling, though, if you do it enough you can increase your chance of being right, but also your chance of being wrong. When you win, you look great, especially for experts in the media, and when you lose, you hope nobody calls you out on television. However, if you lose in a real-life situation, the stakes are certainly higher for you.

In this celebrities scenario, let's also take **context** into account by looking at how the media can manipulate and use images for entertainment, and how some celebrities might use their relationships for marketing purposes.

The media and the celebrities they feature are part of, in some cases, an extremely strategic marketing community. The celebrities are selling something (a film, show merchandise, perfume), and the media use the power of the celebrities' notoriety to create content that attracts viewers to the space where the media are advertising for their own clients. In this respect, the media–celebrity relationship with you, the observer—or they might say "consumer"—is predicated on the process of selling something and cannot necessarily be viewed as a normality of most people's lives. What we see as "real life" for celebrities on the red carpet is often being somewhat curated in certain ways to create engagement and buy-in from audiences, perhaps a little like the way you might curate your own Facebook page or Instagram account, posting only what fits with the impression you want to give.

In *your* "real life," however—unless you and your friends are celebrities and heavily invested in the business of sponsorship tie-ins, sales, publicity contracts and so on—deciding that a couple is on the verge of a breakup based on a fleeting look of contempt would be quite a stretch. You would need to consider a host of other factors, what else could be going on—essentially, context. Real life does not necessarily imitate or reflect life on the red carpet, however much you may identify with your celebrity heroes.

So **what else** might you **ask** and look for that would help you predict a couple's impending breakup? Another body language sign showing that contempt is underlying the negative tone in a relationship is eye-rolling (which we also look at elsewhere in this book). This signal shows disapproval of the other and a rejection of understanding and empathy. Eye-rolling also fits into Gottman's model as it can be a symptom of defensiveness, part and parcel of stonewalling and a sign of criticism. Sticking with Gottman's model, the micro-expressions indicating disgust or anger and potential breakup that may be visible upon close freeze-framed inspection are anger—vertical lines between the brows, brows drawn together, tensed lower lid, tight and narrow lips, glaring eyes, dilated nostrils, jutting lower jaw (as we've noted previously, all three facial areas must be involved in the gesture)—and disgust, demonstrated by a wrinkled nose, downturned mouth and tense lower lip. These signs also display defensiveness, stonewalling, criticism and contempt, all of which create and feed into feelings and actions of disregard, dismissal and the denigration of others' concerns. Importantly, contempt raises your feeling of power and status above the person toward whom you are contemptuous, and holding these attitudes toward someone else leaves little room for empathy.

Empathy involves caring about the feelings of others, showing concern and nurturing relationship bonds. Empathy creates an equal leveling of status. Empathetic behaviors show up as open and positive, such as listening with open body language or gently mirroring the behavior of another, both of which are literally movements toward being in the same viewpoint or similar emotional or cognitive state as another.

It is tricky to get a baseline in our celebrity situation as to what any usual behavior might be. However, as we've done here, you may want to consider how you observe and judge similar personal situations. By witnessing a public display or an analysis of a display, you may be able to observe more critically your own real-life situation and potentially draw parallels, bringing up deep-seated doubts or, alternatively, putting your mind at rest by recognizing contrast.

Ultimately, it could be that the look of contempt may not be directed at the partner but could be for the media, the paparazzi or even the situation itself of needing to perform for them and of course you—the consumer—in an intimate moment. Hey, who's to say they are not breaking up with you, the consumer voyeur of the relationship? Maybe tomorrow you will find out they are leaving the media spotlight and not their celebrity partner.

So here's a possible **new judgment**: Maybe they *are* on course for *so* breaking up—with the pressure of the spotlight.

How can we **test** the media truth or lies around all this? Stay tuned.

QUICK SCAN

S: **Suspending** judgment on your initial instinctual reaction to news media can help you think critically about the images and story being shown to you. Be more descriptive of what you see to uncover what may be fact and what may be biased evaluation.

C: Many photographic images of body language lack enough **context** to truly evaluate the thoughts and feelings of the subjects. But with the right story around the image, a context can be implied that biases your reasoning and thinking about the subject.

A: When you **ask** what else may be going on in the wider context of news, entertainment and commerce, sometimes you can uncover other motives for presenting images to you with a specific narrative around them.

N: Some **new** judgments are impossible to test beyond staying tuned in to the stories that present the behavior to you and see how they unfold.

PART

THREE

FRIENDS AND FAMILY

I know when you are hiding something!

—Your mom

Whether we realize it or not, our friends and family have shaped who we are today. We are to a large extent the product of interactions with friends and family members, even those we may no longer be in touch with.

Our family and early friendships play a vital role in teaching us life skills throughout our key developmental changes, acting as a training ground for how we behave in all other relationships we build. They define our priorities when choosing new relationships, determining whether these relationships will nurture us or not. They provide a network for us to engage with others. Undoubtedly, some of our friends are "friends of friends" or "friends of the family," keeping us in a close tribe of like-minded people.

Though we may possess, enjoy and even cherish some strong bonds with our friends and family, there can be an equally powerful dark side to these relationships. The people who know us best often have the most power over us, and seem to have particular power over our emotional well-being: the power to lead us astray and into trouble, to abuse us at times and even to betray us, whether by design or unknowingly. At the same time they are most likely to stick with us through thick and thin, even when we might be the ones abusing our power over them.

We are powerful in a group with our friends and family, often more powerful than as individuals. Even though at times they can make us feel angry, sad, small, insignificant, powerless, isolated and lonely— whether by ganging up on us over a particular issue, or by posting images all over social media of the great time they are having at just the moment when we are at our lowest—friends and family are undeniably our life-support system. They are as important as the oxygen around us: They can behave in ways that breathe new life into our day, take our breath away with surprise or stifle the atmosphere in a room. Regardless of gender, identification and the bonds they keep outside of our relationship with them, they matter deeply because they know us so well, and we know them. They are more practiced than most at reading the positions we are in and understanding our responses and behaviors around them, most likely because essentially they are most like us. We share with our family elements of genetic makeup and history, and with our closest friends we share and witness some of our most formative and important life experiences. Friends and family often give us a reality check when we stray from the shared ideas, values and beliefs of this most important social group. So they'll call us out when they believe we are lying to ourselves as much as to the group.

It is no wonder we feel it is so easy to read our friends and family like a book when it comes to decoding their nonverbal behavior with us or with others outside our inner circle. And it is no wonder we find it so confusing when it turns out we read it all completely wrong. We need these connections. We are hardwired to depend on them for our very survival, and so the pressure we may unwittingly impose upon ourselves, or have imposed on us by others, also perhaps unwittingly, to keep these relationships intact can often result in our skewing interpretations of the signals we are getting from those closest to us, leaving us drowning in a sea of confusion.

Let's look at some characteristic body language and the assumptions we make during encounters within these relationships to uncover the truth and lies that affect how well we survive and thrive therein.

17

THICK AS THIEVES

It's a night out with your friends, and it appears to you that certain members of the group are secretly whispering to each other. They appear to be shielding their mouths with their hands as they pass comments out of the corners of their mouths. They are avoiding making eye contact with you around these moments. This happens repeatedly, and always among the same few friends. You catch the eye of one of them right after such an exchange and they quickly look down and away from you, their body shrinking back and in a little. Then you see your friends passing knowing looks to each other, maintaining prolonged eye contact, and

➡

then quickly glancing toward you. You try to catch them in the act, and a couple of times catch the eye of one of them in these moments. They respond with widening eyes, slight smirks and nervous giggles before loudly introducing new topics of conversation. What gives? Is it a conspiracy against you? You think with growing paranoia, *What's the big secret? Is it me? Nice friends I have, ganging up on me. They're thick as thieves!*

WHAT IS THE KEY SIGNAL that they are "thick as thieves" and conspiring against you, or at the very least keeping a secret from you? The behavior in this scene is classic blocking behavior. They don't want to show their mouths or their eyes: Their hands conceal the conversation, and they look away from you and down when you try to engage. These defensive body language signs are the clincher for you that they are using their combined powers to close you out of the conversation, and they seem united together against you with their secretive communication.

To start the **SCAN** process, let's first **suspend judgment** and **be more descriptive** of what is going on. You are with friends after all, and hopefully that implies you have mutual understanding, values and beliefs; that you like each other and have respect for each other, and place value on each other's society. That said, what often happens is that we default to negatives when something is unclear; that is, when we are faced with insufficient data, we tend to think the worst. And the body language of blocking, covering mouths, avoiding eye contact and looking away, and physically shrinking away, all in tandem with the nervous laughter and refreshing the conversational focus would seem intended to shut you out, to conceal data from you. With insufficient data you think the worst and feel actively excluded. Your assumption that they are as thick as thieves and keeping something hidden, potentially about you, could be right on the money.

Canting Crew

Why does a conspiracy feel so bad to us? The word *conspiratorial* comes from the idea of a group "breathing together." When our gang of friends seem to behave in a way that bonds them together and excludes us, it can feel very threatening. As if they are stealing away the air we breathe. Usage of the word *thick* to mean "closely allied with" dates from early nineteenth-century England, around the associations of thieves of that era who conversed with each other and plotted together using a conspiratorial and secretive language. Many who were seen as being on the fringes of society or involved in illegal acts in those times habitually used secret words and phrases to talk among themselves. East London's Cockney rhyming slang is a derivation of this, where words are replaced with other words that rhyme and then are reduced, resulting in a singsong or "canting" way of speaking. (Not to be confused with the nonverbal cant of the head when it is tilted to one side.) For example, "Can you adam the porkies from

➡

the pot?" can translate as "Father is lying to us. Unbelievable!" How can this be possible? Let's break it down: *Adam* refers to Adam and Eve, which rhymes with *believe*. *Porkies* is another word for pork pies, which rhymes with *lies*. *Pot* refers to pot and pan, which rhymes with *old man*, a sometimes colloquialism for father. More directly translated: "Can you believe the lies from Dad?"

Similarly, American gangs commonly use secret sign language, often known as "stacking" or "throwing up signs." These signals are an easy way for members of a group to silently identify themselves to each other, mark out their territory or represent their crew on another gang's turf. Using secret hand signals can help indicate who is in the group—or outside it. Whether the hand signals are new or traditional ones reappropriated, groups and gangs past and present use them to covertly communicate, often because they are operating on the margins of society, they hold extremist views and so are outside mainstream society, or they feel under threat by mainstream society and therefore require confidentiality.[1]

Powerful world leaders have also used hand gestures to solidify a brand experience around themselves and their politics; sometimes doing so has caught them up in conspiracy controversies

➡

about secrets or affiliations implied by such usage. For example, the hand gesture commonly taken in the United States to mean "A-OK"—the index finger and the thumb forming an O and the other three fingers held up and slightly fanned—was used with great frequency by Donald Trump during the early days of his presidency, and it became aligned with extremist viewpoints that Trump and his administration espoused. This A-OK symbol is classified by social scientists as an "emblem," meaning you can switch out the verbal "A-OK" for the hand gesture and be equally communicating the same thing, though it's important to note that this symbol (and others) has negative or obscene connotations in many cultures and countries outside North America.[2] Trump's use of it in the United States was widely seen as a shout-out to the American white supremacist community, who commandeered the emblem as a secret signal within the group. Trump's continued use of the gesture was also recognized, though less widely and mainly by conspiracy theorists, as his openly acknowledging membership of a secret society.[3]

While it may be that something is up that you are not part of, is it something good or something bad? Your friends are avoiding meeting your gaze, in fact diverting their eyes from you, which could cause you, on the receiving end of this behavior, to quickly jump to the conclusion that you are being lied to. Additionally, and as you've seen in earlier chapters, blocking signals—here the shielding of the eyes or mouth, avoiding eye contact—could lead us to the assumption that someone is lying to us. However, while these actions may well result in someone or something environmental or psychological getting shut out, contrary to popular folklore, the truth is they do not necessarily go hand in hand with lies and deceit. And even if you detect an additional handful of other gestures associated with lying, like shifty eyes, blinking or (alternatively) a fixed stare, shuffling feet, breathlessness and sweating, you still need to carefully weigh the nonverbal against the verbal when attempting to determine if you are being lied to. And in the heat of the moment, how right will you be? You have roughly a fifty-fifty chance of being right that deceit is at play. So now what?

We need to be most descriptive here specifically of the **context**. You are out with your group of friends, and suddenly you are made to feel excluded by a subgroup of the party. There are more of them than you, and they know something you don't. You are not only outnumbered and excluded but also suddenly feeling less intelligent than the others, all of which will seriously erode your feeling of social power within the group. While you would normally feel comfortable among your trusted friends, it is easy in this situation to feel vulnerable and uncomfortably paranoid about whether they are for you or against you.

So while your assumption about your friends' concealment of something looks to be correct given the blocking gestures you see, your lack of knowledge about what they are concealing, plus your perceived shift in social power, equals catastrophization in your mind. Your thoughts can run away from you, increasingly demonizing the culprits—they now seem like thieves.

In such a moment, stop and take stock of your day. **Ask what else** could be going on for you personally? What biases, insecurities or negative feelings might be running through your mind already that could be swaying your judgment toward the negative? Also, what else could be happening with your friends? Sit back for a moment and think about whether you know anything about the whisperers that may be causing them to behave in that way. Did they come from another event together? Are they going on to another engagement? Do they work together? Are there other points of connection they have that don't involve you that could be the subject of their whisperings? Alternatively, are there any major group events coming up that include all of you, such as a birthday, or a work event that they wouldn't necessarily share the details of with you? It is worth investing a few seconds: you may remember or realize some mitigating circumstance that helps form a **new judgment** and put your mind at rest.

But if this doesn't happen and you really feel no wiser as the moments pass, how can you **test** your assumption that you are negatively implicated in some way, that they're hiding something from you, that they are talking about you and it is bad for you? The decision you make about how to act here will likely be shaped by the power of the social group and your perception of how you fit in. Are you all of a similar status in the group? Are these really great friends, or are some of them acquaintances, friends of your friends? Are you all on equal footing? Whatever the case, you will need to assert yourself if you are to find out what's up, what's the secret, or you'll have a miserable and paranoid night. This can be done by asking them what is going on. However, this may come across as suspicion, aggression, accusation and insecurity. Better yet, harness your negative thoughts; in other words, continue to suspend judgment while you lightly and politely ask what you are missing out on.

Your friends may tell you the answer, or say they'll tell you later, which could mean the subject matter is sensitive in some way, or they are looking at you and concealing information at the same time because they need to share it with you, but perhaps not at that noisy venue. Of course, the other outcome is that you get no answer from them, that they carry on with the shared behavior. You get no joy out of prying, and you end the evening wondering why you are hanging out with this crowd in the first place. At least you know how you can feel in their presence, and how they can and will use their power over you. You can continue to try to get to the bottom of their behavior, but perhaps with just one of them while the two of you are on your own, taking away the social power of the gang against you. Alternatively, you can decide to "suck it up" or ignore it. Or you can find new friends.

BODY LANGUAGE MYTHBUSTER
You Can Spot a Criminal by Their Face

At one time, people believed you could tell a criminal just by looking at their face. Fortunately, this destructive myth is much less popular today than it was during the nineteenth and earlier twentieth centuries, when it was rooted in criminal anthropology, which is the combined study of the human species and the study of criminals. This represented the beginnings of offender profiling and was based on perceived links between the nature of a crime and the personality of the offender, deemed at that time as being detectable through physical appearance.

In the late 1800s, Italian criminologist Cesare Lombroso put forward the idea that criminals were born with inferior physiological differences. His theory

➡

was that crime was located completely within the individual and utterly divorced from the surrounding social conditions and structures. Lombroso and his followers performed autopsies on criminals and declared they had discovered similarities between the physiologies of the bodies and those of other primates.

Lombroso outlined fourteen physiognomic characteristics that he and his followers believed to be common to all criminals. We won't waste the ink on listing these, as they represent the hateful stereotyping, misogyny, bigotry and racism inherent in his work and of the time. Certainly his ideas gained popularity in support of dangerous and extremist ideas such as eugenics and genocide. Their proponents recognized what they saw as genetic flaws to justify sterilization and death. Unfortunately, even today some follow the tenets of Lombroso's theory.

During Lombroso's life, British scientist Charles Buckman Goring was also working in the same area. He concluded that there were no noticeable physiological differences between law-abiding people and those who committed crimes. Maurice Parmelee, seen as the founder of modern criminology in America, also rejected the theory of anthropological criminology, in 1911, which led to its eventual withdrawal from the field of accepted criminology research.

QUICK SCAN

S: When there is insufficient data to make a judgment, your primitive brain will default to a negative one. When you are unsure, **suspending** judgment on your initial negative instinctual reactions can therefore be very powerful in developing a more positive truth.

C: The social **context** in this scenario is your group of trusted friends. Their unexpected behavior that seems conspiratorial against you erodes your feeling of social power within the group.

A: When you **ask** what other events are happening or what relationships you may not directly be a part of, you may uncover more information that helps you form a less negatively biased idea of the feelings and intentions of others.

N: If you have not learned or recalled a reason for their blocking behavior, something to put your mind at rest that you are not negatively implicated in some way, and so have not formed a **new** judgment, the decision you make about how to act may change how you fit into this group going forward.

18

MY NEW BFF?

You are out on your own at a social event in a new community of people you would really like to fit into. While there, you meet someone and cannot believe how much you click. In a purely platonic way, you just know you like them very much, and you quickly discover that you share the same interests and musical tastes, and you even dress a bit the same. You agree on everything. You can't help noticing that you are mirroring each other's actions: You smile at the same time, seem to spontaneously laugh when they laugh, drink when they drink. It's like there is some immediate telepathy going on. You realize they have a big personality, and you

➡

notice because others are looking over at them so much that they seem popular and like a leader in this social circle. They are very charismatic and confident. You feel so lucky that you may have just found your new BFF.

IT IS AN AMAZING and powerful feeling to meet someone with whom you have a clear and obvious resonance, like looking in a mirror and seeing a really great version of yourself. However, how can you tell whether this will be a bona fide relationship or a flash in the pan? Because if it's the latter, what consequences do you risk by overtrusting and oversharing your deepest secrets? It is definitely in your best interests to **suspend judgment** and **be more descriptive** of what is going on as a start to your **SCAN** of this situation.

We look at the concept of mirroring often in this book, as it plays heavily when considering body language. In romantic relationships, mirroring can mark the early stages of infatuation and can be a telltale sign that we are in tune with each other and are mutually engaged. Similarly, when we hit it off with someone platonically, mirroring them—reflecting the other's postures, gestures, sitting positions, tone of voice, talking pace—helps to quickly build trust, connection and intimacy and lets you feel more at ease, comfortable and understood. So in our story, the fact that you and the other person mirror each other shows a desire from both parties to relate, get along and share, all of which uphold your initial assumption that this person will have BFF status.

Also, you may find it a plus that this new friend seems popular.

Others at the event are clearly looking over at them, targeting them in some way with a value or power of some sort. You've seen elsewhere in this book how the leaders in a social group are more often looked at by others in the group, and looked to for behavioral cues. And if they are looking to your new friend as a revered member of the group, chances are you will have lots in common with others in this new community and build more friendships. So far, so good.

INSTANT FRIENDSHIP

TONYA REIMAN is a well-known media personality in the world of body language. She has authored three books: *The Power of Body Language*, *The Body Language of Dating* and *The Yes Factor*. We asked her what key signals she has noticed that indictate people are saying a big yes to being friends.

"As soon as I saw you, I knew an adventure was going to happen," said Winnie the Pooh to his best friend, Piglet.

What do we see in others that allows us to instantly recognize a friendship? Once we have laid eyes on an individual, millions of neurons in our brains are activated to determine if a person possesses the traits we feel are important, such as likability, trust and competence. We compute all the experiences we have had and instantly form an opinion. We label them with an intensely powerful yes or no response, and this entire process begins and ends within one-tenth of a second—in other words, before we have even exchanged a single word with them.

So much of this deduction is determined through nonverbal communication. Here are some of the signals that trigger a positive response:

1. Open and inviting body language, including your posture, expressions and gestures. For instance, holding eye contact with an exposed torso (no folded arms or barriers), and orienting toward the person and smiling indicate you are confident and interested in meeting new people.
2. Getting close to an individual shows you care. Repositioning yourself when you've moved in too close shows you are paying attention to their needs as well.
3. Human odor is a chemosignal we transmit to others unconsiously. Smell is so powerful that people can detect at least one trillion distinct odors, and in doing so quite often mirror the emotion conveyed by the scent.
4. Nodding for encouragement, acceptance or agreement demonstrates that what they have to say is valued or significant to you. One of the most important aspects of communication is fully listening (most people will half listen while mentally preparing their response). If you can make a person feel like they are the *only* one in a room full of others, you can make a friend for life.

People like people who are similar to themselves, as we become influenced by their emotional feedback. The rapport that often comes naturally occurs because of shared commonalities. By being sincere and transparent, you'll bring out the best in everyone you meet and your likability will soar.

However, before you jump right in and invite them over for a BBQ or to watch the game, or even "friend" them on social media, letting them into your world, it is worth taking a critical look at the information you have within the **context** of this situation. And the catch here is that in this new community of people, you cannot help but be less intelligent than everybody else in the room about the behavioral norms and relationships that inform that social context. Essential to remember here is that first impressions are not always accurate and do not tell you the whole story.

You find this potential new BFF to be charismatic and magnetic. Charisma, that compelling, focused and charming quality some people possess that inspires and engages others, can be displayed nonverbally by the Duchenne (genuine) smile, positive eye contact and straight-on torso positioning. Those who appear charismatic can show these signals in a prolonged and consistent manner. These can feel like strong leadership signals, and as mentioned, people tend to follow people who give off the strongest and clearest signals in an environment. And when people display charisma, we think there is a congruence between this display and who they truly are. If someone is bent on deceiving you, though, they may be able to purposely conjure any number of nonverbal signals and combinations of behavior to convey charisma and appear authentic. It is in your best interest to learn more about them before you play follow the leader.

BODY LANGUAGE MYTHBUSTER
Charisma—You Have It or You Don't
Many think those with an irresistible magnetism were born with it. Either you have it or you don't. However, many studies, including one from the University of

➡

Tennessee at Knoxville, found that anyone can display this kind of magnetism. If you want people to perceive you as charismatic, you need to display attributes such as empathy, good listening skills, eye contact, enthusiasm, self-confidence and skillful speaking, all of which are behaviors that can be learned.[1] So although some people may seem to be naturally charismatic, others can learn to be. It is also likely that the naturally charismatic have simply learned the behaviors too. But it just looks natural to you.

What else can you consider and **ask**? Let's look at why others in the room are looking at this person. Not being familiar with the group, it may be impossible for you to assess whether they are looking at your potential BFF in admiration or in worry for you.

Are the others looking over with a sense of pleasure? Are they looking over with a sense of fear? Fear is shown by a subtle facial gesture that includes raised and knitted eyebrows; open eyes; lips tightening with the sides of the mouth widening; and the jaw dropping (mouth opening) slightly.

Why might they be fearful? Well, charisma is a trait seen in some people who can turn out to be really quite dangerous for you, your family and your friends to be around. Other behavioral indicators that they could have a dangerous personality include talking faster than is normal for most others in the environment, agitation, irritability and overconfidence. They don't sleep much, and they might also engage in impulsive, high-risk behaviors such as reckless driving, gambling, excessive spending and high-risk sex.[2]

If you are with someone who is risky, you may get sucked into their high-risk lifestyle. You might be dragged into their problems and find yourself being used or sharing in their debt. They may be looking for an accomplice, enabler or facilitator.

Furthermore, as you are new to this community, you will be eager to find friends, like-minded people and similarities, and you may even be mirroring behaviors that are not usual to you in order to fit in quickly. Anyone who roughly fits the criteria of being a friend for you might get put into BFF category.

Without experiencing the behavior of your potential BFF over time, it is difficult to move forward safely, although your first assumption may still be correct. You can more clearly identify possible risk or the potential for friendship bliss by not leaping in, instead holding back to learn more about this person. Ask others about them. Get an endorsement, a few more opinions of the person. And use the **test** of time. You haven't seen their behavior over time to know if they can truly be trusted or not. You can't compress time to make a judgment, so you need to hold off. The upside of somebody being charismatic is that they can be great fun to be around; the downside is that they can be dangerous. So get more data before you leap into anything with your new friend.

QUICK SCAN

S: What do you see in others that allows you to instantly recognize a potential friendship? How easy is it for you to **suspend** judgment and not jump right in when you feel the friendliness of these very specific signals?

C: In the **context** of the folklore "first impressions are never wrong," no one would ever need to read a book like this or train in body language analysis. To what extent do you think the saying is accurate?

A: Ask yourself what behaviors you think are high risk for you but perhaps not for others. What behaviors do you feel to be low risk that others may judge as high on the risk scale?

N: New friends can take time to be trusted. Old friends have stood the test of time. When new friends behave like old friends, we can be triggered into fully trusting them too early on to say for sure that they are trustworthy. This is a good example of "best-fit thinking," where we make something that behaves *a little* like a thing *exactly* that thing.

19

FOMO

After a little break from social media, you are back at
it and comforted that you actually haven't missed that
much. As usual, your friends have been posting party
pictures, travel pictures and loads of selfies online, but
you notice that some of them, as well as others in their
pictures, are posing with a crazy expression, a new
face pose. It seems to be *a thing*, and everybody knows
about it and is doing it. Whatever the case, it's surely a
passing fad, but it does leave you feeling strangely paranoid and uneasy that you are falling behind the times,
old, out of touch and ignorant; in short, this strange new
trend that all your friends seem to know about is giving
you a case of FOMO—fear of missing out!

SOMETIMES TRENDS IN online body language can make us feel like dinosaurs no matter what our age. In trying to keep up with trends on social media and feeling included online, it's easy for us to sometimes end up feeling out of it, excluded and blindsided. Is that the intention of groups or the people who post on social media? And is it true? Let's **SCAN** this situation, **suspend judgment** and **be more descriptive** of what is going on by taking a look at the powerful trends in online social media body language.

How we show up online will vary depending on the platform. The body language we choose to adopt in our profile pictures sends key signals, whether we are posting on dating sites, other social media or professionally on sites such as LinkedIn. Of course, we may choose to represent ourselves differently depending on the platform. We wouldn't necessarily use the same profile picture for finding a mate on a dating site as we would for displaying ourselves to our friends around the world or for potential employers or clients to see. It's not that we lie or don't give the whole truth about ourselves. Rather, we curate the experience others have of us. The way we stand, what we do with our facial expression and our hands, how much of our bodies we capture in the photo, how we dress and what else we include in the picture will likely vary greatly depending on the context, on how we want to represent ourselves, and with whom and what power we want to align ourselves. There will also be a different feel to a photo that someone else took of us than to one we took ourselves—a selfie.

Let's take a look at the body language we display in selfies, those self-portrait snapshots of life's special moments, often mixed with other iconic elements, that many people post to social networking sites. Selfies give away loads of key signals and information about who we think we are, what we like, what power we have or wish to be aligned with and, particularly if we are careful about it, how we would choose for the world to see us. This body language says something about us at the moment it happened, even in the moments or days before we posted it, and will continue showing something about us, likely with meaning shifting as time passes, for as long as the photo is out there, potentially for years to come. There are all kinds of body language trends on these platforms that we can align ourselves with.

How new is this phenomenon of constructing and controlling our own image? Way before the Kardashians/Jenners set the selfie world on fire, many powerful and famous leaders of history had already paved the way in strategic artistic self-representation, having portraits painted of themselves displaying specific body language that would show off their status and power and drive their propaganda machines. Napoleon is an example of a historic leader, considered one of the greatest military leaders of all time, who used painted portraits of himself in much the same way that celebrities in modern times use selfies. Napoleon was painted time and again as a victorious general as well as a man of culture and intellect.[1] He was also painted perhaps most famously with his hand stuck into the front of his waistcoat. There have been many theories over the years about why his hand is tucked in in such a manner. Was he trying to ease a stomach ulcer, or did he have itchy skin? Not at all. This body language does not tell the story of any underlying physical or psychological condition; rather, Napoleon was choosing to be represented as aristocratic, even though he was born into a lower rank of nobility.

In Napoleon's era, you could boast that you were an important gentleman born into a wealthy family by sticking one hand into the front of your coat. Napoleon as a leader was at the forefront of changing ideas around who was considered nobility. During his reign he changed the system so that he could decide who would become nobility and then awarded certain people with titles, so that being born into an aristocratic family was not the only way to achieve a high social rank. The body language we see in these portraits shows us he was very aware of the power of the image, and he actively controlled how he would be identified by his peers. The hand-in-the-waistcoat pose in portraits was not new but a trend of the time. Napoleon simply and cleverly used it to his advantage to suit his ideology and show his alignment to a certain social rank, to redefine that part of society and show off his power. Certainly, his process of image making proved essential to his ongoing political successes and to winning over leading intellectuals and political thinkers in France.[2]

Painted portraits in the time before photos and smartphones were a sure way to show off power and influence for leaders of empires. The portraiture of Queen Elizabeth I of England (1533–1603) is another great example of someone who had images constructed with her as subject that would show off her royalty and power, as well as the strength and aspirations of the state by presenting objects in these portraits that would have carried symbolic meaning to her subjects of the day.

While monarchs and their court advisors would commission artists to paint portraits showing off the power of the monarchy, artists themselves throughout history have created self-portraits that give a more intimate perspective of the individual. Artist self-portraits give unique insight into the painter's state of mind, as in the introspective self-portraits by Dutch painter Vincent Van Gogh (1853–1890), which have been interpreted time and again as showing his deteriorating state of mind. Self-portraits have also been awarded mystical and supernatural properties, as with the red chalk portrait of Leonardo da Vinci (1452–1519). Italian popular lore tells us that the gaze of Leonardo in this portrait has such intensity that the viewer will become stronger for looking at it, and that due to these "supernatural" powers, this self-portrait was especially protected during World War II to keep it out of the Nazis' grasp.[3]

Nowadays, of course, regardless for the most part of our artistic abilities or even our state of finance, most of us can create the desired look we want in our portraits with the touch of a finger on our handheld devices and broadcast them to the world immediately. As with our examples of historical portraits and self-portraits, the selfie can broadcast details about ourselves of our choosing, give intimate insights into who we are and what we believe, and show what power we hold or would like to hold.

Instagram stars, fashion bloggers and stylegrammers set today's trends in selfie body language and how we use it to show off our power within and to the social groups we fit into or want to fit into. These social media stars have large online followings, and fans emulate their popular poses. What are these poses based on? The body language and looks adopted by the likes of the Kardashians/Jenners and many other popular online style icons, similar to the hand in the waistcoat shown off by Napoleon, do not necessarily tell any secret story at all about their physical or psychological condition. Much of this body language originated on the red carpet and so is associated with celebrity, glamour, wealth and power. Some poses originate from other countries or cultures and are then often controversially recycled in pursuit of more social territory and power.

Let's look at some commonly used body language on social media, largely from North America.

"Skinny arm," or "teapot," is a historically popular female-celebrity red-carpet pose to look skinnier, to show off a dress or to appear more shapely for the camera. In this pose, your hand is on your hip with your elbow pointed away from the body at a 45-degree angle. In the "sugar bowl," you have both hands on hips in a similar pose. In the "crossed ankle," you stand with one leg crossed in front of the other, for a sleek silhouette in your dress.[4] Migrating from fashion magazine to social media via fashion bloggers with big followings, these poses become common practice among the demographic of online followers who copy them in their own photos and selfies, culminating in exponentially higher circulation. These trends show the democratization of the tricks of the trade of celebrity. By feeling closer and more aligned in a very immediate way (by way of copying the body language), we are showing our preference to belong to that perceived "higher" social status or social rank and tribe.

Adopting trendy facial poses is part and parcel of this same aspiration to belong to the celebrity's tribe. Here are just a few of the constructed facial poses in circulation online today:

- **Fingermouthing:** posing with a finger or two around the mouth area, drawing more focus toward the mouth
- **Duck face:** sultry eyes and pursed lips
- **Fish gape:** open-mouthed and slightly toothy high-fashion-magazine-like pose
- **Kissy face:** puckering up the lips and tilting the head up
- **Brow-too-strong face:** an asymmetrical look lifting just one brow, tilting the head and pouting the lips slightly
- **Model pout:** a less exaggerated version of duck face
- **Smize:** closed-mouth almost smile, with lots of expression in the eyes
- **Squinch:** squinting the eyes slightly as if looking into the sun
- **Sparrow face:** opening the eyes as far as possible and slightly puckering the lips, like a bird about to be fed[5]

Online body language poses quickly become easily recognizable and are often used to strike a chord with the celebrity blogger's community of followers. The person posting the selfie may hope to be recognized and noted as being part of that tribe. But if we are not in the tribe or familiar with it, then what? We can find ourselves looking at these poses with confusion, bewilderment and often dislike. We are wired, after all, to default to the negative when we have too little information, so we tend to dislike what we don't understand. So how we are personally affected by the latest trends in online body language largely depends on who we are and what social groups we are in or want to be a part of; in other words, we are just as tribal from a social media perspective as we are in our off-line life.

Also, we are exposed in an instant to so many more cultures and norms on social media than we are off-line, giving us much more information to either process or ignore. We have the potential not only to extend our own realm of influence but also to put ourselves within range for being influenced by so many more people. Anybody who has loads of admiring followers on social media by definition wields loads of power, and like Ben Parker, better known as Spider-Man's Uncle Ben, reminds us, "with great power comes great responsibility." Look at Napoleon: He used a pose normally reserved for a social group other than his own to his advantage, to show his power and influence, and at the same time it was for him and others by and large aspirational; he wanted to stake his claim within that strata of society, and by so doing pushed his influence and showed his power.

Could the same be said of the Kardashian/Jenner sisters' posting pictures of themselves with cornrows and box braids in 2016? The pictures sent shockwaves across social media, and the sisters were widely criticized for cultural appropriation. They attempted to rebrand hairstyles already commonly and predominantly worn by black women, renaming the hairstyles with personalized names, as though they had invented these looks. As one journalist from *Teen Vogue* so aptly stated, trying to "rebrand these historically African American hair looks with cutesy new names in the hopes that others emulate the look is just not cool."[6]

Looking at our scenario, given the **context** that you haven't been on social media in a while, why had you dropped out for a bit? Is it possible you had not been feeling such a part of the group? If that is the case, is it any wonder you don't recognize some of the body language and you feel more out of it? Check in with yourself and decide if this is really your gang anymore. Maybe you feel more drawn toward another group. Changing tribes is painful. Some people never change social groups, but there are many who do.

We can also consider context from the point of view in which the subject is situated in a selfie (increasingly intimate environments) and with whom or what; where the selfie is distributed and how different hashtags cause the selfie to be more widely distributed outside the subject's normal channels; the difference between what we show of our personal selves and the public persona that we have constructed for wider distribution; and how we are increasingly compelled to take and post selfies strategically to be present, part of the conversation and more influential in the online and off-line world.

We can create a feeling of intimacy in a selfie by taking the picture in private locations where we are not normally seen, such as bedrooms, bathrooms and closets. If a celebrity shows themselves backstage or in their dressing room, they create the same intimate connection with the viewer.

If we want to show off an intimate connection with power, we have to show ourselves being somewhat intimate with that person or thing, such as a selfie of kissing the president or kissing a championship trophy. Of course, sports fans posting selfies in which they are kissing the Stanley Cup, the FIFA World Cup Trophy or the Vince Lombardi Trophy, with the winning team surrounding them and cheering them on, also demonstrate close proximity with powerful tribe members or icons. Selfies like this show off unusual access to and familiarity with a normally inaccessible yet highly desirable object, group or person of power.

Similarly, we can align ourselves with a powerful environment to show our relationship to power when we take selfies next to natural wonders: at base camp about to scale Mount Everest, in the mist under Niagara Falls, above the Grand Canyon or atop Mount Fuji. We also do this when we take selfies beside monumental structures: in front of the Taj Mahal, the Sydney Opera House, the Great Pyramid of Giza or the Great Wall of China. Of course, what exactly we communicate to our tribe about our attitude toward our selfie setting will alter from person to person. We can show whether we hold that place in high regard or even that we feel we have somehow gained power over it. For example, we might have championed our way to the top of Everest. Or we may show how we were victimized by the setting, or perhaps that we are champions over the setting by showing an attitude of being aloof, nonplussed or irreverent toward it.

We can also show off our alignment with values or causes we believe in by posting selfies linking us to epic social or protest events (e.g., showing yourself carrying a sign at one of the many historic global Women's Marches protesting the election of Donald Trump or the protests of the Muslim ban under the reign of that same president).[7] Changing the filter on our profile picture may show our support for people or causes; many across the world did just that when they sported the red, blue and white of the French flag to show solidarity with France after the Paris attacks of 2016,[8] or similarly for the attacks on Beirut or Baghdad the same year. In this way, we can display to our social groups what we hold important, our values, rituals and beliefs, by connecting ourselves to events through a selfie or our existing profile picture.

Ask what else you can consider: As we have discussed, online body language is largely constructed in that you generally pose for your selfies or your portrait pictures and so can put some thought into how you look. Here is an overview of camera angles, how they affect your online body language and what it tells others about you:

- **Camera at eye level** with the close-up selfie gives the effect of a parity of height, and so gives the viewer a parity of status in that they are at eye level with you.
- **Camera angle from above** makes your face look larger than the rest of your body, particularly your eyes, which can be helpful if you want to create a more personal or intimate connection with the viewer. Also the mouth will appear closer, again feeling more intimate for the viewer. The body will look smaller at this angle, which can be an incentive for some people who want to make their bodies appear smaller. This angle will ultimately cause the viewer to feel a size or height advantage, causing you to look more submissive as your eyes are looking up, making you look easier to dominate; therefore, you are enabling the viewer to feel potentially more powerful in relation to you.
- **Camera angle from below** the face not only causes the viewer to feel smaller or lower than you, it also displays more vulnerable areas on your body (e.g., the throat/jugular), which can have the effect of making you look arrogant. Taking a photo from this angle can make you come across as dominant, superior or, again, arrogant if it appears you are looking down your nose at the viewer.

One **new judgment** is that it's easy to see just how complex the social media landscape can be to judge and navigate. Its capacity for content means for sure you will always be missing out on something somewhere, so the initial assumption that you are missing out is highly likely but often unavoidable. Here's the important **test**: Is what you are taking part in online giving you what you need? And if not, do you need to take a more active role within it, or to look elsewhere? If you have no intention of changing social groups and want to get ahead of the game, you can try posting a picture that fits in better with the latest trends you observe, doing some research on Urban Dictionary to get ahead of the trends, following the same celebrities your social group does or starting your own trend.

BODY LANGUAGE MYTHBUSTER
The Body Never Lies

We know that nonverbal communication is a response to external environments and also to what we are experiencing internally, how we are feeling and what we are thinking, and so most people at times leak nonverbal cues about how these environments are affecting them. Because people give off these signs about what they are thinking and feeling, and because nonverbal communication often operates at a low level of cognitive awareness, or even subconsciously, people often assume it is more trustworthy and should be believed above other factors. It is easy for people to move from this idea to the theory that we are unable to hide our true feelings. Sometimes this is the case, but nonverbal behavior can also be highly conscious and strategic. How often have you faked laughter, feigned interest, cried crocodile tears or pretended to be angry? Have you been successful at it? Anyone can be deceptive. Of course the body lies, and it does so regularly.

QUICK SCAN

S: You should **suspend** judgment of your instinctual reactions to online behavior. The online world moves exponentially faster than you can, and you often need to create the time and space to consider what you see and how it makes you feel against a wider online backdrop.

C: It is often safe to view online selfie body language within the **context** that it is largely consciously constructed, and the context will shift with online distribution and time.

A: When analyzing another's selfie, **ask** yourself if they have placed themselves alongside icons that project power onto them, as this can powerfully affect your judgments of them as a person and what you think they think.

N: Your **new** judgment may confirm that you will likely miss out in the online world, but you can choose how you can best participate to feel empowered.

20

CONTROL FREAK

Things have been extremely busy for you lately.
It feels as if you have a never-ending number of
work commitments. You're always overbooked,
without enough hours in the day. It's go go go,
e-mails coming and going thick and fast, the phone
ringing nonstop. You know you've been burning
the candle at both ends trying to keep up, and the
commitments and demands just seem to multiply.
You haven't had much sleep or downtime, and you
know you are getting run down, perhaps even a little depressed. Your family is also making demands
on you, and even though you've bumped their calls
and ignored their texts for a few days, your parent

➡

and a sibling show up at your door with groceries in hand. You let them in, explaining that you are extremely busy and have no time to make food at the moment. Rather than understand and give you space, they take a hands-on approach, physically leading you to a chair and forcing you to sit down so they can give you their best advice, which you really don't have time to listen to. You feel pushed around, small, like a little kid. You think, *My family are a bunch of control freaks! They all want to push me around.*

THOUGH WE LOVE THEM, families are annoying at times. They think they know what's best for us, and often they don't hold back in pushing us around and voicing their opinions about how we should run our lives. Even when we are all grown up, they can make us feel like we are little kids, chipping away at our power. Though this behavior may be annoying, let's take a moment to **suspend judgment** and **be more descriptive** of what is going on.

What are the key signals that your family members are trying to control you? In this scenario they push you down, physically make you stay put. This firm, full-contact touching body language certainly may reveal their desire or default mode to control, manipulate and push you around.

BODY LANGUAGE MYTHBUSTER
Nonverbal Is What We See and Hear

When observing body language, though the cues we pick up on visually are of course very important, let's not underestimate haptic cues: those physical cues produced by touch. Our skin, the largest organ of the body, is also a nonverbal sensor. It's loaded with nerves sensitive to pressure, temperature and pain. We receive an endless stream of information about our environment from our skin. Plenty of studies show the beneficial effects of touch to our emotional and physical well-being.

Recent studies also show how touch can often accurately communicate the emotion that motivated the touch, both to the person receiving the touch and to onlookers observing the touch. In other words, we have the ability to decode the emotion informing the touch to a much higher accuracy level than just by chance. The distinct emotions we can accurately identify by touch are anger, fear, disgust, love, gratitude and sympathy, as well as happiness and sadness.[1]

So our skin is a largely underestimated communication tool and certainly a huge part of nonverbal communication. Perhaps that is why the haptic buzz of our mobile phone against us can be so comforting, signaling that our friends and family are reaching out to us with a message on our social media platforms, or so annoying if it's our manager literally shaking us via a vibrating text to remind us to show up with that report.

Our key signal here of touch, an ownership signal, is an integral part of body language. How we use touch indicates the level of connection, preexisting or not, that we have with others. Who initiates touching and how they touch can display to those being touched, as well as to onlookers, who holds the power in the relationship. If we witness someone pushing another down, we may assume the pusher is high status, a bully even, showing off their power and dominance over someone weaker than themselves.

Continuing with our family scenario, another key signal is the gift of food, which may well cost you more time in having to put it away or prepare it, or it may even stress you out when it goes bad in the fridge. Food and sharing meals together, while often a happy and integral part of harmonious familial traditions, and of religious and cultural rituals, often show who has the power and control in a family or community: who goes to work to earn money to buy the food, how much food is obtainable, who has to prepare the food (division of labor). Sometimes we have to eat food we don't like, or have to eat at times we don't want to, or get too much or not enough. Most religions involve fasting at certain times of year. So while your family could be bringing you the food as a gift, the food may also represent your family's leveraging of their power, finding a convenient way to assert their possession of you and control your life.

Power Shake, Anyone?

We can read for days about the handshakes of world leaders past and present, specifically about what leaders communicate to the public in the way they shake hands, how the handshake may be accompanied by back patting or shoulder or elbow grasping, and whether they give the upper hand or take that power handshake position for themselves to take control of others.

Donald Trump's handshakes in the first 100 days of his presidency, as well as being a hot topic of media discussion, showed his very hands-on approach to leadership when meeting with Trump-friendly foreign leaders and political allies, and a hands-off approach when it came to anyone who had apparently earned disdain or impinged on his sense of power.

With his friends and allies, Trump is famous for giving a double-handed clasp handshake and yanking the other person in close, pulling them off balance. This maneuver would not only bring them closer into his territory and personal space but also destabilize them, giving the visual impression of Trump as more powerful and in charge. To what extent this is intentional is hard to say. If intentional, it certainly suggests a Machiavellian approach to allies in that they should be brought in close but kept on their toes.

➡

How did those on the receiving end of this characteristic nonverbal display of power counter this move to maintain and assert visually and publicly their own power? The historic second U.S. election debate with democratic opponent Hillary Clinton in 2016 started with no handshake at all between the opponents, reflecting the animosity between the two and signaling both candidates' attempts to hold on to power. Still, it ends with Trump giving Clinton a quick-grab handshake: He takes her hand and gives it a slight yank in toward himself, then firmly grasps her elbow, perhaps an effort to make her appear to falter. Clinton may have prepared for this type of maneuver and allows only her arm to extend flexibly while staying firmly rooted to the ground, avoiding being pulled off balance, thereby also avoiding any public perception of instability triggered by such a handshake.

Similarly, Canadian prime minister Justin Trudeau appeared to have prepared for the important handshake at his very first televised meeting with President Trump. We see Trudeau emerging from his vehicle and approaching Trump at a brisk pace, with a locked-out straight arm, making it untenable for Trump to pull Trudeau into control, and instead causing Trump to yield and simply hold his own ground. Trump then tries to strong-arm

➡️

Trudeau with an elbow hold, which Trudeau counters with a long, firm shoulder pat, thus taking control of more of Trump's arm, suppressing Trump's ability to visually demonstrate any dominance over him and allowing Trudeau to appear to maintain his ground—and his power.

Let's take the all-important **context** into account to get closer to making a correct interpretation of the body language. If we were to randomly see someone push somebody down, without knowing the context, we would not know if the pusher, the perceived bully, had been repeatedly victimized by the person they pushed, and whether their push was perhaps a misguided effort to take some power back from the habitual offender and stand up for themselves. And while an eye for an eye makes the whole world blind, what is important here is to acknowledge that every moment we witness is the moment *after* something else, and the moment *before* something else—and the more we can understand the backdrop for the actions we see, the more we can make better choices about how to act and work toward resolutions of conflict in positive ways.

The context in our family scenario is that you are busy, tired and overworked. This is the new normal for many in an industrialized and hyperconnected world. With the technology to respond to anybody in an instant at our fingertips, others expect that we will do so, and if we don't, they equally expect that we will miss an opportunity. As a result, we can live under excessive pressure, feeling that we are running a million miles an hour while losing sleep and neglecting our health. In our description here, you are tired and on the verge of getting sick, depressed or both, and so the physical contact and indeed their very presence at your door may well feel more impactful for you or too much to bear.

Also to consider: Within the context of your family, is this a regular pattern of behavior? Do they often show up unannounced and try to control you and your situation? Depending on how you relate to your family overall, looking at their past behavior and your relationship with them may reassure you that they are truly showing up to demonstrate care and love toward you; equally so, it could be the last straw for you of having certain family members show up when you are at your most vulnerable to assert their power over you and so maintain a family status quo in the balance of power.

Ask yourself: In this context, **what else** could be going on? When you are run down, unhappy, tired or in pain, it can be difficult to read and interpret others' body language correctly. Everything can end up feeling negative, and even when people closest to you are trying to help out, you can easily get that all wrong.

One psychological model of human interaction, the Karpman drama triangle, suggests that people respond to conflict or pain by taking on one of three possible roles: the "persecutor," the "victim" or the "rescuer." In this model, the "victim" (represented by one corner of a triangle, with the "rescuer" and the "persecutor" taking up the remaining corners), while possibly not actually a subject of any direct abusive behavior, importantly *feels* like a victim—oppressed, embattled and powerless—and according to the theory, searches out another to take the role of the "persecutor," someone they increasingly see as oppressive and controlling. The "victim" may also search out a "rescuer" figure who supplies a corresponding narrative, suggesting there is a better place to be.[2]

In our scenario, if you are feeling overwhelmed and run down, you may be unwittingly taking up this "victim" role and so perhaps have a bias toward identifying someone who fits the role of "persecutor," causing you to be sensitive to those types of nonverbal or verbal behaviors—the body language in others that best fits this persecutor role. Indeed, you may even distort, delete and generalize the behaviors around you and take them out of context to prove to yourself the theory. Often it takes only an external nudge to trigger a full-blown response; and so in your present overwhelmed condition, the combination of the food, coming into your space and the hands-on touching approach could easily translate that your parent and sibling are persecuting you, controlling you and pushing you around.

So whether unwittingly fulfilling the role of persecutor or perhaps even rescuer, your response to their presence and actions shows that your family is in a position of some control over you. Whether they are intending to be caring and helpful or pushy and aggressive, you feel small in relation to their dominance, powerless against the force of their presence.

Notice how they are physically handling you (the haptic). Is it with soft palms or hard fingers? With soft palm touches—touch that has a light pressure—the neurochemical oxytocin can be released from the skin via activation of cutaneous sensory nerves. These are the soft hand strokes on the skin that we see in self-soothing gestures but that others can perform on us, too, to calm us. Oxytocin is linked to increased levels of social interaction, well-being and anti-stress. If we are handled with a soft touch, we can feel not only better but also more connected with others and less stressed, and we might even become healthier.

Conversely, aggressive touch—for example, poking with the fingertips, especially in sensitive and vulnerable areas of the body—can cause stress. Levels of cortisol rise and levels of dopamine decrease to tell the brain the environment is showing indicators of little benefit and so to prepare for risk.

You now have enough information and insight to think about making a **new judgment** and to **test** whether their surprise visit and their hands-on approach is intended to be controlling and pushy or soothing and comforting. Identify if the touch from your parent and sibling was soft or hard and pushy. If soft, it may be more likely that they see how busy you are and that you haven't been eating, and their intention is not to control you or push you around but to soothe, to help and to care for you. If you distinctly felt sharper fingertips gripping you, you may very well be correct with your judgment that they are handling you aggressively and trying to push you around.

Multiple studies show that human beings need touch to thrive. Newborn babies thrive with touch,[3] children need to be lovingly touched so they can grow up feeling safe and nurtured, and even adults can use a good hug every once in a while. It can be helpful feedback to your family and friends if you let them know what feels too pushy and what feels caring about the way they handle you.

QUICK SCAN

S: **Suspending** judgment often means moving away from strong associations you have with the way you always expect family members and longtime friends to behave, think and feel.

C: When analyzing body language, it is important to discover more about what happened before whatever it was you saw. This **context** can radically change what you think others may be intending.

A: Your physical wellness as well as your mental state can have a powerful effect on the way you judge others' intentions. **Ask** yourself what else about you has a powerful effect on how you judge others' intentions toward you.

N: What is hard touch for you and what is soft touch? Ask others to show you what they think is hard and soft when it comes to touch, and see if this information leads to a **new** judgment about the accuracy of your touch-rating scale.

21

TOO CLOSE FOR COMFORT

You are at a traditional family holiday gathering, and you've pitched in to help with the food. You've left your partner to fend for themselves and mingle with other family members they do not know well. You go to check on your partner after a while, and you see they are hitting it off much better than you expected with one of your siblings, sitting beside them and involved in conversation. This instantly makes you feel relieved, and you continue to help with the food setup. At mealtime, you are back socializing with the group, and you find that now you can't pry your partner away from your sibling. They sit very close, looking seriously at each

➡

other, and when you do break in and get their attention, they both look up slowly, appearing to not
want to break from each other. This is your partner
of some years, so while you feel secure that they
are not going to run off into the sunset with your
sibling, you do start feeling concerned and irritated
because they are eye-locked, faces close together,
and now and then you see your sibling touching
your partner's shoulder. It makes you quite angry
that your sibling does not seem to respect that this
is your partner and to keep their hands off. They are
getting way too close for comfort.

IS YOUR SIBLING HITTING ON your partner? Though you may feel
pretty angry and be a hair's breadth away from making a scene or
becoming a guest on *Dr. Phil*—or ending up in front of a jury—let's
employ the **SCAN** process, **suspend judgment** and **be more descriptive** of what is going on.

A few key signals are powerful here: Your sibling and partner seem
eye-locked, faces up close, and your sibling is touching your partner's
shoulder. Eye contact is central to any discussion of body language and
the topic comes up frequently in this book. The meaning behind the
way one person looks at another person can vary immensely. In the dating section of this book, we looked at targeting with the eyes and how
this may be a signal of attraction and interest; if the targeting develops
into direct eye contact with the other, the sign of attraction and interest
may grow more powerful. We may hold eye contact for a longer period

with people we like, especially if we are trying to figure out if they like us back, though this may take the form of looking back and forth from one eye to the other, literally searching for meaning. Prolonged eye contact can also mean aggression and sometimes takes the form of staring, which may be uncomfortable, until the first one to look away gives up the staring "contest" and the dominant position is taken by the "winner."

When people are attracted to each other, they may stare into each other's eyes, but their eyes also may slightly unfocus, to take in the whole picture of the other, giving the effect of dreamy "doe eyes." Alternatively, to cope with the intensity of an eye-lock, which can become uncomfortable, people sometimes will drift their focus slightly to the bridge of the other's nose, which avoids appearing as if they are breaking eye contact while also reducing tension and anxiety. Prolonged eye contact can also sometimes signal that we are listening intently and are deeply engaged in what the other person is saying.

Back to your sibling and partner: While the eye contact may be an indication they are hitting it off a little too well, it is not a conclusive sign that your reality TV career is about to take off just yet. With that signal there is also the possibility that either your sibling or your partner is showing off the relationship they have with you or the group, perhaps even trying to show dominance. Or they could be having a conversation, possibly about you or the group, that is engaging and interesting to both of them.

Are They Gazing or Giving Me "Evils"?

How can you tell the difference between gazing into someone else's eyes and staring at someone? A gaze ➡

is a powerful visual connection that often arouses strong emotions in the gazer and in the receiver of the gaze. Our gazing at something and not someone will direct others to look at what has caught our attention. Gazing can mean romantic interest, and certainly gazing into someone's eyes and then scanning them down and up can signal desire, though the down and up scan may also indicate judgment about how they look and so display a potentially dominant or negative attitude. In Western culture, a prolonged eye-lock can show off power and superiority and is a nonverbal technique to demand that others believe and obey you. Staring is the wide-eyed relation to gazing, showing surprise, shock and disbelief. Staring can also indicate anger and aggression. Both gazing and staring may spontaneously and naturally happen during deep thought, causing the looker to be stuck in an unfocused look at something or someone while internally digging in their memory or imagination. The appropriateness of both gazing and staring varies depending on situation, culture and sometimes personalities.

However, as we have mentioned throughout this book, it takes more than one body language sign to indicate meaning. Here, the face-to-face proximity is also in play. According to anthropologist Edward T. Hall, our personal boundary reserved for close friends, lovers, children and close family members is somewhere within eighteen inches between us and the other person, whereas we are more comfortable keeping new acquaintances between eighteen inches and four feet away. And if your sibling and partner are closer to each other than six inches, that would indicate they are letting each other into their intimate personal space.

Your sibling is also touching your partner's shoulder. Is it a soft, sensitive touch, or are they poking or prodding them to push them around or make a point? It is not just the type of touch—its pressure and frequency, speed and rhythm—that has an impact on the way we feel. The location of the touch on our bodies is also important. Anthropologist and evolutionary psychologist Robert Dunbar, head of the Social and Evolutionary Neuroscience Research Group at the University of Oxford, produced a map based on his study findings of where touching was acceptable and where it was unwelcome. This study is to date the largest ever done on physical touch, with almost 1,500 participants from Finland, France, Italy, Russia and the United Kingdom. The study found that most respondents were comfortable being touched anywhere on their bodies by their partners. Most people were happy for close friends and relatives to touch them on the head and upper torso, while strangers could touch only their hands.[1]

BODY LANGUAGE MYTHBUSTER
A Kiss Is Just a Kiss?
Though kissing may have originated in the passing of premasticated food from parent to child, mouth to mouth, it has become an intimate act that can show love and caring. Equally, it has the potential to show

➡

ownership[2] and sometimes, as in the case of kissing someone or something that equates to a "trophy" (originally the head of a slain opponent), to show your power over another person or thing. It by no means always signals that attraction and intimacy are sealed by it; rather, it can often be a clear display of ownership power or, on the receiving end, a response to that power. One thing is for sure: A kiss can be a powerful catalyst for us in our relationships and influences how we view the relationships of others.

While we don't often think of them in this way, human lips are the body's most exposed erogenous zone. Packed with sensitive nerve endings, even a light brush sends a cascade of information to our brains, helping us decide whether we want to continue and what might happen next. Think about those times you have brought food to your lips, but the moment it touched them you thought better of it. Evolutionary psychologists at the State University of New York at Albany reported that well over half of men and women say they have ended a developing relationship because of a bad kiss.[3] How is it that such a seemingly simple exchange has the power to influence attraction and rejection so dramatically?

It would seem we can pick up just from the touching of our lips just how suited we might be to produce the healthiest offspring. The lips are able to sense many of the same chemicals found in the distinct natural scent we all possess, a scent that appears to guide us toward choosing a partner with complementary genes that, together with our own, code for a stronger immune system. The benefit may be that if we mate with that partner, children down the line are better equipped to deal with disease.

Let's examine the **context** of our sibling scenario. This is your family's gathering, after all, and your partner, not knowing anyone too well, is an outsider. You will see in other chapters the power of the tribe and the exclusionary tactics that tribe may use to show off the dominance and power of the family to the outsider. The notable closeness could be an effort by your sibling to include your partner, bring them into the fold and accept them into the family circle, and so they are displaying uncharacteristic nonverbal behaviors to build this bridge.

Ask what else you can consider. Touching is an ownership signal that can show dominance and power over someone, and accordingly it is more often the leader in the relationship who initiates any physical contact. Touching can also signal comforting, sharing information, persuading, giving an order or asking a favor. All these indicate the top-dog position, and all are reasonable scenarios if your partner was left to fend for themself at your family gathering, and your sibling stepped in to offer leadership and make them feel more comfortable. Being part of the dominant social group, your sibling would likely feel and display a stronger relationship to power in that context than would your partner.

So while you may be able to consider a **new judgment** that your sibling is trying to be helpful, you need to determine whether that helping out is now verging on overstepping the mark. Given that we often find mates who fit familiar norms for us, including cultural and even genetic similarities, it is quite possible that others in your family may find your dates and partners attractive too. It is the job of families to define spoken or unspoken boundaries.

Test your new judgment by first asking your partner if the conversation and contact with your sibling is feeling odd to them, if it is too close for *their* comfort. Watch them during the conversation to see if they look uncomfortable or are perhaps feeling helpless. Are they hunching over, protecting vital organs, submissively smiling with the mouth but not the eyes to placate the other? If they are returning the eye contact, closeness and touching, then you would be wise to move closer to your partner and make sure you are connecting with them in some way, potentially touching them. Show PDA and make clear your relationship to your partner in front of your sibling. You can ask who your sibling is seeing right now or how their partner is or when they might be arriving. And of course, if you have to, be crystal clear to everyone that the touching by your sibling is not acceptable.

PERSONAL BUBBLE

Body language expert **ROBERT PHIPPS** is one of the UK's best known as he has been resident expert on some of British TV's biggest and longest-running shows, including guest analyst as part the *Big Brother* franchise. If anyone knows the truth about being too close for comfort, it's him. Here's what he has to say about personal space.

Everyone likes their own space.

In fact each of us has our own bubble around us that we don't like others invading. The size of your personal bubble is dependent on your background, where you're from and the natural space around you. People who have grown up in cities and towns generally stand closer together when interacting than those brought up in rural settings.

The general rule is that zero to six inches from our bodies is the most protected area. We don't like letting people into that space unless we know them well: close friends, family and children.

These people are allowed in as we have a bond with them and don't feel the need to protect ourselves, but anyone else must stay outside, which is why some people freak when others touch them innocently on the arm, shoulder or back. It physically sets off their fight, flight or freeze response.

However, just because we allow certain people into our close personal space doesn't mean we always like it! Sometimes these people do things that invade our space and can be very annoying. A mother's squeeze of our cheeks at the wrong moment, a cousin who always nudges you when reminding you of something in your past, a friend who touches you gently on the forearm as they jokingly insult you.

Personal space is always dependent on who you are with and the context of their invasion.

QUICK SCAN

S: Eye contact can mean many different things depending on its nature and duration, and on the context and culture. **Suspend** judgment to get a better look at what else is going on.

C: Look into how your close family use and treat space around each other. This is a **context** that will consistently show up when thinking about their behaviors and body language.

A: Ask who is dominant in the group and who appears to be dominant in the exchange under scrutiny. Touching someone is often a sign showing ownership and power, perhaps giving an order, but touching also signals comforting, sharing information, persuading or asking a favor.

N: New judgments can help you see where you need to step in, setting new or clear boundaries with the people around you. If you don't like a certain behavior, let others know.

22

THEY'LL NEVER FIT IN WITH MY FAMILY

You thought they would have so much in common,
and so you brought your new romantic interest
into the family for the first time. Though you were
understandably anxious to introduce this new partner to your nearest and dearest, you also believed
they would have common ground and really get
along and that your family would see what you
see. However, your new partner, usually lively, confident and charming, suddenly seems awkward, as
well as clumsy and argumentative. The conversations and opinions your new partner passionately
espouses strike the wrong chord even with you
when you see your family's reaction to them. Your

➡

family members are leaning back, looking down their noses and then away from your partner, and appear put off by the way your partner is speaking and using so many hand gestures to make every point. As time passes, the family continue to avert their heads every time your partner speaks. You think, *How did I not see it before? They have nothing in common. My new partner will never fit in with my family!*

TAKING YOUR NEW PARTNER to meet your family for the first time can be a momentous, not to mention nerve wracking, event. It can often mean the relationship is heating up and getting serious. That first meeting between your partner and your family may have a lot riding on it: mutual acceptance and approval, and for some, high hopes that everyone will get along harmoniously.

Let's look at the key signal telling you this harmony is not going to happen and giving you the feeling that your new love will never fit in: You can see your family leaning away, looking elsewhere and at each other, turning their heads away from your partner. Though the messages of nonacceptance seem blatantly clear, and highlight to you that your family is completely opposed to your partner and their opinions, let's use the **SCAN** system, try to **suspend judgment** and **be more descriptive** of what is going on.

Your new partner is lively, confident and charming, and clearly likes to speak using their hands. Some people talk with their hands more than do others. The degree to which the hands are used while speaking varies from culture to culture. For example, Latin cultures, such as people from Italy, generally use hand gestures to illustrate their speech much more so than people of Anglo-Saxon extraction in the UK, who in turn generally use more gestural indicators than people from Asian cultures. This is possibly due to the differences in verbal language structures, where some depend more on nonverbal cues to best communicate meaning. Beyond this, some languages require more syllables per unit of meaning, which requires more neural resources (brainpower) to produce. Hand gestures stimulate the language center of the brain (Broca area) and so produce more activity. Therefore, your partner gesticulating differently or more than your family is accustomed to, though perhaps culturally normal for your partner, may be completely lost in translation in the context of your family, or it is possibly confusing to them. Either way, the gesticulating is making this meeting seem extra awkward, with your lively and passionate partner sticking out like a sore thumb.

Talking with our hands is part of kinesics, the study of human body motion established by anthropologist Ray Birdwhistell, who in the 1960s set out to prove that body movement and facial expression together, what he called kinesics, can be best viewed as learned cultural behaviors and not universal.[1] Subsequently, professor Paul Ekman and his colleague Wallace Friesen went on to research and prove that some body language, particularly facial expression of emotion, is innate and universal and so does not always rely on being learned. They categorized kinesics into five categories:

1. **Emblems**—physical gestures that have an exact spoken word equivalent, though they are subject to cultural variations
2. **Illustrators**—actions that describe, reinforce or accent what we are saying
3. **Affective displays**—gestures that convey emotional meaning
4. **Regulators**—gestures that control the flow and pace of communication

by giving visual (or vocal) cues when it is time to take turns speaking

5. **Adaptors**—actions we make when adapting to environments or circumstances that we are not aware we are making, like hair twisting or pulling an earlobe; these gestures may unintentionally tell something to onlookers about how we are feeling[2]

Kinesics communicate specific meanings with body language; certain elements are universally understood to have the same meanings, and others are culturally specific. When we gesticulate with our hands to emphasize spoken content we are using illustrators, and in different cultures there will be massive differences both in terms of what illustrators mean and the frequency of their use. Put another way, many hand gestures mean one thing to one culture of people and something very different to another. For example, in North America, the A-OK hand gesture translates as "everything is good," whereas in France and Belgium the same gesture means "zero" or "nothing," while in Japan it can be a sign for money.

While we use illustrator gestures to a greater or lesser extent to help communication along, we often use regulator gestures, or cues, as well. Regulators nonverbally control the pace of conversation, signaling when it is our turn to listen or to speak. In some cultures, nodding when listening to someone reassures the speaker that you are listening and want them to continue speaking, while pointing your index finger vertically up may indicate you want to halt conversation so you can jump in and make your point, and moving your hand around in circles can indicate you want to speed something up.

IS IT YES, NO OR BOTH?

In many cultures, we signal "yes" with a head nod up and down, and "no" by turning the head horizontally from side to side. However, for many cultures these signs can mean the opposite or something else altogether. For example, in Greece, Sicily and some Middle Eastern countries, "no" is communicated by a single nod of the head up, but not down. And the Indian head wobble, which is neither a yes (up-down head nod) nor a no (right-left head movement), is somewhere in between, a side-to-side head movement that may confuse anyone not familiar with it. We spoke to **KANAN TANDI** in Goa, India, where she is a body language expert and trainer. We asked her to explain to us her view of this gesture's background.

India is a country famous for its diversity. It is the home of many cultures, languages and arts. I conclude that the "Indian head wobble" originated from South India—maybe originating from classical dances where the South and Southeastern styles for both males and females all have neck (side-to-side) movements, whereas the North and Northeast India don't. In these dances, some as old as 2000 years, this neck movement is considered very attractive.

The Indian head wobble in conversation is predominantly seen in the corresponding states of India, from Southeast to Southwest. In the deep southern state of Tamil Nadu specifically, the up-and-down head nod is almost nowhere to be found, nor is the "no" head movement in that state's more isolated rural village areas.

Typically the head wobble is a gesture of acceptance or acknowledgment. The faster the movement, the greater that acceptance or acknowledgment is.

The effects of globalization and Westernization are encroaching, however. Watch local state channels, their shows, discussions, and you will find very few head wobbles.

Given the different possible meanings of hand gestures depending on culture and geography, it may not be your partner's content, those opinions they hold dear, that is causing a lack of interest or offense, but their nonverbal communication style. If, because of their culture or social group, your partner is gesticulating wildly when talking and if your family is not big on gesticulating, or if your family members use the same gestures but in different ways, they may quite rightly feel they are just not speaking the same language as your partner. The conversation could easily become one-sided and frustrating. One party keeps talking, and the other party can't get a word in. They may be talking over the top of each other, confusing and annoying all parties and making it look hopeless that they will ever get along.

Let's look at our **context** next and the power of the family together, the tribe. Our first tribe, for better or worse, is our family. As we grow older we join other tribes, such as the group of kids in the nursery or daycare, neighborhood friends, school teams, clubs, grade years, university, a sorority or fraternity, groups through a job, pastime and religion, a political group, or a user group and on and on it goes. Many of us are members of many different tribes at the same time: our trade or profession, our department at work, the ball team or pickup hockey group, the weavers' guild, an online gaming community or other special-interest group. Perhaps even the tribe that drives the same car or motorcycle; rides the same type of skateboard, subway train or highway into work; or even listens to a tribal leader on drive-time radio—chances are there are some tribes you belong to that you don't even know you belong to.

And chances are that if you don't think you belong to any tribes, that you are an individual with your own way of doing things, bucking the system and setting the trends, well, join the tribe—there are a bunch of us out there. Some are reading this book just like you and thinking about it in the way you are now.

Tribes share social norms, a common experience and often a common purpose. They have limbic resonance and mirror each other. Every tribe has some shared values, beliefs, rituals, customs, goals, concerns and signals that drive and shape how members of it behave:

Values—what they feel is most important in life

Beliefs—the things they just know, without needing any real or ongoing evidence

Rituals—organized stuff they do together to support their values and beliefs on a regular basis

Customs—other stuff they all share in together (such as clothes they wear and the food they eat)

Goals—achievements they are trying to reach together

Concerns—shared barriers and conflicts

Signals—specific ways they communicate with each other, maybe through a language or dialect, acronyms, vocabulary or objects and symbols that speak to the group alone

Tribes have rules and a hierarchy, and following established normal behavior can ensure you reach a status that will allow you to have respect and influence within the tribe for at least a short time, and in some cases, always. All in all, this context is loaded with opportunities for your partner to get it wrong.

At this moment, your partner is a newbie to your first clan or tribe, and many cues can play out to make clear that people don't get them, and they don't get the group. A tribe will often make in-jokes and use a shorthand of speech and acronyms to show and strengthen their existing bond. In our scenario, the nonverbal displays by the family to show off their bond to the outsider are displays of arrogance—leaning back and displaying vulnerable organs, taking up more personal space, tilting the chin up and so overexposing the throat, which could be interpreted as looking down their nose at your partner. Though these arrogant displays are telling you this is a lost cause, they equally could be the family's collective response to being alienated by your partner's animated and physically expressive method of communication, and not actually a sign that the family dislikes them or their content.

In **asking what else** you need to consider, you must accept that the behavior your family is exhibiting may cause your partner, and you in empathy with your partner, to feel uncomfortable, intimidated, annoyed or like they are being given the cold shoulder. In turn, because your partner is passionate and lively, this may be sparking them into even more energized gesticulating in their communication as they fight to get themselves and their ideas across to your family, trying to prove themselves, all resulting in a downward spiral for you.

Furthermore, those arrogant gestures you see from your family may also be cues that show your family is evaluating this new partner. While they are mirroring each other's arrogant gestures, they are also looking away and around the room, which though a possible gesture of disapproval may also be an evaluative gesture, showing they may be considering the best way to respond.

Therefore you can form a **new judgment** that all hope is not lost, that it might take more time for your family and your partner to get used to how each communicates, to get better acquainted with the visual cues, to understand each other's cultural regulators and illustrators to create a space where they will understand each other better, and so over time be able to recognize the common ground you believe they share. Both your family and your partner need to take a breath and help the longer-term **test** by slowing down the communication to give the tribe members more time for translation.

BODY LANGUAGE MYTHBUSTER
Close Proximity Increases Violence

Can close proximity to others increase the potential for not getting along and even lead to a more violent society? There is a popular view that high population density inevitably leads to violence. This myth, which is originally based on rat research, applies neither to us nor to other primates. If it were true, we would expect Tokyo to be one of the most violent places on the planet, given its high population density, yet it has an incredibly low rate of violent crime per capita. The relationship between crime rate and population appears to be in some cases negative and across the board is statistically insignificant.[3]

QUICK SCAN

S: **Suspending** judgment on your initial instinctual reaction to the judgments your social groups make about outsiders and newcomers can be hard because you are often quite dependent on these groups.

C: Can you put a name to some of the tribes you feel you are a member of? To what extent do these tribes bring a **context** within which you view others?

A: Ask what pressure the context of the family tribe may be exerting on the outsider, your new partner, that may be causing an exacerbation of their tendencies and habits that in turn become harder for the tribe to comprehend.

N: The **new** judgment about how everybody will get along will require some time and patience around forming the new familial relationship and reveal where each party may find challenges.

23

HOUSE ON FIRE!

Your young family has decided to join in on a group holiday with your other nearest and dearest relatives and their families, all of whom don't see each other enough because of busy schedules and different places of residence. For this family get-together, you're converging at a rented holiday home somewhere beautiful and a little remote so you can relax and reconnect. Everyone is pitching in and laughing and joking at the first night's dinner. You are all planning mutually acceptable activities for the holiday, and you will be going to most places together as a group. Everyone seems to be genuinely getting along like a house on fire . . . so far

➡

> at least. It's a great day one of seven. How do you
> know whether this idyllic situation will last?

BEFORE WE OUTLINE the key signals of group harmony that tell you the good times are going to last and the family holiday will not "go south," let's first look at **context** as it will overwhelmingly set the tone for this discussion: This family holiday is on neutral territory. You are not visiting a relative's house—you are meeting somewhere new to all, and this levels the playing field, setting the stage for a possible equal power share, with nobody having home advantage. You are also in the context of the family, a tribe to which you all belong. What could go wrong?

THERE WILL BE BLOOD

If there was a hall of fame for body language expertise, **ALLAN PEASE** would undoubtedly head it up. Allan and Barbara Pease are the most successful body language and relationship authors in the business, with eighteen best-sellers, including ten number ones, and have given seminars in seventy countries. Allan is legendary for having trained Russian president Vladimir Putin in body language skills. So when Mark and Allan chat, you can just imagine the stories they might tell, having both worked with G8 leaders. But instead of spilling the beans on those encounters, Allan tells us how we might best detect if family members will really get along in the context of the family get-together.

For some people, family get-togethers can be a happy, joyful occasion. For many others, however, it's an opportunity for the spilling of family blood, the venting of past grievances and for some family members to explain to you what you really should have done with your life. In a get-together with your friends, they usually show you how much they love or admire you, whereas family members may highlight all your past poor choices.

People who like each other will stand closer together and mirror each other's gestures, facial expressions and voice inflection. Those who don't like or respect you may also stand closer than usual but use contrary and aggressive gestures such as talking with their palms facing downward (authoritative), hands beating time with their words (driving home their point) and prolonged eye contact, like a lion watching their prey. People who are rejecting of your presence or your attitudes might cross their arms (barrier/rejection), nod their head with more than three beats (more than three nods is a "shut up" signal), and their foot or feet may face toward the door or toward another person, indicating where they would prefer to be.

If you have serial family offenders, tell them in advance how you expect them to behave with you and children, and clearly explain how they will be reprimanded if they play up. The main reason your negative old Aunty Mabel becomes unruly is because family members have always allowed it. Reward the offenders when they toe the line and show positive behavior toward others. Regularly touch, mirror and smile at everyone (with your teeth visible), and encourage others to do the same. If all else fails, don't attend the family event. For most people, their list of best friends usually doesn't contain many relatives.

Just because you're related to someone doesn't mean you are obligated to them and have to put up with their rude, aggressive or stand-off body language or behavior. That's why every Christmas vacation, I go overseas to another country.

The key signals telling you this will be the best family holiday ever: open and easy body language showing no fear of attack, lots of smiling from the group, with a genuine Duchenne smile with crinkles at the corners of the eyes, and possibly laughter. Relaxed proximity and mirroring open and positive body language are telltale signs that you can reserve the spot same time next year.

Now let's **SCAN** this situation, **suspend judgment** and **be more descriptive** of other key signals that may be warning signs the fun and games are getting edgy and dangerous: At the beginning of strife, you may notice people participating in self-soothing behaviors, such as crossing their arms or holding onto themselves in a hugging posture. Touching releases oxytocin and makes us feel better. If tempers start to flare, watch out for invasions of others' intimate or personal space (territory) without permission—in other words, a breakdown in respect for each other's boundaries.

If you notice that people are trending toward spending more time hiding out with their electronic devices, this could indicate they are hiding out from the gang or feeling vulnerable. And if they display any of the following signs of aggression, anger or depression, it could signal that the gloves are about to come off: compressed (disappeared) lips, frowns, sneers, snarls and bared teeth. Remember that one signal on its own does not reveal a clear emotion. If you notice others fidgeting, sweating, using jerky movements or smacking their lips because of a dry mouth, this could indicate fear, and so the environment may be becoming psychologically or even physically dangerous if people's needs are not being met or they feel threatened. Finally, watch out for regressive behaviors, or people trying to provoke conflict so they can act out, and of course anyone crying or leaving in a huff, all clear signs that a brouhaha is imminent.

When you look at the list of potential negative behaviors, it can read as a cautionary tale for planning that big family holiday in the first place, and you may decide to stay well clear. But **what else** can you consider that keeps you planning this trip? You may well **ask**, why not just go away on our own? Since the beginning of human culture, we have weighed the pros and cons of being in a group context as opposed to branching out with our single family unit and going it alone. The same need for survival that causes our primitive brains to drive us to fending for ourselves also causes our limbic brains to drive us to be tribal, to be a part of the gang. Both of these systems are judging, while under pressure, the pros and cons of being social versus antisocial, and comparing the advantages and disadvantages of each as if they were getting ready to face Armageddon, as opposed to a trip to the zoo or the family lobster boil, or in this case the family holiday.

Following are some of the positive judgments the primitive brain makes about going solo:

- I can move faster.
- I will need fewer resources and less of each.
- I'll be stealthier.
- I'll face less conflict.

Meanwhile, the limbic system is thinking of the cons of going it alone:

- There'll be no one to look after me.
- I'll be lonely.
- It'll be depressing.
- I'll feel less secure.

The limbic system is also considering all the pros of teaming up:

- I'll get group support.
- I'll have extra resources.
- I'll have a greater sense of security.
- It'll be easier with less work.

But of course, the primitive brain under pressure understands the uncertainties that are poised against all of that:

- Can I trust these other people?
- Is this a winning team?

And, of course, the most pressing issue:

- Will I get lunch?

There really is no middle ground here. You are either with the group or you aren't. And being with the group bestows you with responsibility toward everyone else in the group, all of whom are implicated with the same responsibility toward you. It's a collective. Sometimes this feels safe, and sometimes it feels very dangerous, just as when you go it alone.

There are many people taking part in your family vacation over many days, and so the dynamic may be fluid and changeable. And so whatever your **new judgment** is now, it may also change. Here's a nonverbal technique to keep the peace and keep yourself and others from losing self-control. Many of the trickiest emotions to be around in their strongest forms, such as anger, contempt, fear and sadness, cannot be sustained for a long period of time. They cause too much strain on the body and mind because they are designed to signal to others strong enough feelings to change the environment for the better, right now. If you or a family member are going through a strong emotion, then move yourself or them away from the immediate environment for just ten minutes. You will most likely find that the strong emotions subside, and then you might be able to talk about the problem rather than just nonverbally reacting to the power of it. In this way you may be able to **test** the feelings that are present rather than be drawn into them.

BODY LANGUAGE MYTHBUSTER
Nature versus Nurture!

How big a role do different cultures and upbringings play in body language? There are universal behaviors that are controlled by the primitive brain, which in turn controls emotional behaviors and motivation. There are also behaviors that are influenced somewhat by culture or are totally cultural. All people may unconsciously compress their lips to show that something is negative. We also all eye block—covering eyes with hands or fingers—to control how data comes in through the eyes in the same way compressed lips control data through the mouth. But culture can influence the level to which we perform universal behaviors, such as when we crinkle our noses (as if something smells really bad). In some cultures they can be hardly perceptible, while in others these behaviors look exaggerated and potentially caricature-like to those not a part of that group. Culture can amplify

➡

instinctual behaviors in some circumstances as much as it can suppress them. And of course, there are strictly cultural gestures such as the predominantly modern North American thumbs-up sign, which we don't recommend doing in Egypt, where it is considered a phallic gesture.

QUICK SCAN

S: Suspend judgment if only to be mindful of other cues that support the judgment, or alternatively if you notice clusters of signals that may tip you off to issues that can quickly crop up.

C: A neutral **context** in this scenario of visiting a place nobody has any prior territorial claim to creates an equal playing field and avoids potential negative behaviors from others.

A: Ask yourself the pros and cons of the big group gathering if times get tough. There is often strength and security in numbers.

N: New judgments may happen over the course of the week in this fluid situation.

24

I AM BORING THE PANTS OFF THEM

You just got back from the holiday of a lifetime. You ticked off some places on your bucket list, learned how to order food in a new language, swam with sharks, and even learned a few cool things about yourself. It was a wild ride and will surely go down as one of the best times of your life. Your friends have been following you on social media, where you have been uploading loads of pictures and videos. You get back and cannot wait to tell everybody the stories, show more pictures, share your excitement! However, at your triumphant homecoming outing at a regular haunt with your friends, while you are bursting at the seams to spill, they look . . . not that

➡

interested. Although they listen for a bit, they are
staring blankly, nodding robotically and definitely
glancing around while you are talking. You continue trying to bump up the excitement, keeping
the fantastic stories rolling to hold their interest,
but end up feeling that they are not really listening.
You come to the realization that you are boring the
pants off them.

YOU ARE TALKING but no one seems to be remotely engaged. How
could this be? You've just had the time of your life, and these are your
friends; presumably they'd be excited to hear your tales, so it is worth
suspending judgment and **being more descriptive** of what is truly
going on. Let's **SCAN** this situation to learn more.

What is the key signal leading you to assume your friends are
bored silly? They are staring blankly, nodding robotically and glancing around the room while you are speaking, indicating that what
you say has no power for them—they are bored.

How correct is this assumption? A host of body language signs
can indicate boredom: yawning, fidgeting, breaking eye contact,
eyes glazing over, glancing around the room, eyes squinting, pursed
lips, torso turned away from you, head nodding, responding the same
way over and over so as not to appear rude, shuffling feet or crossing
feet tightly in ankle lock and rubbing eyes, ears or nose. But as we
have seen, gestures often have more than one meaning depending
on circumstances, such as context and the other signals they come
packaged with; for example, rubbing the nose is also associated with

deception, evaluation or disagreement, depending on the situation and what else the person may be displaying.

The signals from the friends in our scenario do fit in with the signs for boredom, so they truly may be bored, but let's first examine **context**. You are all out together at a regular meeting place. There are likely to be other people there too, sitting or standing, walking to and fro, along with music playing, video screens showing exciting sports or other compelling programming—all of which provide distractions that compete for their attention. Even the most riveting actor, speaker or storyteller will tell you how hard a job it is to keep an audience's attention when there are other visual stimuli in the room, not to mention the clicking sound of cutlery on plates or the crinkle of potato chip bags.

As well as the obvious environmental distractions, what about other powerful distractions you can't see, like smartphones buzzing in your friends' pockets, which they may be working hard to ignore? Even when we are in the middle of important, even life-changing conversations, it only takes that buzzing phone or message tone to take our focus away from the conversation and into our own thought processes for a few seconds or more, depending on what we've got going on. *Who's calling me? How many likes am I getting on that post? Did I get back to my assistant about e-mailing that potential cool new client?*

Some people are better than others at staying focused, at being in the moment and not as easily distracted, though the majority of us are challenged. Staying focused is not easy when we are fighting against constant demands on our time and attention as well as the instant gratification digital technology offers us through our smartphones. We don't need to rely on living vicariously through the adventures of others when in seconds on our own devices we can at least visually and sometimes aurally experience adventures from faraway lands and even planets. Our increasing shift toward engaging with entertaining web culture content may be decreasing our capacity to stay focused on the same live subject for any length of time. Science backs this up with research showing that since the boom in smartphone use in the year 2000, the average human attention span has fallen from twelve seconds to eight seconds (so it wasn't that long in the first place!), and in fact those with more digital lifestyles struggle to focus in environments where prolonged attention is needed.[1] However, research also shows we have become better at multitasking and that early adopters and heavy social media users experience increased short bursts of high attention and are better at cherry-picking what they want to pay attention to.

Back to our scenario. It could be true that after briefly engaging with your story, your friends are onto the next thing. Because you are their friend and they like you, they are doing their utmost to show you they are paying attention, but they certainly may be showing signs of strain. You may simply be unaware, as you are riding that wave of your big trip, what you are up against to hold their attention for long periods of time, and you are not alone. But are you actually boring them? Are you dull?

Ask what else you can consider. Your friends are breaking eye contact, staring into the distance, which can often look as if they are glazing over, zoning out. And maybe they are. There is an interesting area of study by neuroscientist Jonathan Smallwood at the Max Planck Institute for Human Cognitive and Brain Sciences in Leipzig, Germany, and Jonathan Schooler, a psychologist at the University of California, Santa Barbara. They are leading experts on mental zoning out, or what they call the "offline mode." Their studies show that people spend about 13 percent of their time "offline," and during this time we are lost in thought, zoned out and tuned out to what is going on around us. Not a bad thing for us, as their evidence suggests that zoning out may be vital to our creativity and imaginative thought, allowing us to freely follow where our minds randomly take us without being distracted by external stimuli, thereby giving us more scope for forming spontaneous and interesting ideas.[2]

You should also consider in this scenario that you are potentially full of great expectations; you are pumped up about your trip and used to a new adventure each day, and so your energy may be shooting through the roof, and honestly you do not want the good times to end. In comparison, your friends have likely been getting on with the day to day of work life, so they may not be riding your roller coaster, and so even though they are from your tribe, may not be mirroring the potentially excited body language you are displaying.

Considering all this, you can form a **new judgment** that while they may be zoning out listening to you—and they've seen the pictures already on social media—as opposed to being bored by you, they could be remembering your pictures, or remembering their own experiences, taking an internal walk down memory lane or visualizing similar experiences. You may be inspiring them.

But if you want to **test** whether they are in some way engaged with your content or totally disengaged, change your body posture by leaning forward or stepping in closer to them and smiling. Do they mirror this move of further engagement, or do they disengage further by moving or looking away? If the latter, perhaps something else altogether is going on; because, if they are good friends, they should be comfortable being in the personal space with you and are primed to mirror you. How about just stopping with your story and asking what they think to see where their minds are? Do they reply with something associated with what you were talking about, or do they say, "Huh?"

BODY LANGUAGE MYTHBUSTER
"I Don't Need to See You to Hear What You Are Saying"

How many times have you heard someone say, "I *am* listening. I may not be looking at you. But believe me, I'm paying attention." Are they being disingenuous when they say that, or can people be truly listening to you even when they don't seem to be giving you their visual attention? Listening to everyday speech is about hearing and discovering potential meaning. If we are listening to poetry or written prose, we have the advantage of hearing in the written words more descriptors, words that create the mood and context. Not so in everyday speech, which uses far less vocabulary and far more repetition of the same words. Meaning is therefore helped along by seeing the words put into context, and part of that context is of course nonverbal. To this point, you are unlikely to get the fullest meaning of what someone may be trying to tell you without taking in some of their nonverbal communication around their messaging.

QUICK SCAN

S: Suspending judgment helps you remember that any one signal, like the apparent signals of boredom seen in this scenario, can have multiple meanings depending on the context.

C: Check the **context** for other stimuli that may be competing for your listeners' attention.

A: Ask yourself if someone's behavior has *anything* to do with you. You may feel important to the scenario, but sometimes you are not as big a part of it as you think.

N: Thoughts live in people's heads, so you cannot know them for sure, but you can make a **new** judgment that your friends have already seen part of your journey on social media and may be feeling more introspective or inspired to take their own journey.

25

LYING THROUGH THEIR TEETH

A new acquaintance asks you out for early evening drinks and snacks. They seem great, like they could be a potential close friend. Though you don't know them well, they've told you they are in an unhappy relationship. As you're having drinks, they seem a little overinvolved in texting someone. They explain they are just dealing with a work issue. After a while, someone you don't know shows up and sits at your table, a work colleague of your friend. The texting has stopped. The two of them seem very familiar. They are chatty with each other, leaning in toward each other, having long bouts of direct eye contact, and both seem a little giddy. You can't help but feel suspicious that something is going on, and you are also feeling like a third wheel.

Eventually the colleague steps out for a minute, and you ask your new friend if there might be something up romantically with the colleague and if you should perhaps leave. You freeze when your friend says, completely surprised and angry, "How could you even think that of me!" They are outraged that you would suggest they were the unfaithful type. Their eyes snap wide open and their mouth starts tightening up as their nostrils flare. They blink quickly and repeatedly, their shoulders rise up and their hands shoot out in front of them, their palms pushing toward you. All in all, it seems a shockingly severe reaction to what had seemed obvious. You instantly apologize while scrambling to figure out how you could have read the situation so badly.

A few weeks pass, and you hear through the grapevine that your friend and their partner are breaking up and your friend is having an affair with that same colleague. You are annoyed with yourself that you didn't stick with your gut feeling, and wonder how your friend managed to convince you their behaviour was "innocent" when they were clearly lying through their teeth.

WE ALL WANT TO BE ABLE to tell when others are lying to us. However, lying is often extremely difficult to detect, even for crime professionals.

We are generally all capable and practiced at lying. Lying is one of our most important social skills, as is telling the truth. Both lying and telling the truth can empower us. Both can deliver pain to us or others. Lies can be necessary. Some lies can be just as empowering for the person being lied to as for the person doing the lying. People often lie so as not to hurt or offend others, to avoid conflict, to placate others or to raise their status or self-esteem. And then there are those cases as with the story of the emperor's new clothes when everyone is complicit in a moment of deceit in order to support or maintain the accepted status quo. The majority of us are practiced liars but are bad at detecting lies.

Those times we find out we've been lied to may make us feel at the very least mildly insulted and potentially extremely disadvantaged or even disenfranchised. By lying, the liar grabs the advantage and the power and deprives us of it. They manage this by purposefully giving us some alternative, inaccurate description of the world, knowing that by our buying into their false rendering, they will stand to gain power, advantage and benefit. In these cases they may not care how we are affected, and sometimes they are purposefully putting us at a disadvantage to raise themselves up. In our scenario you have additionally been gaslighted: The new friend led you to believe you were totally in the wrong, using denial, misdirection and lying. These tactics by the liar destabilize and delegitimize your belief in what you see to be true so they can keep some power. Let's **SCAN** the scenario. You know you were lied to and so it's too late to **suspend judgment** in the moment, but you can **be more descriptive**, investigating the fallout and what went wrong.

You believe your new friend has been lying through their teeth. They have lied while seeming to be completely sincere. The key signals that duped you in that moment into believing their lies are the sudden emotional displays, a combination of surprise, anger, defense and aggression to your question, when their eyes snap open wide in surprise, their mouth tightens as nostrils flare in anger, while their hands come up in a pushing-away gesture. These displays powerfully disrupt the flow of conversation and the regular pattern of socially appropriate behavior in the moment, and so they stand out and demand you pay attention. You get blindsided, lose your moment for mindfulness and critical thinking and buy into their protestations. You jump to conclusions not based on adequate body language evidence in the moment; you think they are surprised and then angry by what they have taken as a bold accusation, but they never actually give the full expression of either emotion.

According to the Facial Action Coding System, a tool for describing human facial movements, surprise looks like this: Both inner and outer parts of the brows rise up, the upper lid rises slightly and the jaw drops. So while in our scenario the eyes do pull open, rather than the jaw dropping, the mouth tightens up, suppressing a different emotion. The nostrils flare, which often accompanies anger but does not describe it on its own, and the hands up are a blocking gesture, which can also be a regulator gesture to signal to someone to stop talking.

BODY LANGUAGE MYTHBUSTER
Looking Up to the Right Means They're Lying
Does the direction in which someone's eyes look give away that they are lying? The idea that looking to the right indicates lying, while looking left suggests truth telling, is shown by research to be false.

➡

The University of Edinburgh completed three studies to show there is no definitive correlation between the direction of eye movement and whether the subject was telling the truth or lying.[1] However, it is fair to say that eye-accessing cues (unconscious eye movements) do indicate an internal search for or retrieval of information, or creation of data, information and memory.

And even though you may not, in the moment, be able to bring to mind the Facial Action Coding System, the facial gestures of surprise and anger are the same across the globe, and so you may be able to recognize them in others. But in our scenario, you witness a complex and confusing mix of sudden displays, not enough of either anger or surprise for you to tell which for sure. In hindsight, now that you're being more descriptive of all the signals, a number of these displays could be associated with discomfort, anxiety, protection and concealment, and so in the right context might tip you off to the person's dishonesty or at least defensiveness to try to cover up their dishonesty—for example, the blocking gesture with the hands, the shrug for protection, the high blink rate (an increased rate of blinking is often cited as a sign that someone is potentially lying, worried or stressed). Verbally, they evade the question by not answering it. You questioned them as to whether it would be better in that moment if you left, and they responded by demanding how you would ever think they would be a cheater, an extreme reaction that deflects the question. What causes even more confusion is that the reaction is sharp and powerful, taking you by surprise, and its severity accompanied by the hands pushing you away causes you to back off.

Looking at **context**, the power of their response has drawn you into a context of threatened social exclusion. You had hoped this person would be good-friend material, part of your group, someone potentially sharing common ground. To save your hoped-for friendship, you allow yourself to believe their lie, and in that moment you become complicit in their story. It takes two people for a lie to work: the sender of the lie and the receiver of the lie. In this sense, you, the receiver, comply with the lie in order to save the future relationship. Don't be too hard on yourself, though, as the shock caused by their fast and extreme show of surprise and anger could have shifted your emotional state, making you more compliant.

In a normal, friendly social context, you are just not expecting this kind of shock tactic. Were you a criminal investigator, you would be looking for opportunities to instigate moments like this, opportunities where body language might alert you to the gravity of the potential deceit. As always with finding the most important nonverbal elements, the key can be sudden change, and not necessarily the specific actions on their own.

SIGNALS OF INTEREST

With so many body language signals indicating stress, blocking and discomfort that are associated with the act of lying, experts often pick a favorite area from which to start working to form a foundation for their analysis. Take for example the area of micro-gestures, popularly associated with the TV drama *Lie to Me* and based on the brilliant work of Dr. Paul Ekman and Dr. David Matsumoto. Here, a whole world of deception detection was cleverly spun around one nonverbal concept, micro-expression. **ERIC GOULARD** was the first person in France to become a certified master of micro-expression recognition through his training under Dr. Matsumoto, an acclaimed psychologist and body language expert. Here's what he says about the points that interest him most when he analyzes a situation.

> When we talk about humans, we think about controlled and uncontrolled behaviors. The desire to be honest, or on the contrary to cheat, lie or manipulate, sometimes gives rise to interesting signals. I stay very attentive to automatic reflexes, including micro-facial expressions, but also body freezing and flight or fight movements, as well as stress reactions and breaks in eye contact. I am always on the lookout for an orientation reflex. This movement of a single shoulder appears when the person wants to turn and run. Feet can betray you, as well as other gestures. But what I like above all are the breaks in visual contact: this moment when there is so much information to manage that the brain needs all its energy to focus it. There are also other signals, such as dry mouth, shown through the desire to drink, and the tensions visible in the arms, neck, shoulders, etc. My favorite is when the person says, "I really love what you do!" And at the same time you observe a micro-expression of contempt appear on their face!

Of course, whatever you may rely on or choose as a focus for determining lies, remember that practiced liars or people who really need a lie to work for them can cover or counter almost any of the tells of deceit. In our scenario here, it is easy to miss the shrugged shoulders that come from protecting vulnerable areas of the body because of the push blocking gesture that took attention away from it. You might have missed the rapid blinking, which—when set against the relaxed baseline before your question—could indicate stress around the subject. And it would be very easy not to consciously detect the micro-gestures of fear (eyebrows raised and pulled together, raised upper eyelids and tensed lower eyelids, lips stretched horizontally) that caused you to freeze because they were instantly masked in your friend's face by the widening of the eyes to feign surprise and the lip suppression masking the widening of the mouth.

Ask what else you should have paid attention to that could not be so easily masked. Where do liars eventually fall down and betray their deceit? Often, in the structure of what they say and the story they give. Look for whether they distance themselves from the hot spots of the story, split hairs when challenged on elements of the narrative, decline to answer questions, change the subject or tone, protest a question, stall on getting to a point by giving extraneous information or are unable to recount the story out of chronological sequence. Also, you can be linguistically tipped off when they direct you toward exterior social qualifiers: "Ask anyone about it," they might say—or they might try to give a character reference for themselves by pushing the focus onto you, saying you know they would never do such a thing, or measuring probabilities by saying they are not likely to do that. These linguistic alarm bells avoid the test of questions that are clearly answerable with "yes" or "no" and instead use other negatives, such as "I never do that." In our scenario, the response of "How could you even think that of me?" not only evades the question but also employs a powerful social lever by suggesting your viewpoint is not aligned with their viewpoint and so the relationship with them is at risk, bringing in that context we looked at of threatened social exclusion. And it is most likely the power of this social cohesion that causes you to stand down your assumptions against your better judgment and comply with the deceit.

EXPERT FALLIBILITY

Here's some advice from our friend and colleague **SCOTT ROUSE**, a body language analyst (and also an expert reader for this book), who teaches military and law-enforcement personnel about interview and interrogation techniques.

"You've been gathering information and tips, old wives' tales, stuff from movies and things you hear in TV shows, and even secrets from so-called experts. And guess what? Most of that information is incorrect or incomplete. Yeah, I know. It sounds crazy. But I promise, it's true.

When I was a little kid, I watched a TV show about a spy. He knew when someone lied to him because they broke eye contact when they answered a question. And that went for everybody he talked to: men, women, children, other spies, you name it.

All through junior high and high school I thought that was true. And I told other kids about it too. Had I known that wasn't the case at all, that it wasn't true and had no basis in reality other than "that's what everybody always says," then Kevin Hojenackie, to this day, wouldn't hate me.

In the seventh grade my jacket was stolen and Katrina Brooks assured me Kevin was the perp. So I asked Kevin, "Hey, man, did you take my jacket?" And he looked at me and said, "No. I didn't. I don't want your jacket." Then he looked away as he said, "I've got a jacket cooler than that one."

That's when I KNEW he stole it. I threatened him and told him he had an hour to give it back and if he didn't I was telling on him. The hour went by and he didn't give it to me, so I told on him.

Not long after that, John Shannon brought me my jacket and told me he and my brother, Mitch, took it because they thought it would be funny. To make a long story short, it really embarrassed

Kevin, as he had never been in trouble before. Even though I apologized, he never spoke to me again.

But wait a minute . . . What about the infallible body language cue that told what's his face, the spy, when somebody was lying to him? That was my introduction to the truth and reality about people handing out bad, unresearched information concerning nonverbal communication to anybody and everybody and not caring or thinking twice about doing it.

In our scenario, we are way past forming a **new judgment** and testing it. The person had done such a good job of shocking you into compliance with their deception that you were in a fantasy world until the moment you discovered the truth, that they had lied to you. We do not usually embark on social gatherings with people expecting antisocial acts. You are there for the society of it and therefore normally, unlike someone who works in lie detection, not on guard to uncover duplicity. The lesson to learn from all this is that if you are tipped off that something may not be right when someone you don't know that well exhibits surprising behavior, even if you go along with their version of reality, you should be cautious in going forward in the friendship and giving them your trust. Deceivers can display many nonverbal cues, both gestural and structural, to maneuver you into complicity, to avoid a risk or win a reward, so keep some safe space for yourself for further observation if another version of the truth rings true for you, regardless of what that particular person says.

QUICK SCAN

S: You are past **suspending** judgment in this scenario. Lies can blindside you, taking your power away, and you discover the truth after the fact.

C: The **context** in this situation is the threat of social exclusion. You play your part in the lie to avoid being ousted or marginalized and to keep the status quo.

A: To help determine whether someone is lying, **ask** yourself what distancing or diversionary tactics they may be using, and listen for linguistic alarm bells.

N: You do not have the luxury of making a **new** judgment in the moment, other than that this friend may not be for you. You can learn when you are shocked by confusing behavior to pay attention to it and reserve a little more personal space and time before investing further time or trust.

26

PERSONA NON GRATA

You have been getting together socially on a regular basis with the same crowd for some time. You always have fun when you see each other, and though you don't hang out every day, you have lots in common and generally feel genuinely comfortable with them. However, you are at a party you were invited to at one of their homes and get the feeling people are avoiding you, moving away when you move in to talk. It feels as though they don't want to engage in any kind of conversation with you at all and are giving you the cold shoulder. You start feeling a little self-conscious, worrying there is something putting people off. A smell, perhaps?

➡

Something stuck in your teeth? Did you unwittingly embarrass yourself in some quite unforgettable way at the last get-together? You manage to break into a conversation with two members of the group, but as you are speaking you cannot help but feel that although they are quietly listening, they are looking down their noses at you. You see one of them wince! And then as you leave the conversation, you catch them sharing a look, and one of them rolls their eyes. You think, *Oh, I get it, I'm persona non grata—they all hate my guts!*

HOW DO YOU GO from being accepted by your peers to suddenly feeling like you are in the doghouse—persona non grata, unappreciated, unaccepted and unwelcome? One moment you are feeling the love and the next you feel in your gut that they hate you. What are the key signals in this description that have set you off? Looking down their noses, wincing, the eye-roll. Though you may want to leave the party immediately to lick your wounds, step back for a moment to **SCAN** this situation (not too tricky as no one wants to talk to you anyway), **suspend judgment** and **be more descriptive** of what is going on.

The eye-roll, a covert signal sent between your friends that you just happened to catch, is often a sign of contempt. The meaning of the eye-roll in body language terms is shifting, meaning how we use it changes over time as we age. Babies will naturally roll their eyes away from us when we no longer hold any interest for them. Younger children will show boredom by rolling their eyes. For teenagers, studies show that the eye-roll is often deliberate, part of a nonverbal package to target others, more often employed by females but also by males, to show aggression toward someone, sometimes in an attempt to cause exclusion.[1,2] In adults, studies have linked eye-rolling to contempt and as such may be symptomatic of a relationship ending.[3] Other studies show women in particular will often default to eye-rolling in response to annoying, belittling or sexist humor.[4]

When seen in tandem with other gestures, eye-rolling is considered to signal contempt or annoyance, that we are fed up, sometimes looking for solidarity in response to annoying stimuli. So collectively, the key signals here are (1) wincing—a display of physical pain on the face when there is no physical discomfort but instead a psychological or social one; (2) looking down their nose—which as mentioned earlier, unless someone is shortsighted and trying to get a better look at their phone screen, is a sign of arrogance; and (3) the eye-rolling, all of which seem to point clearly to disapproval, discomfort and contempt. That's gotta hurt.

It seems you are being given the cold shoulder. Again, this turning away of the shoulders and torso can show disinterest or aloofness, but taken with the other signs here could signal contempt. Historically, the term "giving someone the cold shoulder" describes a lack of acceptance or hospitality, particularly to an outsider or a guest. So if others are physically turning away in addition to the other body language displayed, chances are your presence is no longer desired.

Let's take a look at the **context**: You are at someone's house that you have been to before, and you've been in this social group for a while. You will in part share with them similar values, beliefs, rituals and customs; in short, you are at a party with your tribe. As you see in other chapters, members of the same social group, as well as having limbic resonance and mirroring each other, have rules, hierarchies and also ways of signaling loyalties to each other to maintain the strength and feeling of cooperation in the group.[5] And seeing the shared eye-rolling behavior behind your back, and all the group joining in pushing you out into the cold, giving you the cold shoulder, you are becoming aware that you are now outside the group.

Ask what else could be going on. What does not add up here is that you were invited to the party. So unless you are the target of a particularly cruel joke, things were fine fairly recently. With this in mind, you are correct to suspend your judgment that they hate your guts, though perhaps you have said or done something to make you persona non grata, at least for the moment. Replay in your mind any significant conversations or physical interactions you had thus far during the evening, any arguments or perhaps strong political or ideological viewpoints that may have singled you out as out of line with the ideologies of the group. Check yourself for any antisocial behavior in the context of that group and their familiar ways of being. Did you drink too much and behave in an unwelcome fashion? Loudly scoff at a tweet by Donald Trump, not knowing your friends suddenly all just turned supporters? Brag about the superior power of the newest iPhone in the company of android loyalists?

It is easy to form a **new judgment** of the situation if you can put your finger on any divisive or highly controversial discussions you had, the news of which may have spread around the room. There is still every possibility that your tribe likes you but finds your particular point of view over an issue abhorrent. It is easy to mix up signals that may be about your viewpoint with signals about you personally. You can **test** the veracity of your new judgment by easing into another conversation and completely changing the subject, for the time being anyway.

BODY LANGUAGE MYTHBUSTER
Fidgeters Are Hiding Something

Fiddling with your hands for no apparent reason may be the displacement of emotions and thoughts that are unexpressed, anything from excitement or boredom to frustration or relief. It can be a self-pacifying behavior where the physical movement creates a stimulus that calms us in times of anxiety. Or it can just be a way to shift parts of the body to make us more comfortable after being still for too long. In no way can it be seen as a sure indicator of deceit. Besides, if someone really wanted to hide something from you, don't you think they would be able to control their hands for just a while to get away with it? Without this ability, poker players couldn't bluff. Undercover cops would be instantly exposed. Most relationships would be irreparably damaged forever.

QUICK SCAN

S: When nobody wants to talk to you, it's the perfect opportunity to take a moment to yourself, breathe and **suspend** your judgment that your friends now hate you or want you gone. Think about what you know about when people use the body language in question, in this case the eye-roll.

C: A party with friends at a friend's house you have been invited to is the **context**, and that implies you share values and beliefs.

A: Ask whether you crossed the tribe. Why did they invite you, then?

N: Form a **new** judgment by replaying the conversations you had, noting with whom. Did you upset someone with social power in the group who has been spreading the word? How can you fix it?

27

INVISIBLE ME

Family members are taking no notice of you during family discussions, and they are making decisions without you. Everyone is talking past you, interrupting and talking over top of you. Nothing you say has any weight or bearing on anything, as nobody even appears to be listening to you. You feel small and insignificant, like you are not even there. You are invisible to them.

IN YOUR FAMILY, do you sometimes suspect you are a nothing and a nobody? Let's **suspend judgment** and **be more descriptive** of what is going on.

The key signal that is making you feel small, insignificant, powerless and invisible is that nobody appears to be listening to you; they are interrupting, talking over top of you and carrying on like you are not there.

When we feel small, we often minimize our size and impact by displaying submissive body language. Submissive body language involves gestures that make us look like we are caving in, looking defensive, reclusive or indecisive—in short, powerless. Adopting submissive postures shows that we prefer not to take power but to give it over to others, that we do not want to be in control. We not only take up less space and try to look small, we also avoid making noise. We take up as little nonverbal real estate as possible, be it physical, aural or temporal.

We may display submissive body language when we feel fearful toward whoever has power. Or we may fear for ourselves being responsible and holding power. We may be in awe, or completely admire someone else, or we may have low self-esteem, deep insecurity or simply a lack of motivation to act.

Submissive postures display the opposite of dominant ones, postures that take up space, sound and time. If someone moves loudly and decisively through a territory over sustained periods, you'll notice them. So the opposite—submissive body language—may look like this: cringing to appear smaller and less threatening; head bowing slightly; the chest caving in; "doe eyes"—that wide-open and innocent gaze mirroring the "startle" of the freeze, flight, fight, faint system or fear; hunched shoulders showing passiveness and even sadness while defending the neck area from attack. We may even look physically unbalanced, like we could be pushed over.

Crossed, defensive postures can also show submission or indecision. When you cross your body you hinder your ability to move, and therefore although you may feel less vulnerable, you may look and even feel more passive.

In the **context** of your family, it looks like everybody else is dominating the available space and leaving little room for you. Perhaps you are simply toeing the line, keeping the status quo, being the small fish in the big pond and playing the lower-status part you have always played to keep balance in the power dynamic. If this is the case, what does the rest of the pond look like? They are talking over top of you, literally standing and talking over your head, showing a heightened stature. They are interrupting you and dominating the airwaves as well. Other body language that displays territorial dominance includes spreading out, leaning in, bigger hand gestures, bigger facial gestures, open arm gestures, more eye contact and longer direct gazing, all of which take control of more real estate. Regardless of what they are saying, they are bigger, louder and taking up more time.

Ask what else could be legitimately adding to your feeling of being dominated and so feeling small. Have you been spending more time on your smartphone or other electronic devices lately?

While we are reminded often that social media can make us feel blue and lonely as we bear witness to others having the *best life ever*, what of the physical and psychological impact of always holding and staring down at our screens? Body language expert and TED Talk sensation Amy Cuddy explains a correlation between the bad posture so many of us experience from using smartphones—what she calls iPosture, also referred to as iHunch by New Zealand physiotherapist Steve August—and the psychological damage and changes in behavior that result. Citing studies that link depressed postures to lower self-esteem and mood, greater fear and more negative verbal reactions to questions, Cuddy's research finds that the "slouchy, collapsed position we take when using our phones actually makes us less assertive—less likely to stand up for ourselves when the situation calls for it."[1] Of course, as none of us are likely to give up our smartphones or other devices any time soon, Cuddy recommends that we do specific exercises and stretches to counter the iPhone slouch. Or save up for those visits to the osteopath.

While you can form a **new judgment** that you are of course not actually invisible but perhaps not taking up enough space within your family, what can you do to **test** this theory and claim, or claim back, some of your power? Try immediately taking up more physical space. First off, sit up straight. If you are at a table, move your chair back six inches so you are taking up more room and showing off more of a physical presence to others at the table. Place your hands on the table so you are taking up that territory as well. Place your smartphone on the table and push it away from you to take up even more territory and also to keep yourself from reaching for it and hiding away with it. Stand up when you are speaking or making important points. Make eye contact with the other members of your family. All these postures will make you appear more assertive.

However, if you are concerned about looking aggressive as opposed to assertive, avoid putting your hands on your hips or putting both your hands on the table and leaning over in close proximity to others. These gestures are both easily taken as an overt display of upper body strength and so could misrepresent you as aggressive, getting you further dismissed or shut down by your family. You may have a better chance of being heard and listened to if you engage with the clan by commanding some space in a calm and assertive manner, without appearing aggressive. The best way forward is to test the theory, get feedback and decide what's next based on that.

BODY LANGUAGE MYTHBUSTER
Body Language Changes Your Hormones

Many readers will be familiar with the incredible talk given by Amy Cuddy at the TEDGlobal 2012 conference: "Your Body Language Shapes Who You Are." Her talk, which went viral, details the research findings of Cuddy, and collaborators Dana Carney and Andy Yap, on the feedback effects of adopting powerful (i.e., expansive) versus powerless (i.e., contractive) postures—otherwise known as "power posing"—and concludes that holding power poses affects the body's hormone levels, causing a rise in testosterone and a drop in cortisol levels.

With science evolving at an exponential pace, those findings were later shown to be inconclusive. Power posing has not been scientifically proven to affect our hormones as the researchers initially thought. What remains clear to Cuddy, and millions of others who have adopted these power poses, is that the effect is indisputable and powerful. Cuddy now calls it the "postural feedback effect," and her key finding, which others in the world of body language can attest to, is profound yet simple: Adopting expansive postures causes people to feel more powerful. It is not necessarily why it does so that is important in this case, but that it does, regardless.

In an interview with David Biello for TED Science, Cuddy says of her older research, "As sticky as the power-posing-for-two-minutes idea is and as much as many people feel it has helped them, it over-simplifies the broader idea—that how we carry our bodies affects how we feel about ourselves, how we interact with others, how we perform and so on. My unintentional oversimplification may have allowed people to miss the forest for the trees."[2]

QUICK SCAN

S: Suspend judgment and see how expansive you can be with the space you take up. How minimal can you also be? Does it change the way you feel? How do you think others will think about you in these different positions?

C: In what **context**, if any, do you most regularly dominate the space or feel that you minimize your presence?

A: Ask what other elements in your environment may be affecting how you minimize or maximize your physical presence in the world.

N: How would you like to be more of the time in terms of how visible you are to others, and what **new** behaviors would you need to produce to test whether you can be that? When might you be able to start these behaviors?

PART

FOUR

WORKING LIFE

I never worry about what the people at work think of me.
—Nobody honest, EVER!

We can't really avoid work. Our current civilization has been built on the work of all others so far, and we can recognize our development in the early tools central to our evolution. Where would we be without the flint ax or the bone needle?

But if work is so important, and has got us so far, why should it be such a stressor? Although many people are engaged and motivated by their work and even form lasting friendships in the workplace, more and more of us are taking time off because of depression or anxiety, or just to spend more time doing what gives us more satisfaction.

Work is necessary and can be extremely stimulating and satisfying, but the circumstances of work can alienate us from the people we are meant to be working closest with, who are indeed the people with whom we may spend the majority of our waking hours. And of course the majority of us rely on exchanging our work for money so we can get what we really need and want, the most powerful resources of food and shelter, and good times for ourselves, our families and friends—the people who matter most to us. To help us accomplish this sequence successfully, the relationships we have with our colleagues start to matter as much and sometimes even more than the relationships we have outside of work. Although we may let ourselves off the hook, and our friends and families may forgive us, if we can't supply what they need because of challenges we are facing, our work colleagues may not be so forgiving during challenging times. It may be the continued good feelings of those workmates toward us that facilitate our ability to succeed and to earn what we need. And as we spend increasing amounts of our time working or at least being accessible to our work colleagues on our mobile devices, we end up spending a considerable amount of our time in their company, and so how we relate overall is important to everyone's well-being.

If we can predict the thoughts, feelings and intentions of our coworkers, whether we are face to face or communicating via video conference, phone or e-mail, then we may be able to better build and stabilize our relationships while increasing the resources we give out and our share of the benefits. Let's take a look at how we can detect the truth, the lies and the power plays at work and truly win a greater piece of the pie.

28

I ACED THAT INTERVIEW—
SO, WHERE'S THE JOB OFFER?

You recently interviewed for your dream job. From the moment you walked into the building, trying to keep your cool and focus, you were put at ease. Things could not have gone better. Everyone, from the receptionist to the HR folks and your potential manager, was happy and truly smiley toward you—very genuine—and even the CEO, whom you passed in the hallway, gave you a welcoming handshake. During the interview, your interviewers looked directly at you and seemed positive and engaged, nodding in agreement with what you said, making you relax and giving you the confidence to wow them with your expertise and ideas.

➡

They often looked to be genuinely smiling when you were talking, and they were obviously listening well to you because they asked great follow-up questions. You saw them looking at each other and nodding, seemingly receptive to your ideas, wanting to learn more. The interview was lengthy, and you left on a real high, feeling confident that you got the job. You can't stop talking to your friends about how great the organization is and how fun and friendly the people are. "They loved me!" you say. But after a few days and no word from them, you are starting to sweat and wonder why they haven't called. You think, *They've got to call! I totally aced that interview!*

THIS SCENARIO WILL BE FAMILIAR to many of us who leave an interview feeling like we definitely are going to get the call, only to be shocked and confused when we do not. While it may be true that you aced the interview, let's **SCAN** and **suspend judgment** that the interviewers are giving out positive signals about you and **be more descriptive** of why you made that assumption, and what happened in the interview, to try to clear up some of your confusion.

The key signals from the interviewers that you aced the interview: clear and positive looks, including genuine smiling; looking at each other and nodding to each other; and listening. First off, the smile here is described as "true" and genuine. The Duchenne smile, as you read elsewhere in this book, where the eyes crease up in the corners, is a true smile of pleasure, one that can show support and encouragement, as opposed to other types of smiles, like some half-smiles, which can imply the smugness of negative judgment and superiority, or a tight-lipped, closed-mouth smile, often described as secretive or polite.

The interviewers in this scenario are also nodding, which as we discuss in other chapters can express different feelings, like boredom or, if the nodding speeds up, a desire for you to stop talking in order for the person doing the nodding to jump into the conversation. However, other telltale signs would also show up in that case. For example, if the interviewers are nodding and trying to conceal boredom, they may also be yawning or trying to hide yawning; fidgeting; and looking around the room or turning away, their eyes glazing over. This is not the case here, as the interviewers are described as positive, looking at you, nodding and smiling, all pointing to signs of encouragement and the use of nonverbal regulator cues to get you to talk more. They are listening, which includes all of the above positive signals, and they are angled toward you, maintaining good eye contact, and often look as though they are tilting an ear slightly toward you. So far, it would seem you are right about their positivity.

All these positive signals toward you within the **context** of the job interview seem to speak volumes about your bright future with this organization. Job interviews can sometimes be run by people who want to come across as aloof or tricky and so are cold or smug or judgmental, wanting to test you, making you work to grab their attention and in turn the position. Interviewers like these can create a foreboding interview environment; they may be transparent about your competition for the position to make you feel you need to "dance for your dinner," conducting the interview with a kind of "treat them mean, keep them keen" power play. The opposite is true in our scenario. The interviewers compel you to relax, to speak more and share ideas, allowing you to take your time, clearly providing a safe and relaxed environment where they will get the best out of you, and you can show your individuality and the power you can bring to the table. Which seems to have worked. Why haven't they called yet, then?

Ask what else could shed light on why you didn't get the call when you came out of the interview feeling so certain about your success. Not only are positions at organizations difficult to land, but organizations often find themselves competing with each other to attract the best and brightest candidates. They are making a sizable investment in their workforce, after all. They want the best employees, so they are creating an environment that is super friendly and welcoming. Right down to the genuine smiles? As we've said before, contrary to the folk wisdom that you can't fake a real smile, almost everyone can successfully fake a true smile in the right circumstances. They are in competition for you. Your skill set is in demand. Then again, there are other people competing with you who share your skill set, and the organization wants the top talent.

You came out of that interview feeling you had aced it but also motivated to tell your friends how amazing the organization is, how friendly. Many organizations want to be seen as the best on every level, from the public's perception right down to the potential entry-level employee. No matter who they ultimately offer the position to, they want that job candidate to accept the offer immediately, not be ambivalent about doing so because they're faced with other offers from more welcoming organizations. Consider also the trend of organizations becoming increasingly customer-focused, with brands working to ensure integrity of user experience at every interaction. The behavior of the interviewers is as much an expression of the company brand as is their product or service. They may be putting on a great show.

Furthermore, having a satisfied and motivated workforce is increasingly linked to overall success for the organization. We need only look at consistently top-performing organizations that make the Great Places to Work list every year to see the direct correlation between a fulfilling work environment and the organization's growth, profitability and stock performance. As Michael C. Bush, CEO of Great Place to Work, notes, "The new, largely uncharted business territory is about developing every ounce of human potential, so that organizations can reach their full potential . . . All companies—including the Best Workplaces—face the challenge of creating an outstanding culture for everyone, no matter who they are or what they do for the organization."[1] Research shows that the more inclusive, diverse and consistently great the workplace, the stronger the revenue growth. All of which means that many organizations are actively engaged in working toward this goal—in our scenario, even down to the CEO being more hands on.

BODY LANGUAGE MYTHBUSTER
Always Give a Firm Handshake

The definition of a good handshake can be different depending on the culture and the situation. Handshakes last a few seconds, and within those few seconds you can make a lasting impression of the power you possess. Here's how you execute a classic North American/European business handshake: Slip your hand all the way into the other person's hand until the web in between your thumb and index finger meets your partner's, and then clasp the fingers of the other person. Bring your and your

➡

---

partner's hand up and down two or three times and then let go.

Other countries and cultures tend to have less firm handshakes, such as those in China and other Asiatic countries. Misinterpretation of the interest and power being shown can often occur when the two parties involved in the handshake do not fully understand the culture or the situation and can end up giving the wrong impression.

A study in 2013 by the Weizmann Institute of Science found that handshakes engage our sense of smell. Researchers noted that the study's participants not only unconsciously sniffed their own hands but did so for a much longer time after shaking someone's hand.[2] Though handshakes are thought to go back traditionally to checking if someone has a tool or weapon in their hand, these findings also hint at its evolutionary origins: Handshaking might have served to convey odor signals, and such signaling may still be a meaningful, albeit subliminal, component of this custom.

You can now form a **new judgment** that perhaps you are not exactly perfect for the job, but the interviewers displayed such positivity toward you because they were displaying their brand values, showing off the organization as an upbeat, amazing, accepting and positive environment in which to work. You need to accept that you may have misinterpreted how they show off their excellent workplace environment for positive feelings about you, even though you likely performed extremely well at the interview.

Your initial reading of their positivity is therefore not wrong, just misdirected. They have likely behaved in much the same way toward every other candidate for the job. To **test** this theory, ask around or even do some online research to see if other job candidates describe a similar experience. It is an amazing organization. Everybody is showing their best side, and that includes you showing your optimism.

We hope you get to work there. It sounds like you fit in and it would be a great place to work, but you need to keep cool until you hear a real "yes" from them. Maybe drop them an e-mail to say it was great to meet everyone and see if you can get feedback on the interview, find out when the final decision will be made and when they'll let you know.

INTELLIGENCE IN THE HAND

Organizations use many avenues of intelligence to find the best candidate when it comes to filling some of the most important positions. Our friend **JAMIE MASON COHEN** is a handwriting analysis expert who uses his skill to help organizations develop their employees to reach their full potential. Here's what he told us about the "body language" of our handwritten words.

Handwriting is a projection of the unconscious mind. It's your personality on paper. Handwriting analysts believe you can tell how an individual wants to be seen by the world through the unconscious act of signing their name. Your signature is your personal brand; it's the authority you project in the world.

Cursive handwriting is sometimes referred to as frozen body language because your brain creates the image of what you want to express and your fingers carry out the directive of your mind. By identifying what certain written traits look like and mean, you can gain instant insights into how you come across to others. Small neuromuscular movements are the same for every person who has that personality trait. Micro-movements are so tiny they need to be visually frozen to be identified; handwriting is an example of this visually frozen movement.

Your social aptitude: It's in the size and slant. A shy and socially withdrawn or introverted person may display small, cramped letters that slant to the left. This individual is signaling to the world that they prefer a quiet night at home to a loud, gregarious party. They may appear to someone who doesn't know them like a snail who doesn't come out of its shell too often. Accountants, auditors, scientists, engineers, computer programmers, fighter pilots and possibly surgeons may display small, left-leaning and angular writing. The writing also correlates to a personality type that rarely displays emotions easily. To project a more dynamic, charismatic public persona, practice signing your name larger, in the center of the page, with a slight upward slant. A grander, bolder signature equals the physical manifestation of a more outwardly confident image. It gives others the impression that you see yourself as a leader comfortable with being the center of attention or taking the lead in a new project at work.

Direct and clear communication: It's in the loops of your circle letters. Handwriting that displays middle-zone letters free of interior double loops represents integrity. Double loops that pervade writing may show that a person doesn't feel safe telling certain people the truth about something going on in their life. While writing, you may consider bringing some nonjudgmental self-awareness to the unnecessary loops that you are making in the circular shapes such as "O," "A" and "D." It may help bring a new perspective as to why you may be withholding the truth in a particular situation.

High self-esteem, ambition and goals: It's in the height of the t-bar. A high, strongly written t-bar from left to right shows that a person values themselves and their ability to plan ahead to achieve their goals. If the t-bar is softly drawn and fades out quickly, it may be beneficial to change this stroke. The next time you are taking notes in a meeting, consciously write strong, high and long strokes on the top half of the t-bar to project an enthusiastic and powerful level of self-esteem. It can generate enthusiasm and help positively shift one's mind-set by changing the neural pathways that correlate to a specific trait. The high t-bar also reflects the unconscious belief of setting strong and clear personal boundaries, of fearlessly facing change, and signals to the brain to take calculated risks in the direction of where someone sets out to go in life.

Barrier to trust—illegible signatures: If your signature is illegible, it may be a sign that you have a desire to be seen but not known. You are projecting to the world that you are a private person who desires to keep your identity hidden. It could also be seen as an obstacle to intimacy and connecting with others. To solve this, take the time to write out every letter in both your given name and your surname to display more openness, approachability and presence.

QUICK SCAN

S: Suspend judgment on what your interviewers' smiling and positivity might have meant to investigate whether it was just for you or their modus operandi.

C: Look at the **context** of the organization's brand and what external image they may enjoy or aspire to.

A: Ask what this organization and others like it may be keen to project and how the interviewers reflected this in the interview.

N: While you may not get this job, you likely did a great interview but were not quite the right fit. Asking for feedback is a great way to test a **new** judgment.

29

THEY HATE MY WORK

There's been change in your organization that has meant annoyance and complication for you. Trooper that you are, you've been putting out your usual exceptional work. It's just that now they all seem to hate it. Take the latest project. You worked diligently on your part of it and were in overdrive getting it done, with all the new responsibilities and changes you have had to cope with at the same time. When the team gets together for the progress meeting in the makeshift boardroom late in the afternoon and you present your stuff, people are wincing and grimacing, frowning, slumping over and sharply exhaling, and rubbing their faces.

➡

Someone even does a facepalm and groans. *This is so painful for them*, you think. *They obviously all hate my work.*

FEELING LIKE YOUR WORK isn't appreciated or hitting the mark, particularly when you are giving it 110 percent, may make you angry or depressed and can certainly be a knock against your confidence and self-esteem. But is it true that your colleagues hate the work you are producing? **SCAN** this situation. Let's **suspend judgment** and **be more descriptive** of what is going on.

Hate is a strong feeling of extreme emotional dislike and may be accompanied by a collection of body language key signals indicating anger, disgust and hostility, as you've seen in other chapters. For anger: vertical lines between the brows, brows drawn together, tense lower lid, tight and narrow lips, glaring eyes, dilated nostrils, jutting lower jaw, the head tipping down to protect the neck with the chin. All three facial areas must be involved in the gesture. For disgust: wrinkled nose, downturning mouth, tense lower lip. And for hostility: the energetic display of some or all of the indicators for anger and disgust, along with a readiness for physical aggression. This could be clenched fists, raised voice with downward inflection, feet stamping to stamp out the object of hostility or the torso turning away from the object of hostility, looking to avoid the hated thing.

Your coworkers are frowning, certainly one of the signs of anger and disgust; however, as we have noted previously, knitted eyebrows that make up a frown on their own do not necessarily equal anger. If the frown combines with wincing and grimacing—wrinkled nose, eyes squeezed shut, mouth twisted—these body language signals are associated with pain, either physical or psychological.

Add to that the slumping over and the sharp exhaling, which suggests that the wind is getting knocked out of their sails and they are experiencing an exasperated, sinking feeling. Slumping over and letting the air out of the lungs shows they are deflating, and submissive to power or pain, as opposed to energetically pushing back against it in anger or hostility. Let's not forget the groan either—an expression of or reaction to pain. Alongside the slumping and exhaling, they are rubbing their faces, a self-soothing gesture. The facepalm, also a blocking gesture, suggests hiding, maybe in fear or shame.

So far, although you may be right on the money that your colleagues are experiencing a strong emotion, hate does not fit the description. Though a couple of the signs may be associated with anger, there are not enough accompanying signs to suggest it fully, and there are no energized postures of aggression or fight, usually associated with anger or hate.

BODY LANGUAGE MYTHBUSTER
A Pictograph Says a Thousand Words

In 2015, the president of Oxford Dictionaries, Casper Grathwohl, described *emoji*, the company's Word of the Year, as an increasingly rich form of communication that crosses language barriers. "Emoji have come to embody a core aspect of living in a digital world that is visually driven, emotionally expressive, and obsessively immediate."[1] An emoji, the small digital image or icon used to express an idea or emotion in electronic communication, and its precursor, the emoticon, both function within text-based communication along the same lines as nonverbal cues in face-to-face communication. Now in any social media situation, we can qualify the meaning of our text or indeed replace the words with graphics that show a picture summing up how we are feeling. But how well do they really function to show the feelings we want to communicate? Are these cool little pictures really getting across what we think they are?

Studies such as that by Hannah Miller and colleagues from the University of Minnesota find there are plenty of ways to misinterpret emojis, with their increasingly nuanced graphics. One of her main findings was that since emojis render differently on different platforms, there can be vastly different interpretations of the same emoji. She notes that Emojipedia, a website serving as an encyclopedia for emojis, lists seventeen such platforms, such as Apple, Google, Microsoft, Samsung and LG, which means there may be at least seventeen different renderings for a given Unicode emoji character.[2] Miller concludes that emoji usage between different platforms can create an environment ripe for misconstrued communication. Furthermore, the research found that even when used on the same platform,

➡️

the same emojis were interpreted by users completely differently. One example she cites is the
Apple emoji for "grinning face with smiling eyes,"
where some people surveyed found the emoji to
show positive emotion, while others thought it was
more negative. So the digital equivalent of nonverbal communication may be just as likely to give us
the wrong impression as an in-person interaction.
Being mindful and using critical thinking is the key
to getting it right when interpreting words and emotions expressed via emojis! ¯_(ツ)_/¯

Well, it's certainly something, this reaction to your work. Is it
you? Is it them? Is it you *and* them? Let's look at the **context** to shed
some light on this. You are meeting with the team members, each
of whom is working on different aspects of the project, so you will
have shared goals and objectives. However, any group ties you may
have shared previously have been transplanted into a new dynamic
environment, potentially against an overwhelming backdrop of
change, and you are all experiencing something like a twister effect,
where things are not how they were before, where your entire team
is now trying to make sense of how any of your work is going to fit in
with the new standards and direction. In other words, you're not in
Kansas anymore.

A new working order has every chance of causing pain and confusion as people attempt to navigate the new system and potentially
repurpose themselves within it. Most organizations will experience

change multiple times, needing to innovate and adapt to realities that are constantly evolving and developing as society changes at an ever-increasing rate. The stress and uncertainty that accompany organizational change are well documented, and one thing we can count on is that organizational change can be difficult, causing daily negative feelings for many employees.[3]

Ask what else is going on. Our description here kicks off with how you feel about the organizational change. You are annoyed and confused, and furthermore you feel you've had to work extra hard through the difficult times. Being on a team or in a department or a silo with others with whom you have worked harmoniously before may not be enough to keep you working harmoniously after a big change, what with a new regime and new rules, systems, managers and staff and with that, new pressures. But you feel you've been a trooper, which suggests you feel solidarity with the team.

Chances are you are not the only one with these feelings. But how much are you wearing your annoyance like a scratchy shirt, looking uncomfortable and irritated, sighing, rubbing *your* face and burying *your* face in your hands? Are others in the group simply mirroring your body language? Do they in fact feel the same as you? And lastly, are you operating in a makeshift room at the end of the day? A cramped, physically uncomfortable environment after a long hard day may be the final straw that causes everybody, including you, to become and to therefore look exasperated and beaten down.

So the **new judgment** is that your coworkers do not hate your work per se but, like you, are feeling exasperated and annoyed. You may all be mirroring each other's body language, which speaks volumes about the pain and hardship you and they are experiencing as your organization transitions. How can you **test** to know for sure, though, to then try to improve the situation, not just for you but for your coworkers as well?

There is no way of presenting your work outside of the change that is currently going on. However, you could try to present your next lot of work in a different environment, and at a different time of day, to see how people respond. Make sure your body language is upbeat and optimistic. You cannot control the macro-environment, or in other words, the change in the organization. But you might be able to control something of the micro-environment—for example, the room you are presenting in, the time you are presenting and your overall body language. If you get the same negative results at that point, ask your coworkers to pinpoint the elements of your presentation that are causing them distress. If after all of that they are still doing the same thing, it may well be that your behavior itself is overbearing, too much for your coworkers to take given the changing landscape, and perhaps you can attempt to transition yourself into an area of the newly realized organization that may be better suited to your strengths.

QUICK SCAN

S: Although your coworkers are showing strong signs of something negative, you need to **suspend** judgment, particularly of a strong emotion like hate, and evaluate all the signals.

C: Organizational change can easily create a tense and fractured working **context** for everybody.

A: Are you alone in experiencing the pain of the organizational change? **Ask:** Is it you? Is it them? Is it you *and* them?

N: If you make the **new** judgment that your body language may be influencing others, that they may be mirroring you, then simply change your behavior and see if others change theirs with you.

30

BIG DOG

You are in charge of appointing a new sales leader for your organization, and you've interviewed a wide range of excellent candidates. Then this one candidate shows up with way less experience than all the others. They're relatively new to the game, but strangely, right off the bat your gut is telling you this is *the one*, that you can trust them to get the job done, lead the team and sell, making loads of profit for the organization. They already look like the person in charge. They're square jawed and athletic, upright and confident. They dominate the space and the conversation, taking up more space and time by speaking slower and clearer than

➡

281

anyone else; their words are weighty and seem important. They also show excellent signs of listening. They look pleasant and smiley, with good eye contact, a loud voice and a firm handshake—this person will be a powerhouse that will let nothing stand in its way. They'll command the team, and they will be great with customers. Just like you right now, you think everyone will respect them. So what they lack in experience compared with the other candidates they make up for in spades by showing up like the big dog. Time to offer them the job there and then?

EASY, TIGER! LET'S STEP BACK and take a closer look at all of this.

The "big dog" is a person, entity or organization that is powerful, notable, prominent and important. In the workplace, there is often someone who shows up stronger than us and that everybody seems to look up to as the natural born leader, who gets those promotions before everybody else, who seems to shine and always be on the right track. That's all certainly very powerful.

SCAN: Let's **suspend judgment** that this big dog is the right person for the job and **be more descriptive** of why you are thinking that. You need to get this right, after all. This employee is going to cost the organization potentially hundreds of thousands of dollars, and this job candidate has less experience than all the others.

Let's look at the key signals giving you the gut instinct that this powerful big dog should get the job over the more qualified and experienced candidates. First, they are giving plenty of dominance signals, such as taking up more space and thereby claiming more of the available territory and power, dominating time and soundwaves by taking longer to speak and being loud and clear, giving their words a weighty and more important quality; they are athletic with a firm handshake, showing strength and power; they are upright and so look tall, again dominating space and showing power through height, which translates to confidence; and they have powerful eye contact, acknowledging that they see and hear you and are not afraid to meet your eyes.

Let's look at other key signals through a lens of evolutionary and social psychology. The key signals arise from both "static" and "dynamic" cues. A review of the work of evolutionary psychologists by Eric Hehman and his colleagues highlights how "cues related to evaluations of ability tend to be relatively static and structural rather than dynamic and malleable."[1] In other words, we tend to judge someone's ability based on static cues, meaning facial structural appearances: the innate bone structure we are born with and generally cannot alter much, except perhaps through surgery. However, we tend to judge someone's intentions by their dynamic cues, meaning how we look as a result of how our musculature has developed to show our individual expression of emotion. Dynamic cues could technically change if we were to greatly alter the way we physically show our emotions over time. Here in our scenario, the big dog is square jawed, a set-in-stone static cue.

Our primitive brains are overwhelmingly biased to perceive dominance and power, possibly aggression, in those people who have square jaws. To be specific, and as Hehman explains, those with a high facial width to height ratio (fWHR), or a wider bone structure from the outsides of the cheekbones between the upper lip and the lower brow, are potentially four times as likely to be perceived as dominant and aggressive when in fact they may be only nominally more dominant than average. In other words, though we think they are fantastically dominant, in reality they are more likely to be only just slightly more dominant than anybody else.

High fWHR is associated with higher levels of testosterone. The static facial cue of the square jaw tips off our primitive brains to the higher levels of testosterone present in that individual. Over human history, we have evolved with an innate understanding that the higher the testosterone, the stronger, more persistent and higher risk-taking someone will be, and so our gut response is to fall into line. As Hehman summarizes, early humans would have learned to quickly assess the ability and potential threat of other humans, given that intense early competition within groups is thought to have had a major impact on our evolutionary development.[2] So here in our scenario, because you are likely to have an instinctual response that the square-jawed person will be more capable than others and go that extra distance to win the day, you award them power and status and help them on their way. Your theory about their long-term professional credibility is simply a response to their immediate physical power.

Dynamic cues from the big dog also lead you to see them as more able-bodied. They look pleasant and smiley, thereby appearing positive toward you, helpful, friendly and not overly aggressive in their dominance. It feels like they have good intentions toward you, and you extend this behavior into a vision that they will show good intentions professionally. However, it is important to keep in mind that predicting they will perform well professionally is an extension of your theory that they intend well toward you and is likely a response to your relief about this, given their perceived power. You think, *They're powerful and they're going to be nice to me, so that's good.* You then default to making everything about and around them also good. You create a halo of positivity around them. You may even start to placate them in order to keep them well-intentioned toward you.

You may do this for your own physical safety or to prolong the idea you have about them. Often, once an idea feels true to our instinct, we will unconsciously construct a world that upholds it, even if that world is inaccurate or at the very least extremely biased.

The **context** sets the stage to seal the deal regarding your assumption that this person is right for the job, compounding the favorable conditions for the square-jawed jobseeker as well as your predisposition to have a positive gut response to them. In our scenario, the context is the job interview. You are the one responsible for hiring the new salesperson for your organization. Your own job may even be on the line. You need to hire someone who will meet and hopefully exceed expectations, helping the organization as a whole, but also essentially showing the rest of the organization that you are great at your job. You are hoping to find a winner, that leader who will be able to handle the trickiest customers and get the sale, making everybody look good. The big dog shows up with what hits you right away as obvious ability, power and good intentions, and you are predisposed to respond to their cues.

Ask what else you should consider that will either make you review the other excellent job candidates again or go with your gut and hire the less experienced one. You need to recognize that you are making a prediction about the big dog's future performance based on your primitive brain's snap judgment response to them now. With their high testosterone and with all the right dominant body language, the big dog is able to dominate you in the moment. Of course, there may be an excellent chance that the big dog will make the same impression on your colleagues and will make a real impact on clients. However, you need to consider whether these traits indicate they will also be dominant in future sales situations and longer sales cycles. The truth is that they do not necessarily indicate this at all. Over millions of years, people we perceive as dominant have enjoyed more power in the moment, often during moments of conflict or transition, such as this one. You have no indication, however, that this individual will maintain their dominance in situations over time. You don't know yet whether they will be able to maintain long term the power of their credibility with customers or clients and build lasting relationships with them. Remember, by deciding they are the one for the job right off the bat, you are responding on a primitive level to their dominant traits by placating them in the moment. Your primitive brain is not thinking about how you will work with them over the next decade. The primitive brain does not care about the future—it only cares about right now.

BODY LANGUAGE MYTHBUSTER
You Can't Put in What Nature's Left Out

No matter what gifts we are born with, it can often seem like others have an advantage over us and we're never going to be able to compete. The good news is you can make the first impression you want in your résumé or online professional photograph with a smart use of the camera angle and lens. Danielle Libine, a contributor to this book, gives excellent advice on how to take a photo to show you at your best in her work *A Photographer's Guide to Body Language*. For example, using a shorter focal length when taking your picture will make your face look thinner, while using a longer focal length will make your face appear wider. In other words, your face will look more filled out if you take the picture from farther away and zoom in, as opposed to taking a picture of your face up close. And as we've seen, the width of the face will have an impact on how others, including potential employers, will perceive your competence.[3]

So the important **new judgment** you can make about the big dog is to recognize that you are awarding them status and ability based on their innate physicality, which is translating into credibility that at this point you really cannot prove. However, with their good use of dominant body language, they could prove to be the real deal for the job. The **test**: This is definitely the right time to do your homework. Our thin-slice judgments are not necessarily correct over time. Size matters and ratios matter, but they are a quick guide to performance. Yes, if you hire this person right now, they may win the fight, but where will they be in three to six months, let alone two to five years? You cannot allow the brainstem to do long-term planning. The brainstem makes its best guess now and does not conduct long-term strategic planning or strategic hiring.

Study their résumé. Although their past employment may be unrelated to the job right now, note how often they moved on, to get clues about whether they had longevity in any work environment. This is a great example of when you need to follow up on references and have productive conversations with their past employers, team members and even customers. If you do your homework properly and things come up smelling like roses, then you can go with your gut instinct, because it isn't just a gut instinct anymore.

WORKING WITH DOGS

Mark Bowden first met **VICTORIA STILWELL** at university in England. They worked closely together for three years, and both ended up writing, broadcasting and training others in behavior. However, Victoria, as the star of the hit TV series *It's Me or the Dog*, is best known for helping dog owners positively train their pets. With canines having lived as partners alongside us humans for at least the last 15,000 years, it is no wonder they are often seen at work with us. In her book *The Secret Language of Dogs*,[4] Victoria tells us the most important nonverbal signals to look out for from your canine friend.

Dogs have a rich physical and vocal language that is as complex and subtle as our own. Although most people understand basic canine communication, vital signals and language are often missed or misunderstood, causing friction and at times damaging the fragile human–animal bond. Understanding canine language and communicating effectively with dogs is vital for building a relationship, helping them learn and strengthening the bond.

Play signals: Dog-to-dog play includes active and repetitive behaviors that mean different things when performed in different contexts, but in general, play helps dogs gain experience and develop important life skills that promote good physical and mental health. Play can be something of a mock battle in which dogs rehearse physical actions they might need in life, and good play is all about winning and losing the game by "self-handicapping." It's all about give and take—being able to roll over as the other dog dives on top and then to reverse the situation—and keeping the play roles equal. A play bow, where the dog goes down on their front legs with their behind in the air, is used to elicit play as well as to signal to the dog or human that the following interaction is still just play and not battle. Dogs might also mount each other during play. This is usually not an aggressive act (unless the mounter is trying to bully and the dog being mounted takes umbrage) but a good rehearsal for future sexual or dominant behavior and actually helps make aggression less likely.

Appeasement signals: Dogs have a rich language of appeasement—signals that are consciously and unconsciously utilized to change behavior in others and keep the dog safe, as appeasement can help prevent and decrease the likelihood of aggressive behavior. Appeasement signals include muzzle licking; head turning; flattened ears; lip licking; lifting a front paw; low tail carriage; wagging tail; tail tucked between the legs; curved and crouched body; submissive urination; and belly flip, where the dog flips over quickly, exposing the belly. It's important to note that with the belly flip, the dog is not asking for a belly rub but is signaling withdrawal from interaction.

Pain signals: Managing your dog's pain can be hard; because dogs don't speak our language, it is often difficult to find the source of pain or even recognize that your dog is in discomfort in the first place, as the signs can be so subtle. In general, if you notice a change in your dog's behavior or your dog starts moving in a different way (often known as "pain guarding," which takes pressure off a part of the body that is painful), this could be a sign of suffering. Reluctance to be groomed, difficulty getting up from a resting position, change in body posture or normal walking gait, excessive licking, coat changes and changes in behavior are all signs to look out for that might indicate your dog is in pain.

QUICK SCAN

S: You make judgments about people based not only on their looks but also on the cues they give and the sounds they make. **Suspending** judgment gives you time to unpack these details and also shine a light on your own biases.

C: The stakes and resulting stress around any event can create a **context** that affects nonverbal communication and the judgments you make about what you see and hear.

A: Ask how likely it is that the behavior you see now is an indicator of a longer-term trend.

N: Your own **new** judgments may not affect how others will judge. Just because you have new insights about a person does not mean that others will automatically have them too.

31

NEVER GOING TO SEE EYE TO EYE

One of many managers at your organization, you walk into a meeting with a manager of a different department who is of equal status to you. Your departments are totally separate and run completely differently, but because of changes in the business, you now have to meet for the first time and plan how your departments will work together. You go to their work area, and from the moment they beckon you to sit down on the comfy sofa opposite them, you get the impression that this working relationship will be anything but comfy. You can't tell if their face is in a smile or a grimace, but they are certainly looking down at you, with

their chin sticking up, and there is an air of arrogance about them. You hand up to them the hard-
copy of your plan; they frown down at it and at you
and jab their finger at proposals written on the
paper as they rattle off the associated challenges.
You get the overwhelming feeling that this working
relationship is going to be tough going, and that
you and they are never going to see eye to eye.

GETTING OFF ON THE RIGHT FOOT with a colleague is not always
easy. Even before you get going on the real work, you may first need
to work at negotiating around some big egos, which can translate
into territorial protection and aggressive, arrogant and undermin-
ing behaviors. But does this really mean you will you never see eye
to eye? Let's **SCAN** this situation, **suspend judgment** and **be more
descriptive** of what is going on.

Let's review the key signals giving you the feeling this relationship is
doomed: The other manager's reaction to you is at first ambiguous in
that you cannot tell whether they are grimacing or smiling when you
meet; then they respond to your work with arrogance and aggression,
chin up, looking down at you, frowning and jabbing their finger at your
work. Not a great start to a harmonious working relationship, for sure.

First off, are they smiling or grimacing? As you read elsewhere in
this book, there are many types of smiles. There is the Duchenne
smile of genuine pleasure, where the corners of the mouth rise up,
as do the cheeks, thus forming crow's feet at the outside of the eyes.
There are also fake or social smiles—for example, what is dubbed the

Botox smile, where the eyes don't smile but the mouth does. This smile is common with people who feel they have to smile to fulfill the social norm, but they themselves are not feeling the pleasure of the situation. This type of smile looks forced, insincere or downright painful, closer to the look of a grimace, as in our scenario. In this case, the other manager may have been trying to look and act welcoming to you, and the strange forced grimace may be displaying that there are problems for them around that. Studies have shown that people will often try to smile even when they are in clinically painful situations, and they may attempt to smile more the better they know the person administering that painful procedure. Smiling through pain may be our instinctual attempt to strengthen social bonds and so limit the painful activity.[1]

BODY LANGUAGE MYTHBUSTER
A Nod Always Means Yes
It is very important for us, as social animals, to feel accepted by the group and also to accept others, to hold our groups together. While head nodding can show encouragement to others and indicate agreement, it can also be a signal of appeasement—placating someone—without necessarily agreeing with them. Head nodding is also quite often the result of isopraxism, the natural mirroring of another's behavior. In a group setting, it is sometimes both contagious and unconscious. Often those at the top of the social hierarchy can experience a room full of

---

people nodding their heads at their idea and assume everyone agrees with them, only to discover later that no one accepted the idea or even understood it. And a completely still head can mean "We don't get it," "We don't accept it," "We don't agree" or "We don't like it" just as much as does shaking the head from side to side.

Back to our scenario, in which the other manager quickly displays what appears to be negative body language: Chin pointing up here may suggest defiance and can certainly look threatening. When the chin is raised slightly, it shows off the carotid artery in the throat; as well as appearing taunting to the other person, it looks arrogant, as the raised chin will often be accompanied by looking down the nose. Furthermore, a more prominent chin display can often be associated with a physically more pronounced jaw, a trait that can arise in anyone when levels of testosterone are increased over a long period. The hormone testosterone causes the jaw and eyebrow ridges to become more prominent. Furthermore, higher testosterone is associated with higher risk-taking. Human beings have evolved to understand this on a primal level; it is embedded in many cultures that when we see the display of a raised or jutted chin, we should beware. Even if testosterone levels are not abundant, our response to this physical feature is ingrained, and so we would respond to body language that aggressively shows off that feature with concern. In our scenario, sensing the aggression of the other manager may make you feel the need to steer clear or alternatively to gear yourself up for an altercation.

Also in our scenario, you see them jabbing their finger at your work. Pointing a finger targets people, places, things and even personifications of ideas, beckoning the onlooker to direct their focus in the direction of the object being pointed at. We need only look at representations of finger-pointing in art and culture to see some common targets and underlying meanings. For example, in religiously inspired art, there are plenty of examples of the subject pointing upward toward heaven or a deity. And many countries have used direct fingerpointing in military propaganda posters, the finger targeting and singling out the onlooker to sign up for the military. Pointing directly at someone signals "Hey, you!" or "I want you!" Finger-pointing can also implicate or accuse: "He did it!" Witnesses on the stand in a court of law are told to physically point a finger at the guilty party, certainly an accusatory gesture that may help sway a jury to decide that a defendant is guilty. Pointing the finger can also be seen as holding or using a symbolic weapon, as in our scenario. The manager pointing at the target of your work and then jabbing a finger at it would suggest symbolic violence. They are stabbing at your ideas and potentially would like to end them.

So by being more descriptive, you can confirm your feeling that they are aggressive toward you, potentially feeling threatened and defensive. And you can justify your relatively primal response to their body language as you jump to negative conclusions that you will never get along, never see eye to eye.

However, the **context** of this meeting is one that is new to you and perhaps to them too. You do not normally work together, your departments are completely different, and you have entered into their department, their territory. First off, this is a tribal situation where both parties might feel some strong and unconscious feelings around each other. There are plenty of large companies that have split up into siloed groups with different values and goals, even beliefs about the world. You may feel you are a member of a tribe that values creativity, and now you find yourself alone in a group that values only metrics and measurables and distrusts anything imaginative. Or maybe you are a blue-collar worker from the shop floor, part of a group that values the team you work with, as well as your life outside the organization, and now you are with white-collar management, whom you believe value their individual progress and 24/7 dedication to the company above all else. Furthermore, our unconscious minds go to work when we walk into unknown territory: We can get a strong feeling of discomfort. We may feel unwelcome, at a disadvantage, even threatened. We often know we are not with our usual tribe because the signals around us are unfamiliar. Different icons on the walls, different clothes, different patterns, rhythms and timings of movement all support the verbal indicators that we are potentially not among friends, and that others have the advantage of being on their familiar home turf. But are these differences really insurmountable?

Ask what else is going on. You went into the other manager's workspace and were invited to sit on their comfy couch prior to the obvious displays of aggression, which would indicate they initially tried to offer you comfort for the meeting, and with it hospitality and a potentially positive outlook to kick things off. The comfy couch puts you physically lower than them—they are not on the couch; they are sitting in a chair opposite you looking down at you. You are looking up at them, and so they instantly have a height advantage and physically dominate you. From your point of view, they are looking down at you and will appear dominant. And if they are slightly raising their chin, this will likely look like a bigger gesture from where you are sitting. The height advantage they have may be feeding into their feelings of dominance and superiority as well, exacerbating the imbalance of power on both sides. Hence it is potentially your orientation to them in the space (opposite and below) that may trigger strong judgments about them that they are arrogant and antagonistic.

Importantly, they do not direct their aggression at you, but instead at the work you hand up to them. And think back to their pained smile: Could this be a social bonding smile around the psychological pain of change? Taking all of this into account, your **new judgment** could be that they dislike some points in your work or the process but do not dislike or feel aggressive toward you personally. They seem to have been quite specific in targeting the problematic points with the finger jabbing. They are likely wanting to negotiate some of your ideas. Tensions are likely to be running high, what with the future of the organization to some degree depending on your cooperation and getting to useful outcomes in the meeting. The pressure is on. And importantly, you are sitting with a physical disadvantage, being lower than they are, looking up at them, in a territory unfamiliar to you.

How can you **test** this theory, and retain some hope that you will ultimately see eye to eye? Though there is some risk of moving into their territory or personal space, you may be better off getting up from the couch, finding a chair and sitting at a more complementary angle to them—for instance, a 45-degree angle to where they are sitting and not at an adversarial angle, which sitting opposite can seem like, making a face-off more inevitable. Once you are physically on the same level and not lower and opposite them physically, you can bring your attention to the paper, looking at it from the same point of view as them, and help direct any conflict into the proposals on the paper (i.e., the work), rather than toward each other personally. If there is conflict, you can now physically move it away from issues of personality or tribal allegiances and punch it out on paper. Be prepared to even get nonverbally aggressive yourself with the paper, but not with your colleague. Don't be shy to scratch out proposals and start again. Find ways of sharing the tools and the space; give the other manager your pen with which to alter text or write suggestions where they see problems in the work. In other words, by mirroring their attitude but keeping the focus on the work and not the personality or potentially antagonistic group they represent for you, you move into an influential state and get into the flow with them. That is the best foundation here for you to be persuasive, moving them to the best results for you, for them and for everyone involved.

THEY DON'T EVER LOOK YOU IN THE EYE

Our friend and colleague **EDDY ROBINSON** is a noted Anishinaabe artist, musician and speaker who educates non-Indigenous people to seek out a deeper understanding of what it means to be Indigenous as part of a path toward reconciliation. Here's what he told us about the nature of some North American Indigenous nonverbal behavior and assumptions and historical stereotyping about Indigenous people that stand in the way of better understanding and communication.

If arms are folded they are the chief. Hollywood and corporate America took full advantage to popularize this idea into probably one of the most recognizable Indian stereotypical images of all time. However, this stoic chief pose is totally fictional, even down to the idea of the chief system itself, which is something that was forced on many Indigenous communities in North America. Indigenous leadership of course existed but not necessarily within the notion of one person solely leading the community.

Indigenous people won't look you in the eye: Wrong again. Indigenous people use eye contact like anyone else. The one difference that may be notable is that whereas a common practice within some non-Indigenous cultures is to look directly at someone and hold their gaze when listening, alternatively in some Indigenous cultures, in respect and attentiveness to the meaning of what another is saying, listening can happen from a holistic place: emotionally, mentally, physically and spiritually, and so the listener may not be making long eye contact while listening carefully to someone. This non-eye contact is not an indicator of disrespect or indifference; indeed, it could mean the exact opposite.

However, one could argue there may be some non–eye contact as a direct result of hundreds of years of institutionalism and oppression. There is no denying colonization happened in North America. And so, whether you are Indigenous or not, most times when visiting an Indigenous community for business or pleasure, you may be greeted with a sense of distrust. When visiting an extremely oppressed community, the indicators of distrust may be more obvious to the naked eye.

Dr. Martin Brokenleg, an author and psychologist in the fields of trauma, resilience and Indigenous youth, talks about a process of recognizing trauma within Indigenous youth through an Indigenous lens.[2] I believe this viewpoint can be placed over many communities that have been oppressed or have endured colonization to some degree to help understand the nonverbal communication we might experience within them:

Casing—The first level of interaction when engaging with those in Indigenous communities is like any other feeling-out process. Is this person safe? What position of power does this person come from? How are other people interacting with this individual? Crucial nonverbal and verbal data are collected during this stage.

Testing—After the person has been scrutinized, people slowly begin to engage the individual in small increments, but with distrust. The person is tested with conversations intended to trigger anger or other deemed unsafe behaviors. If the person exhibits these, then they will not be trusted.

Predictability—Often the trusting relationship is not entered into until there has been enough truthworthy behavior over time to merit it. Therefore trust may take longer to build than with other groups.

QUICK SCAN

S: You need to try to find a way to make this new working relationship productive, so it is in everyone's best interest to **suspend** judgment that that will never happen and look at what pain could be hiding behind the grimace.

C: You are in uncharted territory, an unknown and potentially unfriendly **context** in a different part of the company with a different way of doing things.

A: The other manager did invite you to be comfy. **Ask** yourself if they may feel tense about the meeting and the new arrangement. Also, notice the disadvantages of sitting lower down.

N: The **new** judgment you can make is that there is still hope, with better meeting-room planning, better positioning, better and more friendly body language. It's likely that neither of you is the problem, so focus on getting the work right together.

32

COLD FISH

You bounce into work with great news for the organization. The reaction from your manager? Completely deadpan. Another day, you unfortunately have to share some bad news; yet again, you get a deadpan response. Now that you think of it, you've seen your manager both hire and fire people with exactly the same level of emotion every time: zero, zip, *nada*. The lack of emotional response in your manager's face is making you feel like anything could happen to anyone at work and there would be no obvious signs or clues. This is making you feel worried about your job security. You have no way of predicting what could happen to you, and it's

➡

> making you feel anxious and at a disadvantage, and
> all because your manager is such a cold fish.

DOES YOUR MANAGER'S deadpan expression mean they are emotionless, hard-hearted, cold and unfeeling? Let's **SCAN** this situation by **suspending judgment** and **being more descriptive** of this key signal that led you to this conclusion. Their deadpan face could be described as neutral, relaxed, seemingly expressionless, a face in repose, the facial muscles neither stretched nor retracted, seemingly emotionless. With no information about how they are feeling visible on their face, their expression provides no visual triggers that can help you get a theory of mind about them, to attribute a mental state to them, to infer what they are thinking or feeling. Here with no theory of mind, no knowledge about what emotion, whether positive or negative, your manager may be feeling at any given time, you assume they are as cold as a fish—and, to go along with the negative connotations that implies, that they are hard-hearted and unfeeling. Because you lack visual information about how they feel about you, you default to extreme negatives about them and their intentions, assuming the worst.

In this situation, the lack of emotional information about your manager is powerful. It makes you nervous, and so you catastrophize that your job could be on the line and you'll be blindsided because you will have no way of knowing from their body language cues. Without enough data, your primitive brain defaults to negatives. You're powerless in the face of this seemingly emotionless human. Given your manager's seeming lack of emotion and therefore incapacity for empathy, how can you have any job security, let alone relate to them?

BODY LANGUAGE MYTHBUSTER
Autistic People Don't Have Empathy
Many people think that people with autism have trouble with empathy. This misconception often gets tied up with the misconception that those with autism have no feelings. This is an area rife with misunderstanding, based on a lack of knowledge. Making matters more confusing is a lack of accurate insight into the meaning of the word *empathy*.

Empathy is the ability to step into another person's shoes, so to speak, to feel what they're feeling. Research shows that people on the autism spectrum have different degrees of impairment when it comes to picking up on what other people are feeling by means of observing others' body language and tone of voice. But this does not equate to any lack of feelings that people with this condition experience.[1]

Modern theories of autism, such as the intense world theory, argue that in some ways, people with autism relate intensely to the feelings of others— so intensely that their experience can be overwhelming or even painful. Like everyone else on the planet, those on the autism spectrum will have varying levels of empathy, but the idea that having

➡

---

autism always means you have no empathy is simply inaccurate.

Research on cross-cultural facial expression, such as the work of Paul Ekman, shows that some people, and this is true regardless of culture and gender, are capable of experiencing emotions without showing any visible facial expression of the emotion; in some cases, only through technology can we detect the subvisible pattern changes in their facial activity indicating their emotional response. Ekman also notes that a lack of facial activity in expressing an emotion in a variety of circumstances could partly be due to the different ways the emotion has been called forth, with what speed and in what context.[2]

Following from this, other research, like that of Rana el Kaliouby at her organization Affectiva, shows big differences among gender, age and culture in how frequently people express their emotions. Using technology that uses computers to detect and interpret human facial expressions, el Kaliouby and her team analyzed hundreds of thousands of videos of facial expressions and coded them with Facial Action Coding System (FACS) action units in the development of their emotion recognition technology. According to their research in the United States, women are 40 percent more facially expressive than men; in the UK there is no difference in expressiveness between genders; and people who are fifty years and older are 25 percent more emotive with facial expression than the under-fifty crowd.[3]

How emotions are experienced and expressed can largely depend on the **context** in which the stimulus for the emotion takes place. In some workplaces, the expression of strong emotions is frowned upon or considered entirely inappropriate. In our scenario, all your interaction with your manager takes place in the context of the working environment. This context for some will just not be emotionally charged, nor may it even have the potential to stir up strong feelings. Additionally, in many societies and cultures, it is taboo to show emotions in the public arena at all, let alone in the workplace, and there is fear of serious condemnation and reprisals for doing so. So just because someone does not show emotion in the context of the workplace or even in public is not a clear sign that they do not show emotion in other contexts, with family or friends, say, or in the privacy of their own company; nor is it a sign that they simply do not feel emotions. It is important to make the distinction between experiencing emotion and expressing it, and to recognize that some people certainly experience emotions but will suppress or conceal them in certain contexts.

Your Boss May Be a Psychopath If . . .

Antisocial disconnections with others can often show up in the psychopath's inability to take part in contagious yawning, according to findings from tests at Baylor University's Department of Psychology and Neuroscience.[4] So if you are presenting to a room full of yawning workmates but the boss is not joining in, then maybe they are dangerous, maybe they have had more coffee than the rest, or maybe they are the only one interested in what you are saying—the truth could be any or all three.

But **ask what else** could be going on. Neural differences can cause some people to not experience emotions quite the same as do others. Underlying conditions such as post-traumatic stress can cause people to filter out emotions because their experience of them is too extreme. Some people grow up in conditions whereby feeling or expressing emotions is too dangerous, and so to survive they have suppressed them. For many people who are forced to learn over time that if they show their feelings, they will be at a disadvantage, we can conclude that they may be careful to ensure that nobody will see them.

You can form a **new judgment** that just because your manager is not showing you their emotions, it does not necessarily mean that they are not experiencing any. The deadpan face may cause feelings of unease or mistrust in others, and that often holds true even if the person is verbalizing their emotions but still not showing the outward signs of experiencing them. People who do not show emotion may have difficulties getting promoted to leadership positions, where people skills are essential, or indeed making transitions within their organizations or onward to other work environments, because they can appear to others as untrustworthy and so a risk. Once again we see here that the popular notion that the body does not lie or that the truth will come out in our body language is just not true. Although technology can detect movements in muscles and in some circumstances changes in hormones, to the naked eye, which means for the majority of us, there are plenty of circumstances where the body can and will lie, as in this scenario where your manager is not showing you what is really going on for them.

The problem is that it is easy and tempting to assume that if we can't see a person's emotion, then they have no empathy. We have a tendency as humans to ascribe meaning based on our expectations. Devoid of information, we can easily assume insensitivity and bad intentions toward us. However, if you consider what the baseline activity is for your manager—they hire people and they fire people—it may be that they have the exact right skill set for these responsibilities.

How can you **test** your new judgment that your manager in fact does have feelings and empathy for others? This is more of a social test: Think about behaviors or events you have seen your manager engage in or instigate that are social. Have they ever arranged a great holiday party for employees, or even brought in doughnuts and coffee? It may be that you remember occasions where they behave with sensitivity to the emotional experiences of others in the workplace, even if they do not show that they are feeling emotional themselves. They may remark positively on others' enjoyment, which is a sign they do understand emotion and have empathy for others. Look out for emotional words, caring actions, social actions—there are more indicators of emotional attachment and social ability than just someone wearing a happy face or a sad face.

TOUCHY FEELY

ANDERSON CARVALHO is our go-to specialist in body language for communication and influence in Brazil. He has created the largest online body language congress and is a coach to political and corporate leaders, CEOs, communicators and athletes in South America. Here's what he has to tell us about the most important specifics of body language when it come to South American versus North American social behavior.

When we analyze body language variations, the biggest difference between North and South America is the physical contact. In South America, the interpersonal relationship has physical contact as a strong characteristic: shaking hands, touching the shoulders, and hugs and kisses on the cheeks between close friends and family. Whereas in North America, hugs and kisses, even between those with very close social and family bonds, can be disconcerting and feel like boundaries are being crossed.

When greeting a person from South America, male or female, start by shaking their hand and maintaining eye contact. Generally, if the person you are greeting is of the opposite sex, wait to see how they act toward you. The person may give you a hug, expressing sympathy for you. If this occurs, reciprocate in the same way. If the person you are greeting realizes you have rejected a hug, they may feel rejected and have some antipathy toward you.

For South Americans, there isn't much difference between professional and personal boundaries. However, during a business conversation, avoid any physical contact but keep good eye contact.

At the end of a meeting, when leading another to the exit, you may put a hand on the other's shoulder, as this is considered a sign of conducting the other. For the person being conducted, this act represents protection rather than the suppression and dominance that this style of physical contact may feel like to a North American.

QUICK SCAN

S: When there is insufficient emotional data, it is very easy for your instinct to default to negative assumptions and even catastrophization. **Suspending** judgment when it feels like there are catastrophic implications can be very hard to do indeed.

C: Context can be a barrier to someone feeling comfortable or even appropriately displaying emotion to you or to the group. This may be the context of the current work environment or the context in which they grew up.

A: What else do you know about the area of neural differences in people that could affect the way you need to look at body language? Who can you **ask** for more detail or experience of this?

N: New discoveries around emotion and displays of emotion are ongoing. Just because you don't *see* that someone has a feeling does not mean it is not there.

33

THEY'RE GONNA BLOW!

You are chatting with a coworker about a work-related topic in the cafeteria. You have been engaged in conversation for a little while, and you notice they are contributing less and less to the conversation and are starting to frown. You keep on talking, assuming they are focusing hard on the many very useful points you are raising, and so you also focus more and get more intense about the subject at hand. You look away as you pause to breathe, and when you look back at them you notice their breathing has become more pronounced and rapid, and their skin looks like it is getting hot. Additionally, they now are wearing

➡

a very pronounced and set frown. Their nostrils
are flaring, and they have an intense glare in their
eyes, which are also narrowing slightly, as are their
lips, and their mouth is held a little tightly shut. You
suddenly catch on. *Uh-oh, they are looking pretty
angry. What did I do? I must have said something
to really upset them. I'd better watch out—they look
like they're gonna blow!*

IT IS UNSETTLING to say the least to unintentionally upset someone
to the point where they may explode in rage. Is your coworker going
to blow? If so, this could happen very quickly, but you can still **SCAN**
the situation by **suspending judgment** and **being more descriptive** of
what is going on.

The key signals in our scenario are the frowning, rapid breathing,
glaring eyes, narrowing of the lips and appearance of being hot; so
let's unpack where the power of these gestures lies. Frowning, as we
note elsewhere in the book, or the eyebrows pulled inward and downward, can indeed be a sign of thinking deeply, but if accompanied
by other anger-related signs can certainly point to anger. The rapid
breathing is a result of the body's systemic reaction to potential physical conflict, to fight: Our adrenal glands push adrenaline and cortisol through our systems, which causes our blood pressure, breathing,
heart rate and temperature to increase—and, voilà, your coworker
appears to be hot. The nostrils flare to accommodate increased oxygen flow. The skin tone may also turn red (perhaps more obvious in
lighter skin tones). Also, the pupils will dilate, the eyelids will narrow

to protect the eyes, and the gaze will become targeted, all of which you may be seeing in those glaring eyes. The narrowing of the lips is a strong signal of the building anger but also of further escalations being suppressed. Though your coworker may be intensely angry, they have not yet exploded. They have not moved into any physical action in order to alter the environment, to jump into the conflict and resolve it; in anticipation of that, they are keeping their mouth shut tight.

BODY LANGUAGE MYTHBUSTER
Seeing Red Is Only a Metaphor

Some people really do see red when they are angry. A study at North Dakota State University found that people who display signs of aggression and hostility are more likely to choose the color red when presented concurrently with a choice of colors.[1]

Anthropologists have documented the association between anger and aggression and the color red, finding this association is shared across all cultures.

Evolutionary psychologists theorize that the connection may stem from our hunter-gatherer ancestors, who linked the color with danger—when searching for food they would have been on the lookout to avoid poisonous plants, dangerous insects and other potential threats.

A study by researchers at Rochester University found that the association of the color red with danger might still have a positive effect: It could make us respond faster and more powerfully. Our brains are programmed to tell our bodies to flee when faced with someone turning red with anger, meaning we get a huge energy burst. Andrew Elliot, professor of psychology at Rochester, observes: "Red enhances our physical reactions because it is seen as a danger cue. Humans flush when they are angry or preparing for attack. People are acutely aware of such reddening in others and its implications."[2]

All signals considered, there is little doubt that your coworker is remarkably angry. But you assume they're going to lose it, freak out, explode with rage. What happens to behavior when the lid blows off the anger and they let it all out in a rageful fit? Rage is an extreme exacerbation of angry feelings that turn into rageful behavior, looking like an uncontrollable physical display of anger and frustration: Faces uncontrollably distort with rage; we fly into a fit of rage; we jump up and down with rage; or we rage at others—the word's use as a verb showing the active behavioral quality of rage as opposed to the more held-in feeling of anger. Rage can be a reaction to a threat and is sometimes associated with the fight or flight response. In addition to the anger signs we have already discussed, if someone is about to act out in rage, they may well be clenching their fists in order to protect the fingers and create a more impactful tool of aggression with the hands. Also, you may see them getting more grounded and stable in the lower part of the body (lowering their center of gravity) in preparing for fight.

Are they glaring at you? Are you the target of their growing anger and hostility? Regardless of whether it was something you said, or the way you said it, or the situation, if they are targeting you, you are in their firing line and will need a course of action.

But what if they are not targeting you with that glare, but someone else? Regarding the **context**, is there anyone else or any situation in the room that may be causing your coworker's negative reaction? Has the environment changed since you started chatting together, has anyone new entered the room or has something got to them more than to you, a disturbance, something disruptive, others arguing or behaving rudely in the communal space? Their growing anger may relate to the goings-on within the context of the room and have nothing to do with you at all.

Canine Calm

Some people find it calming to have pets at work. The Google code of conduct states that "affection for our canine friends is an integral facet of our corporate culture." And at Amazon, around 2,000 employees have registered their pets at its headquarters in Seattle so they can take them into work with them. Having a dog at work can create an atmosphere that feels warmer and more sociable. If someone's feeling a bit down in the dumps or stressed out, they can spend some time with the dog. And having a dog to walk can give workers a reason to get outside for a break and some fresh

➡

---

air. But scientists believe the major source of people's positive reactions to pets comes from oxytocin, a hormone whose many functions include easing stress and stimulating social bonding, relaxation and trust. Often when humans and dogs interact, oxytocin levels increase in both species. Just as with human-to-human contact, stroking the body with the hands, eye contact and simple play have much to do with this effect. All of which, if done human to human in most workplaces, would likely and rightly mean a trip to HR, warnings or instant dismissal. Nonetheless, all these interactions can help slow the heart rate and decrease anxiety and anger arousal levels.

Whether it is you or the behavior of others that is the catalyst for your coworker's potential outburst, examining the context further should shed some light on how likely they are to erupt. You are at your workplace in the cafeteria. Most places of business, regardless of industry, will likely and to varying degrees have implicit or written codes of conduct—rules and regulations that may completely prohibit violent or aggressive physical or vocal outbursts. So it is highly likely to be taboo for anybody to erupt in a rage. So, in seeing your coworker suppress their anger, you may be witnessing their better judgment kicking in. That said, within the organization specifically you are in the cafeteria, a context within the context. You need to think quickly: Are there precedents or social norms whereby the cafeteria itself is a zone where employees are free to storm around, blow off steam, smash it up and let it all out? It may be that in this particular part or room of the work environment, it is considered by the group socially acceptable or even normal to express rage. Is the cafeteria the place people can regularly go to have a temper tantrum? If so, maybe your workmate will be feeling free or even empowered to act out and you will see the volcano blow at any second. But if the space is not considered anger-management HQ, you could lay a good bet that the power of social norms at your organization will restrain them from an explosive emotional display. In many if not all workplaces, there is a massive risk of expulsion from the organization in fully raging out within any part of the work environment and thus causing coworkers to experience fear, threat and possibly long-term trauma.

However, for some people, keeping the lid on such extreme feelings may translate into pain of a psychological or physical nature: Depression and post-traumatic stress disorder, as well as cardiac stress and hypertension, are linked to, among other causes, repressed rage. Your coworker may be in this moment weighing up the risk of not lashing out and expressing their rage versus the risk of so doing and the likely social, professional and legal consequences.

Ask what else you need to consider. Can they or can they not control their impulses? Many people suffer from a serious lack of impulse control, in some cases pathologically. There are many well-documented anger disorders; one example that is directly related to impulse control is intermittent explosive disorder (IED), where the sufferer cannot resist aggressive impulses even when they involve serious attacks on people or property.[3] Forensic psychologist Stephen A. Diamond, an author in the subject area of anger disorders, describes these more generally as "pathologically aggressive, violent or self-destructive behaviors symptomatic of and driven by an underlying and chronically repressed anger or rage."[4] These incidences of rage outbursts can be habitual but can also appear as if out of nowhere. In both cases, they are often triggered by an insult, rejection or stressful event that has let loose the deeply repressed intense feelings of anger within the individual.

In our scenario, if you have a history of working with this person, and this behavior is something new, there is a good likelihood they will be able to check in with norms of social boundaries in this situation and keep a lid on it. However, if they have displayed rageful behavior before, then they are likely to display this behavior again. Whatever the cause of their rage, unlike with throwing the dice, where rolling a one means you now have statistically less of a chance of rolling a one again even though the probability remains the same, with behavior, if someone has done it before, even if it ended badly for them the first time, they are still likely to engage in the same behavior again. As we often say, in behavior, once is a pattern.

So your **new judgment** may be that although your coworker looks like they are about to boil over, they may be unlikely to engage in this behavior in the workplace.

But how much would you like to **test** this? What's the cost if your new assumption tests false? Can you recover from a test that is positive for rage? You could throw caution to the wind and poke the bear a little more if you like, or . . . stop talking. Take a breather. Give them some time and space, and make sure your breathing is calm. They may pick up on a calm breathing rhythm, which may in turn take the edge off their anger. And after everything has subsided (take a few hours or even a few days), you may want to talk about what made them angry—or you may not.

RUDE HUMANS

If you do keep dogs at work, be sure you are maintaining a low-stress environment for your canine friend. Take account of how our longtime friend, dog behavior expert **VICTORIA STILWELL**, imagines the experience of being a pet as told from the dog's point of view:

"Humans are notorious for being rude, confusing and inconsistent. They also have really high expectations that they themselves can't follow. They expect you to come preprogrammed to sit, stay and come back to them when told, even if they're calling you to come back when you are having the best fun—playing with other dogs or chasing small fluffies. When you don't respond, they get mad and tell you how bad you are. Apparently they don't understand that dogs also say, "Just a minute."

People are also really bad about invading space. Even if they don't know you, they come up and touch you. They think they're being friendly, and most of them are, but it's weird when a complete stranger comes close, bends over, stares at you, shows their teeth and extends their big paw to pat you on top of your head. Then when you show them your teeth, they back away and get angry and upset that you weren't nice to them. Just be aware that when they approach you like that, they are trying to be kind.

And the hugging! Why do they have to hug so much? Apparently hugging in human language is an expression of affection, but what humans don't understand is that hugging means different things in dog language. We put our front legs around something only when we are about to fight, and I'm sure if people knew that, they would stop hugging us really quickly. We sometimes enjoy hugs from people we know really well, though, but only if we like being that close.

QUICK SCAN

S: Seeing someone show physical signs of extreme anger in the workplace may look and prove to be scary. At what point is it not safe enough to **suspend** judgment? Think of how you might describe to a friend, date, partner or colleague the process of suspending judgment and being more descriptive.

C: Are there **contexts** in your workplace considered safe zones to blow off steam?

A: Ask whether this person has any history of erratic behavior or violence.

N: They may be able to control their emotion, but with this **new** judgment, give them and yourself a breather and leave them to collect themselves.

34

THIS MEETING IS A WASTE OF TIME

You have been asked to get your team together to brainstorm strategies, innovations and solutions to certain challenges. You bring in the group, the pastries and the coffee and ramp up for an exciting session. Some people are naturally more vocal than others, and conversations are taking off. However, you are very keen to hear from everybody, so you are trying to keep the floor open for all. Someone is looking as if they want to chime in, like they have something important to say. You see their eyebrows repeatedly flashing up, their mouth opening, and they sit up straighter and lean in. But when you offer them space to speak, they sit back, lower

➡

their eyebrows, drop their gaze and say, "No, I
don't have anything to add." This makes you feel
insecure about the group dynamic, the direction
the conversations have been going, and instead
of just ignoring the quiet one, you become con-
sumed with what they are thinking and become
perplexed about what they aren't saying that
clearly they would like to say. You become certain
that others in the meeting are not getting value
from your facilitation. The atmosphere of the
whole group feels to you like it is turning sour.
*That's it, it's doomed! They all think this meeting
is a total waste of time.*

SURELY MANY OF US HAVE BEEN in meetings that prove to be a complete waste of time. But are you correct that everyone is feeling *your* meeting is a waste of time? Are you correct that the meeting is doomed? Let's **SCAN** the situation, **suspend judgment** that it's a disaster, and **be more descriptive** of what you are reading from that one individual who is sparking your fear.

Key signals give you the impression this person wants to speak— to bring in the power of their voice: Their eyebrows flash up, their mouth opens, they sit up straight and lean in. The eyebrow flash can mean a variety of things, depending on context. German ethologist Irenaus Eibl-Eibesfeldt researched the eyebrow flash extensively throughout different cultures, and his and other research indicate it is accepted in many cultures (but not all) as a way to recognize and greet someone, a signal we share with other primates.[1] In our scenario, the eyebrow raise draws your attention, and it is accompanied by a forward lean and an open mouth. These signs together can look like regulatory gestures—that is, gestures showing that the person is listening, or encouraging the other person to keep speaking, or in your case, signaling that they would like to take a turn speaking. A gaping mouth (so long as it is not a yawn) could be a regulatory gesture indicating they want to jump into the conversation.

BODY LANGUAGE MYTHBUSTER
Yawning Means You Are Tired

Yawning is typically thought of as an indicator of fatigue, but in reality the causes of yawning remain a mystery even after continued scientific scrutiny of yawning. One theory is that yawning brings more oxygen to the lungs, but this has largely been discredited after observations of fetal yawning (there's no oxygen in the womb). Another mystery of yawning is its contagiousness. Studies have shown that yawning can trigger a contagious response in up to 60 percent of people who are exposed. It even affects dogs![2] Some scientists propose that contagious yawning may have helped our ancestors coordinate times of activity and rest. Another recent experiment suggests yawning may be an attempt to cool down the brain.

However, when you invite this person to speak, they lean back, drop their eyebrows, lower their gaze and verbally let you know they will not be adding their two cents right now. What else do those body language signs communicate? Looking down and lowering their eyebrows could signal they are concealing something or disapprove of something; both keeping the eyebrows lowered for a long time and lowering their gaze may also show that they feel insecure. Additionally, lowering the gaze could signal guilt or submission to power. All in all, you are getting mixed messages or an incongruity in their nonverbal messages. The person looks like they need to speak but then say they don't. Is it you, or them, or you and them?

Rules and Regulations

In this book, the term *regulators* describes a collection of nonverbal expressions and gestures that in live settings help us control, cue and understand conversations better. We all use regulators, in every country and culture, but there are certainly variations in use depending on the geographical and cultural context. Regulators include many aspects of body language, such as eye contact, touch, hand gestures, head nods or head shakes, facial expressions and vocal cues.

Regulators communicate many things to us during conversation: that we should keep talking, stop talking so someone else can speak, speed up,

➡

---

slow down, change the subject or end the conversation, and even that we are not listening and
we're out of there! More symbolic regulators are
a result of cultural or social norms, and again the
interpretation of these largely depends on context.
For example, a badge of office that someone wears
in one country may nonverbally indicate to people
how to behave in that person's presence, perhaps
a sign not to speak unless asked or allowed. An
action that may seem innocuous to some, like
handing someone who is crying a box of tissues, in
some contexts could be a strong signal or warning
that it is time they stop crying, or alternatively in
another context, an invitation to let emotions fly.

Looking at the **context**, you invited this group of individuals to join you in your brainstorming session, a creative endeavor, and you do not know what the end product is going to be. Though cognitively you know your process and may feel confident and excited, unconsciously, you're very much on the lookout for problems. You are in uncharted territory, after all, uncertain of what is going to happen. And stress could be adding to the underlying feeling of uncertainty, as you likely need to produce something of value from this session. Other people and the organization are likely counting on you. You are under pressure, though you may not feel or be aware of it. Just because we don't know what our biases are doesn't mean they don't exist. In the spirit of conducting a useful facilitation, you may be overlooking or overriding the negative backdrop of anxiety, stress and uncertainty to achieve your goal. And though the majority of the group is creating a positive atmosphere through supportive signals, you cannot stop your primitive brain from focusing outside of that majority and on the one person giving off confusing and therefore negative signals.

By prioritizing that negative data point of one, **ask what else** is happening. You are getting rattled and confused and creating a theory of mind about the entire group. The confusing signals are moving you to default to negatives—when the primitive brain lacks information, it defaults to negatives, an evolutionary survival mechanism. In this situation we could also call this a "squeaky wheel" bias. Your focus goes to that one person not joining in. The majority are complying with your situation, but a minority is not, and so you make rules about the entire event around their activities. **Ask** yourself, is this really fair?

As the other members of the meeting seem to be happy, interested and contributing, it's fair that you can form a **new judgment** that the meeting is going well and not a waste of time. To **test** this, simply check in with the majority of the group—do they look interested, energized, confident and motivated? If so, then let them carry on riding the wave of creativity, and something of value will come out of the session. If the person making the confusing signals is an equal member of the group and not the person who ultimately wields power over your group or the organization as a whole, then as the group facilitator, you need to serve the needs of the group and stay on course to achieve the desired outcomes for that session. There is every possibility that this person's thinking aligns with the group and they are eager to pitch in, but the ideas keep coming out from others too thick and fast for them to catch up, and this in turn could be causing them to feel insecure about not contributing enough or fast enough. Maybe they feel there is a risk. Find a less socially risky place for them to contribute. You can get to the root of their behavior offline from the group.

Emojis as Our Digital Regulators?

When we are in conversations that lack regulators—nonverbal cues that help the flow of conversation—we sure can tell the difference in how those conversations play out. Think about being on a conference call. Often we are speaking to many people in different environments, and we cannot see or often hear them properly to be able to take their cues of when it is our turn to talk, or not, or to whom. We lose those helpful cues that also show how people rank, and we may easily talk right over the person with the power. Surely we've all been in a phone meeting with someone who just will not stop talking and we can't get a word in, or with a person who keeps interrupting, or with a person who pauses awkwardly and we are never sure if they are finished speaking. And some people do not talk at all, often because they lack information about what others on the call are feeling, or who they are within the context. So long as we pay attention to them, regulators helpfully indicate to us the time to be active and the time to be passive while in conversation. A certain balance between the roles of the speaker and listener makes for a healthy and often useful conversation, one with good rapport.

How do regulators translate into the digital world? With e-mail, like its predecessor, snail mail—both within the domain of the written letter—punctuation serves as a regulator for letting the reader know the beginning, middle and end of our thoughts, as well as what we want to emphasize or question, and to what degree. With both types of mail we control when we are finished the message, and then it leaves us to travel geographically or digitally to the receiver. And though all written letters are subject to misinterpretation, still we have at our disposal the tool of punctuation and control over the timing of send and deliver as regulators of a sort.

Text chat becomes a little more tricky, as messages can quickly pile up on top of each other and it can be difficult to correctly follow the thread of the conversation. It is easy to muddle up the sequence of thoughts as texts pop up fast and furious, and we respond to one idea as the next one is already arriving. Punctuation is not as easy to use as a regulator in the quick-and-dirty world of texting. Fortunately, people can create clear nonverbal indicators with emojis, using them to signal the end of a unit of meaning and how they mean it

➡

to be received. We can end a unit of meaning by inserting an icon, such as a smiley face or a pile of rainbow poop, to finally say, Here is the feeling that underlines the text; there you go. In this respect, emojis and emoticons can be considered the regulators of computer communication.

However, studies on emoticon and emoji use reveal, perhaps unsurprisingly, that just as our facial cues or expressions may vary in usage and meaning from culture to culture, so too do our text-based and pictorial representations of these emotions.[3] To maximize our clarity of message in our online world, we need to consider the cultural background of who we are communicating with, just as we would in person, in order to communicate effectively with emoticons or emojis. We need to bear in mind that the way we type an emoticon or which emoji we choose will not always mean to all people what it does to us and our community.[4]

QUICK SCAN

S: Imagine you were teaching someone else about reading body language and the **SCAN** system for thinking about the meanings of body language and behavior. How would you help them understand the importance of **suspending** judgment? How might you explain to them the use of regulators in triggering a judgment about how another wants to join a conversation or control it?

C: What, from watching people's body language, do you now understand about the importance of **context** when it comes to knowing what people are really thinking? How might someone's culture control the context that their regulators should be viewed in?

A: Ask yourself how your online conversations with others might get compromised in meaning. How might you help someone understand the importance of nonverbal communication by explaining what nonverbal meaning can get left out online?

N: What advantage would someone get from your teaching them your new understanding of body language so far? What **new** ideas do you think you have gained so far that you think would benefit others?

35

LOOKS LIKE A WINNING TEAM

You are looking to hire a crack team from outside
your business to move a tough project forward fast.
You've seen some competent groups give pretty
much the same pitch every time—but then this one
crew comes in and although it is pitching the same
spec as all the rest, you are getting the strongest
gut feeling ever that this is a winning team. But
here's the odd thing about it: You can't figure out
why! There is nothing you can pick out in anyone's
individual body language that helps you understand why you think this team is a winner. All you
know is that the feeling is all pervasive. It's just a
great group that you'd do anything to be part of

ACROSS COUNTRIES, ACROSS CULTURES and across sports, there is universal body language of pride. Research by the University of British Columbia shows that both blind and seeing athletes around the world all make the same body language expression when they win a race, which is notable partly because blind athletes often have no visual reference of this winning body language. This body language of a winner is classic: arms and hands above head, mouth open, face pointed up toward the sky, exclaiming in triumph. But in our scenario, how can you tell this team will be experiencing that kind of win anytime soon? What is sweeping you along with the sensation of power and success?

You can certainly **SCAN** this situation and **suspend judgment** right now that this is for sure the team for you, but you cannot **be more descriptive** of what exactly went on here. It is fair to say it is overwhelming, yet you are unable to detect or describe physically what is happening. You only have a feeling.

Let us offer the key signal you may be unconsciously picking up on here: an overall display of complicity. The individuals are woven together into one fabric by a process only they know. The energy they exude is born out of the many subtle micro-movements that are either overwhelming, because of the multitude of data, or not easy to detect because they are so specific to that team. They are tribal signals that only the members recognize both consciously and unconsciously.

Why do they need these many and sometimes secret codes?

Teammates operate in environments or in a **context** where factors rapidly change, and so need to be able to closely read each other's movements. Typically, this means they must effectively and seamlessly communicate with each other nonverbally. This surely goes back to our hunter-gatherer times, when groups had to cooperate quickly and silently to win food and evade danger.

BODY LANGUAGE MYTHBUSTER
Hands Behind Your Back Shows Power

For a long time, some presentation coaches have advised people that hands held behind the back is a nonverbal sign of power. It is similar to a Prince Charles and also Prince Philip (his dad) posture, also sometimes called a regal stance, which suggests the person is royalty and as such does not want to be touched. Unfortunately, adopting this posture doesn't necessarily mean you would inherit the social power of the aristocracy who habitually pose this way.

Research shows that most people find this posture untrustworthy. So, unless you are recognizable royalty, putting your hands behind your back will not make you look superior. Generally, when your hands are hidden from view, people will be mistrustful of you because they cannot see what you

➡

are doing or holding back there. This is why showing the palms of your hands is a great way to
establish rapport—you're showing you have nothing to hide. So keep this in mind when you get into
position for that office group photo: you will generate more positive and trustworthy feelings about
yourself and the group by showing more of your
hands, not less.

There are subtle momentary gestures that can be used effectively
as shorthand communication between team members. The eyebrow flash is something humans do instinctively when they want
to attract attention and show they are known to the other. It is a
signal that says I recognize you. We are part of the same group. Torso
tilting, where the center-of-gravity navel area is clearly directed
toward someone else, is a clear signal of being engaged or wanting
to engage with the other. Athletes who want another team member to openly engage with them ensure that there are no barriers
blocking their torsos. This shows the deep level of trust on the field
in a high-performing team. The chin salute is a super subtle way to
acknowledge and point, particularly compared with a finger point
with a direct hand, or a fully extended arm indicating direction.

Sports teams also use the tools of their trade to make subtle gestures to each other. A basketball team will handle the ball in a way
that instructs others of the play or indeed bluffs the other team as
to the direction the play is headed. A group of negotiators will use
the subtle movements of a pen to tell another to make a low offer.

A construction team may use the rhythm of their hammer strikes to organize a group "tools down" and take a break.

Team members study, train, work, eat, fail, succeed, laugh, cry and sometimes even bleed together. That creates immense opportunities for bonding. Through the power of proxemics and haptics, teammates can have much higher rates of touch than even the closest friends. Team players also maintain smaller distances between each other; they stand close together, huddle together in a corner of the meeting room, cram in lunch together in a tight little diner; share tight travel spaces and even accommodations. Of course, with this comes frequent body touching and close proximity during the game, regardless of what it is. Connection with others lowers the sense of risk. A connected and motivated group can be more powerful than the strongest individual. Their proximity and touch will stimulate more oxytocin among them and so keep them calmer in stressful situations. Teams that use a high degree of proximity and touch and that literally stay tight under pressure and do not fall apart have a greater success rate.[1]

With any great team, uniformity (the many forming into the one unit) can be seen in their dress. With a set uniform or dress code, they are cut from the same cloth so to speak. They are familiar to each other by their mirrored outward appearance as a symbol of their internal communal values, beliefs, goals and concerns. They may have badges of office to show their rank in the tribe or specialization of skill, knowledge or years of membership, but ultimately, regardless of their individual station, they stand in each other's shoes.

Body Language of Losers

Those who lose a specific challenge, like a game or a match, also tend to display a unique body expression. Losers do not learn this expression by observation; it arises from innate human programming. Losers roll their shoulders in, hang their heads low, wear pained or sad expressions and clench their hands into fists of defeat. As the adrenaline and excitement leave the body, it wilts in sadness and frustration; the effect is similar to a balloon deflating as its air slips away.

Ask what else you have not been able to pick up on about the crack team. Possibly most important is that they literally are together in a sort of conspiracy. They breathe together. If you were to look at their breathing patterns, you would find that they are synchronized. The group is like one organism. You share the same space and are influenced to breathe with them; as hormones can be emitted from many areas of our bodies and absorbed by others, chances are you are also absorbing the high levels of hormones floating in the air around them and getting under your skin as they shake your hand. Their group sense of risk tolerance will be due to both experiences that have affected them cognitively and a combination of high levels of oxytocin and testosterone. They feel like an indestructible posse—the word *posse* deriving from medieval Latin and meaning "power"—and it is literally rubbing off on you. This is an overwhelmingly powerful nonverbal communication that you simply cannot see. Indeed, it is so powerful, you will not just breathe with them but chemically you may feel in league with the group. And of course now you want this to be permanent. It's quite addictive. If you can't buy their help, you for sure would like to badge up and be a part of it all somehow. And who can blame you? It is great to be part of a strong team. You feel needed and protected. Well, here's the issue. This tribe is tight, so maybe you cannot join, but you can trade.

One **new judgment** is that you can't be part of the crack team but you can engage them for the work. But how do you **test** the promise of performance your instinct and now new insights are giving you? You can find out how long they have been together. Teams can be costly to support and maintain, so you can bet if they have been doing this a long time, or even for longer than other teams or groups you have interviewed, they must have something of a secret sauce binding them together. What is a benchmark for "long enough to trust them"? Well, of course that can alter sector to sector. But remember that the Beatles survived only eight years as John, Paul, George and Ringo. How were they a great team and arguably the most important popular band ever? "We were four brothers," says Ringo. "There were only four people who really knew what the Beatles were about," says Paul.

QUICK SCAN

S: Suspending judgment and being more descriptive can be hard when you can't quite put your finger on what to describe. But you *can* describe further the feeling you have of any situation, to kickstart being more mindful.

C: You can look out for a **context** of complicit team behavior when a feeling about a situation hits you in a big way.

A: Ask yourself if you are getting an overwhelming feeling because many people are sending the same signal at the same time.

N: When and where has your own body language been influenced or governed by a group? In answering that question, what, if any, **new** insights and judgments does it bring for you?

36

SO, YOU THINK YOU'RE THE BOSS

You have recently transferred to a new area in your
organization, and so far everyone seems friendly
and cooperative. But each time you meet with the
group, there is always this one person who starts
off by sitting up really straight and tall, glaring
around at everyone else. They spread out their
laptop and cell phone on the table, and to take up
even more of the available space, they lean their
elbows wide and then steeple their fingers together
in front of them. Every time someone else puts
an idea forward, this person purses their lips and
squints. They dominate the conversation by jump-
ing in on top of other people's ideas with their own,

➡

and when others are talking they slightly turn away
and look down or elsewhere, not making eye contact with anyone in those moments. And, worst of
all, at the end of the meeting they stand up, fists on
hips and legs wide apart, and deliver their recom-
mendations to the group, finger-pointing at each
and every person. You can't help regarding them
with annoyance and utter disdain, but you wonder
if it's just you. You ask around. Everyone has been
thinking the same thing about this person: *So, you
think you're the boss?*

EVEN THOUGH IT SEEMS quite clear in this description that this
annoying colleague wants to control the meeting, take power and
be "the boss" (originally a uniquely American term, from the Dutch
word for "master"), let's **SCAN** this situation and **suspend judgment** to
be more descriptive about what they are doing, how it reads and how
they make others feel. Importantly, does their body language tell the
truth about the situation? That is, are they actually gaining the power
they want? Will their behavior make them the boss, or are they in fact
losing the interest of everyone around them?

This would-be boss displays many key signals of dominance and
superiority. They start out the meeting by delivering a healthy dose
of direct eye contact, meted out to everyone to establish the power of
their dominance, as if to show that they are the top dog. Then, when
others speak, they turn and look away, not making any eye contact,
effectively demonstrating they are not listening to anyone else, a sign

of disrespect. They show height dominance over everyone else by sitting up very straight and tall, to get higher and show off power and their feeling of superiority. They claim ownership over much of the table surface, going so far as to spread their devices around as if saying they own the land and "Keep off."

Additionally, they cut in when others are speaking, laying claim to more of the airwaves and showing off their dominance and superiority by breaking the social rules of not interrupting. They not only show with their body language that they are blocking out listening to others but also make facial signals that undermine the ideas being put forth by others at the table: steepling their fingers together, squinting their eyes and pursing their lips. The steepling sets out to display intelligence; the squinting shows off their discomfort or stress at listening to the ideas of others; and the pursing of the lips, which involves pulling their lips inward from all directions tightly—not to be confused with outward-protruding puckered lips as in a kiss, or even pointing with the lips—indicates a negative evaluation or judgment, disapproval and, across most cultures, disagreement with what is being said. At the end of the meeting, they take a superhero "power pose" of standing with feet apart and fists on hips, as if that will seal the deal for them— as if everyone they point a jabbing finger toward will start applauding their power and might. Instead and unsurprisingly, the collective response to this display is annoyance and utter disdain.

Pursed Lips or Pointing?
Using the index finger to point, though widely understood in the Western world, is not universal.

In fact, pointing with the lips to target or to draw others' attention toward something is a commonly used gesture in many cultures around the world. In central to northern Ontario, Canada, many Indigenous people signal by pointing with their lips. The Anishinaabe (Ojibwa) word for "over there"—*iwidi*, pronounced "eh-weh-day"—even allows for the mouth to produce this directional pointing gesture as it is being said. Other examples and variations of lip pointing can be seen in Filipino societies, as well as in other parts of Southeast Asia, the Caribbean, Australia, Africa and South America.[1] So, be mindful not to mistake someone pointing with their lips for someone pursing them in disapproval or puckering them with affection.

Of course, every one of us has come across some form of these "alpha" practices and accompanying theories about leadership—mainly, that if you display these dominant gestures, you will be seen as the leader. In our scenario, why is it not working? The would-be leader in the story is certainly playing out those alpha "leadership" behaviors, and yet, you do not feel particularly good about this person based on how they are acting. You are not buying what they are selling. Why is their alpha leadership behavior making them so unlikable in our scenario?

Let's take a look at the truth and lies of the alpha theory about leadership, and how they play out within the context of our story.

Some popular research has many people thinking there is a universal set of power behaviors that top dogs naturally show, and we can all follow along to get ourselves those leadership roles. This idea of alpha body language stems from social dominance theory, derived from European behavioral research into captive wolves. In a nutshell, a study of how wild wolves behave when put into captivity transformed into theory about domestic dog behavior and then human behavior. While none of the original behaviors seen in the captive wolves can scientifically be viewed as normal for wild wolves (because of the situational differences), the behaviors that scientists at the time linked to dominance—without any logic or real evidence that they reflected human patterns of behavior—were theoretically taken to accurately describe norms of human behavior. This approach is analogous to drawing inferences about leadership dynamics in wild wolf packs by studying imprisoned humans. Though there may be some accidental correlation, the species, society and situation are radically different, and we should expect some quite inaccurate theories and practices to emerge. Garbage in, garbage out.

Nowadays, after years of more carefully constructed studies, we understand that in some species of social mammals, every member of a group has a place in the hierarchy, while in others there is a dominant leader or codominant partnership over a group of subordinates that are equal in power to each other. Humans are even more complex: We belong to more than one social circle. A person who is a follower at work may be a leader within their interest group that meets up each weekend, and then positioned somewhere between the two in any of their many virtual tribes; the leader in their workspace may now rank well beneath them in this context. Human social dominance is complex. One size does not fit all in all circumstances; while one behavior can win you power and status in one context, it may be the very same behavior that demotes you in another.

Now let's put the would-be boss's alpha behavior into **context**—a group of coworkers meeting in the work environment, where those top dog behaviors are not met with a resounding whoop from the crowd. Progressive and harmonious work environments are increasingly built on a calm and assertive state of synchronization—one that will enable leadership through establishing common ground, fostering community and respect—and on power-sharing. This is becoming increasingly ingrained in the workplace, and even in environments that are traditionally hierarchical and old fashioned, change is afoot. For many organizations, the new best practice for the most successful working environment involves a culture epitomized by ideals of autonomy, equality, diversity, community, sharing and respect, where employees feel inspired to pitch in and give their best ideas and practices for the greater good of the organization.[3] Plenty of research backs up the correlation between this description of work environment and culture with not only more contented and motivated staff but also an increase in profitability.

This context of the workplace landscape therefore may be at odds with the would-be leader displaying top dog alpha signs, the kind of leadership traits that suggest a domineering and arrogant leader who will aggressively throw their weight around and demean others by showing they do not care what others think. The environment of politics can differ completely from that of the work organization in terms of what leadership qualities resonate for the public. In politics, particularly for populations in times of crisis or threat or who largely feel disenfranchised, we see time and again how it is just this aggressive show of dominance and power that may be able to win the day in a leadership race. But in our scenario, as in many modern workplaces, we are often not looking for a pushy and aggressive leader who does not value our ideas or even want to hear them, who demonstrates they are better than us and who makes no secret of the fact that given the opportunity, they would squash us under their heel. Rather we are looking for sharing, cooperation and teamwork.

In this context, their dominance displays have made us feel disdainful of them. Their actions do not fit the community's values. Though they may feel they are truly putting across all the "right" signs of alpha or dominant body language to show their leadership abilities, the theory behind it is built on a lie, and the place they are performing the tactics don't value those actions.

What else can you **ask** yourself to consider in this scenario? In terms of demonstrating leadership behavior, what other choices do they have? Would you prefer they go in the other direction, minimizing their use of space, caving in and looking down, shrugging their shoulders in a show of either indifference or uncertainty, biting their nails anxiously, showing less dominant and more submissive behavior? Would that inspire you? No, of course not. The behaviors required to perform as a good, modern leader are not binary but are more complex.

So your **new judgment** could be that regardless of whether they want to be the boss, your colleague does not have the slightest idea of how annoying their behavior is, how it is alienating all their coworkers and may just as likely alienate the upper management who could instill them with power. It is so not the route to getting what they want. One way to **test** this would be to politely make them aware of the effect their communication style is having on others; for example, send them a link to an article on best practices in team communication. However, if they ignore you and persist, everyone could refuse to work with them, thereby both proving to them and showing upper management that you will not be bullied into submission.

MY WAY OR THE HIGHWAY

Our friend and colleague **JANINE DRIVER** used to read body language every day to stay alive. She spent over fifteen years as a federal law enforcement officer within the Department of Justice. Now she is CEO of the Body Language Institute and has taught body language skills to, among others, the ATF (Bureau of Alcohol, Tobacco, Firearms and Explosives), FBI, CIA and DIA. Here she talks about the three "determination moves" to avoid using if you do not want to appear too bossy—even if you are the boss.

Maybe you're like me, or know someone like me, who demonstrates "I mean business" or "It's my way or the highway," with an increase in pressure instead of a decrease in pressure. Just ask my husband, or any of my former bosses when I worked as an investigator with the ATF—they'll all tell you I can be a real peach. I'm just one of those people who meet pressure with more pressure; I may pull my lips in, make a fist under the table, tilt my head and use intense jabbing illustrators, or thrust my head forward with a tilt, as if to say, "Helllllllo, did you hear me?" While I don't scream with my words, my determined body language shrieks *I'm the boss here, people*—even when I'm not!

In a study published in the *Journal of Experimental Social Psychology* in 2009, researchers examined how increasing pressure by making a fist affects feelings of assertiveness. Participants, some making the "rock" gesture and others "scissors," answered a series of questions to measure their assertiveness. While the researchers found that men making a fist reported feeling more assertive than those making a neutral gesture, the women did not report the same feelings.

Why the difference? Increasing pressure in the form of a fist activates ideas of power or control in both genders, but each gender might make a fist under different circumstances. Researchers argue that, for most men, physical aggression is a means to gain power, whereas for most women it is an expression of lost power—a last resort.

As you might imagine, when I make a fist, pound the air or

thrust forward, I do *not* make for an inspiring boss or respected and followed leader. So after decades of working for someone else, I left my government job and created my own company, where I get to be the boss of at least myself. I use my increase in pressure movements to persist against difficult odds and resist pressure, justify intent, follow my beliefs and convictions, and build resolve to support *my* favored course of action.

QUICK SCAN

S: Suspending judgment on popular behavioral ideas can be a great way to find the real and sometimes more complex truth in body language in any given situation.

C: Look at the "idea" of a certain role, think about what present or past **context** it may have worked in, and highlight for yourself how these have changed and evolved, and the expectations of behavior with them.

A: Ask what other possible ways someone can realistically behave in a situation. How far on the opposite end of a spectrum could they go?

N: Should you always test a **new** judgement? When is it worth the risk, or laternativekly more valuable for yourself and the community to make a bolder statement to assert yourself: How far do you go?

37

HAND IN THE COOKIE JAR

The secret sauce of one of your company's most important experimental technologies has been leaked to a competitor. You pull the team leader into a meeting room in order to investigate who exactly is on the other company's payroll. You want to find the mole. First spin of the wheel and . . . jackpot! Though they say they are not involved in any way, they are looking guilty as hell. And although you have not actually caught them with their hand in the cookie jar, as they sit in the meeting room slumped with their head in their hands, their body language says you absolutely have. They are guilty. You know it. They know it. They are the prime

➡

suspect. You have caught the perp. Now to move to confession—you are the closer!

LISTEN, SHERLOCK, if determining guilt were as easy as following a few "how to read body language" tips on the Internet, then we would not need a criminal justice system.

However, body language plays a powerful role in triggering our assumptions about how guilty someone may be. Indeed, body language will influence a jury, even when the evidence alone should be telling them about someone's innocence or guilt—and what their punishment should be. For example, one report for the *Emotion Review*, "Remorse and Criminal Justice," noted that a defendant's ability to show remorse was one of the most powerful factors in criminal sentencing, including capital sentencing; it noted, however, that there is currently no evidence that remorse can be accurately evaluated in a courtroom. In other words, there is no numerical "scale" of showing remorse. We all think we can tell when someone feels shame and remorse and so may jump to the conclusion that they won't be likely to offend again, but there is little evidence that remorse is correlated with future law-abiding behavior. In fact, there is evidence that remorse is often conflated with shame, which is actually correlated with increased future criminality.[1]

But in our scenario, how can you **suspend judgment** and **be more descriptive** to get closer to what the truth may be?

First, if you have learned anything from other chapters in this book on truth and lies, let it be to not fall foul of what Paul Ekman calls the Othello error. In general, you would expect someone under some kind of investigation, and being hauled into a room and questioned, to be under some stress if they were guilty, as much as you'd expect them to be under some stress even if they were not. Stress can elicit many of the following behaviors or **key signals**: nail biting, lip suppression, feet wrapped together or a generally tense body; self-soothing gestures or an increase in manipulators such as rubbing the face or the back of the neck, the arms, the legs, hand wringing, even self-hugging; maybe some pacing, fidgeting, tapping with fingers or legs, or moving the whole body toward exits; and some bigger physiological indicators like sweating, fast breathing rate, wide pupils, high blink rate, pale skin, dry mouth resulting in dry-looking lips and lip licking, a swallow reflex, a clicking sound in the voice and even just a generally stressed-sounding voice tonality and cadence.

Well, there's none of this in our scenario. So what are you seeing that is triggering your theory of guilty?

Let's look at the actual feeling and concept of guilt as the backdrop—in other words, guilt itself as the **context**.

Guilt is the cognitive or emotional experience that occurs when a person believes or realizes—accurately or not—that they have compromised their own standards of conduct or have violated a personal, societal or universal moral standard to which they ascribe. Guilt is a common feeling of emotional distress that arises when our actions or inactions have caused or might cause harm to another person, whether physical, emotional or otherwise. Guilt occurs primarily in interpersonal contexts and is considered a pro-social emotion because it helps us maintain good relationships with others. It is a signal that keeps going off in our heads until we take the appropriate action to remediate the wrong. Each internal signal might be brief, but compounded they can add up to a nagging sense that you should have done something differently, and if it is too late to repair, then you can be internally wracked with guilt. The outward expression of guilt is often said to be the look of shame.

The evolutionary theory for why this display of shame exists is that it helps maintain beneficial relationships and may be a function of reciprocal altruism, where one party temporarily displays less fitness in order to bolster the fitness of another or others, with the expectation that the others will act in a similar manner toward them at a later time. Therefore, if a person shows shame when their behavior has had a negative impact on others, the community is less likely to retaliate. A demonstration of shame shows you are contrite, and this increases survival prospects for all. We believe the person who feels guilt is less likely to do the deed again, and their display of shame is designed to elicit a decrease in punishment by their community. So long as the community does not punish unfairly and is willing to forgive eventually, this display of shame and resulting community response may work to rebuild trust on both sides. Of course, whether fair treatment in punishing wrongdoing is actually accomplished by the community, or in fact perceived as fair by the guilty party, may be a major determining factor in the likelihood that the offender will be repatriated to the community or, instead, become a repeat offender. However, it is no wonder jurors respond to a show of shame with more leniency in punishment; it is our social instinct. So, shame makes it possible to forgive and can help hold the social group together.

Of course, there are a multitude of relationships and social constructs in which, knowingly or unknowingly, people will trigger guilt and shame in others to powerfully influence, manipulate and control them. Strategically deployed displays of any one of the panoply of emotions, such as sorrow, anger, disgust or contempt, when used in particular contexts, may show an abuse of power by triggering strong responses of shame, and by so doing elicit extreme psychological pain and in some cases accompanying physical self-harm. Some parents say, "I just need to give my kid a look" when they feel the child has done something wrong. Depending on the type of "look"—potentially one of disapproval, reproach, contempt, disappointment, surprise or all of the above—and the context in which it is given, the parent may or may not understand the depth and power of the resulting feelings of shame the child feels, which has every chance of causing emotional pain or even secret self-inflicted physical pain; and to our point about incidences of the guilty party reoffending, it may not stop the unwanted behavior but instead cause the child to repeat it.

Bad Dobby! Bad Dobby! Bad!
Guilt and shame can cause you to self-punish. The Dobby effect—a phenomenon named after the head-banging elf in the Harry Potter books—refers to a psychological tendency for people to employ self-punishment around feelings of guilt. In one study, students who were made to feel guilty after depriving other students of lottery tickets (worth only a few dollars) were actually willing to give themselves electric shocks to signal their shame and remorse.

So **ask what else** is in the body language of shame. Certain blocking gestures characterize shame, as in our scenario where we have the classic "hang the head in shame" as one blocking gesture and then the "head in hands" over the face and further building on that. A subtler blocking cue showing shame is resting the tips of the fingers on the side of the forehead. More extreme examples of blocking are characterized more generally by avoidance of the person they feel shame around; this avoidance goes beyond, for example, eye contact avoidance through eye blocking or looking away and can be seen by the bigger gestures of avoiding occupying the same space, staying away from the shared office by taking a sick day or leaving town. This of course shows up in the virtual space as well. We can see it in some online ghosting behaviors where someone feeling shame may disappear from their social media scene for a time. Often it takes someone in the online community to call them back into the fold by asking if they're OK. A thread of shame, and forgiveness, may follow to bring them out of self-inflicted virtual exile.

But here's the most important element of all this: Does a display of shame always signal an admittance of guilt? We understand that some perpetrators may never feel guilt or shame, but do we feel guilt only if we are actually guilty? Can someone feel the empathic guilt of another while having nothing to do with the guilt-provoking event themselves? Is it possible for someone or a group to feel the guilt of another individual or group that has transgressed? Well, of course it is. We are social and so we have mechanisms for feeling what others may be feeling regardless of whether we were involved in the acts that caused the feelings. We empathize with guilt and shame. We often even feel shame for acts our ancestors were guilty of decades or centuries before our time and for which they themselves showed no remorse.

Some of us are more prone than others to feeling guilt. Guilt-prone people assume they have harmed others when they have not. With a low threshold for feeling guilty feelings, our guilt alarm may go off when it maybe does not need to. As a result, we end up feeling guilty about how we may have adversely affected others when further investigation would reveal we actually have not. Many of us feel the disapproval of other people when it is really not there. Sometimes we read in their nonverbal communication a hint or minimum specification that leads us to assume they are feeling disdain, sorrow, anger or contempt toward us. This triggers in us extreme guilt, and we may display signs of shame. We not only may end up wrongly saddled with the blame but also risk traveling around with the heavy burden of guilt on our backs. And the real guilty party? They may be getting away scot-free!

The power of the feeling shows up in the body's response against gravity, hence the term *heavy with guilt*. One study found that feeling guilty makes people assess their weight as being significantly heavier than it actually is, and in such cases they respond to physical activities as requiring significantly more effort than for non-guilty-feeling people.[2]

BODY LANGUAGE MYTHBUSTER
Shifty Eyes Means a Bad Person
Eye avoidance is often wrongly associated by the general public with deception. But nothing could be further from the truth. Aldert Vrij, author of *Detecting Lies and Deceit: Pitfalls and Opportunities*, found that people who habitually lie actually engage in greater eye contact.[3] Why? Because they know we look for this behavior and they want to make sure we are buying their lie. A truthful person may let their eyes wander off because they are not motivated to convince, only to convey a story.

Eye aversion happens for many reasons, both personal and cultural. For instance, you may derive

---

great personal comfort in recalling facts or an emotional experience by looking away from someone and looking down or focusing on something distant. Additionally, in some cultures and groups, it is instilled in children that when they are in front of authority, they should show respect by averting the eyes. But how would this look in the context of a trial where someone in the jury just read an online article on "how to tell they are lying" and took the bit about shifty eyes as gospel?

In fact, deceit may not look at all how we think it is going to look. The confidence trickster does not so much engage in behaviors that display overt confidence as gain our confidence by offering something they can see we want. Often they do this by lowering their own status to give us what feels like an advantage. They give us a feeling of power. Therefore, don't expect a con artist to come to you looking like they have all the power. Rather, be aware of how your interaction with them may instill in you a sudden surge of powerful or superior feelings. Practiced con artists take advantage of our weaknesses around the power we may not possess but that we long for, and so manipulate feelings we may have of loneliness, insecurity or poor health; they also prey on our pride or simple ignorance.

So you can now have a **new judgment** that just because someone may be displaying some indicators of shame it does not mean they are in truth guilty of the act you are investigating. It is possible for someone to *feel* guilty of a crime and not factually be guilty. Moreover, it is possible for a *victim* of a crime to feel guilty and of course be not at all responsible for what has happened to them. What **test** can you use to determine if they are actually guilty or not?

Easy! It starts with the Latin expression *ei incumbit probatio qui dicit, non qui negat*—the burden of proof is on the one who declares, not on the one who denies. This is the principle that a person is considered innocent unless proven guilty. This principle keeps any society that uses it safe from its own snap judgments. So the onus is on you to gather more intelligence and hard evidence; where the stakes are high, you need to be thorough and not just go with a hunch.

BASIC DRIVES

Should you find yourself in the interrogator's seat at your organization, we have some excellent advice from **GREGORY HARTLEY**, a trusted colleague from the world of human behavior and body language. His expertise as an interrogator earned him honors with the United States Army. The Department of Defense, Navy Seals and federal law enforcement agencies have all relied on his knowledge. Now he also delivers help to the business world. Here's what he told us about getting to the truth in this context.

I left a world where truth is in absolutes, actionable and can mean life or death for someone.

The modern corporate world shares little with that world. So how do I use the skills I brought from intelligence? Frankly, the two worlds are identical, with human drives, egos and interaction playing equal parts in a soup of obligation, duty, self-preservation and reward.

In the interrogation room, there are roles and expectations set out by culture and media. In the modern corporate world, the same is true. You just cannot use the same "bright light in a dark room" theatrics.

Human drives still are the key ingredients, so go back to basics. From Maslow's hierarchy, we know a person needs to be part of a group and then establish esteem. It is one of these two drives that causes the person to be deceptive or do something less than above board to begin with.

Take a few minutes and design a plan that plays on the person's ability to stay in the group or lose face. You can then use a handful of tools that did work in the interrogation room, things like:

1. Ask for more details than the person has provided or can provide.
2. Listen intently to what the person is saying and notice when their words stray from a normal pattern.
3. Look for increases in body language indicators.
4. Listen for *verbal bridges* (a phrase coined by Jack Schafer), phrases like *and then*, and don't allow the person to hide time.
5. Be specific in your questions and expect specific answers.

At the end of the day you will find that most folks want to be honest and will tell the truth if they believe it will be better for them. Most of the time they have gotten into the situation through trying to gain esteem or belong. Help them belong or gain esteem through your ploy and you will be surprised at the result.

QUICK SCAN

S: "Innocent until proven guilty" is how many societies **suspend** their judgment so as to try to ensure they punish only those truly at fault.

C: Just because someone feels guilty does not mean they are. **Context** can be the lens through which you are looking at someone's actions. In this chapter's scenario, you need to suspend your judgment of the context of guilt.

A: Ask what other contextual lenses are available to you. Innocent until proven guilty is one such lens.

N: A dangerous test of a **new** judgment can be to directly accuse someone. Gather your evidence and present it to another person who is not involved, to test their reaction to it.

SUMMARY

YOU NOW HAVE MORE than enough to go on to assess body language and make more considered and accurate judgments about what others are *really* thinking. You can now more astutely separate truth from lies, not only in what you read and watch about body language through the media but also from the behaviors you yourself witness.

You have a simple method for thinking about the displays of power, and responses to displays of power, in the behaviors and body language you see.

You know how to be more observant of others by first **suspending** your judgments and being more descriptive about what you see, sense and feel.

You are now more mindful of the **context** that surrounds the body language you see. You are also understanding of a more complete nonverbal picture that includes not only what is seen but also what is heard, felt and touched, and the dynamics at play in all of this. You now are able to take into account what is there but also what is missing, and how all of this fits into time and space. You are now mindful of yourself as both a context and a filter for all this nonverbal information and so recognize that how you feel and think will ultimately define your instincts about what others intend toward you and your theories about their state of mind.

You can **ask** what else is happening in and around a situation and what else you could or should know about it. You can ask for another viewpoint. You can ask for expert opinion. And you can even ask the person you are reading for their angle, to truly understand the moment from multiple positions of perception.

And finally, once you have taken a moment to critically sift through the nonverbal information of the particular scenario, you can refine your judgments or change your mind by forming **new** judgments and take action on new ideas, which may be beneficial to everyone.

This, quite frankly, is a critical thinking skill most of us don't use enough. You will now have this powerful tool to help uncover the truth and lies of what people are really thinking. Use it wisely. But most of all, enjoy it.

BONUS BLUFF

NO DECENT BODY LANGUAGE BOOK would be complete without a few words on poker tells, one of the most romanticized aspects of gambling and of body language. After all, learning to read other players' signals both increases your chances of winning and reveals a secret code to tell you everything they are thinking.

Seductive though this idea is, there is the deeper reality: unless you understand the power of your own hand, winning will be sheer fluke. No comprehension of another's mind will be more powerful than knowing the value you hold.

But other players will try to get you to question yourself. Or as they call it in poker, bluff you. They'll want you to think you have less than they do. Or they'll want to con you into thinking that you have more. They'll want you to either fold or risk more than you should.

So, if you think you may have way more to learn in order to ace the game—be it in the high-stakes professional poker world, a friendly game with your crew or trying to impress the love of your life at a casino date night—then you're right. But should this stop you from playing?

If you wait until you understand enough to do something tricky with total surety, you'll never even get going. Or as our longtime friend the British writer Shaun Prendergast wrote to us on our wedding day: "We must kiss the dice as we begin / unless we take the risk we cannot win."

Take what you have, and fly with it.

LEARN MORE

KEEP LEARNING MORE about the TRUTH and LIES of body language at **www.truthandlies.ca**.

Online video training in body language and presentation skills can be found at **www.truthplane.com**.

Mark Bowden's highly entertaining, informative and interactive keynote speeches and training seminars teach audiences around the world how to use winning body language to stand out, win trust and gain credibility. To have Mark Bowden speak at your next event, train your people or even train you personally, visit **www.truthplane.com** and contact **info@truthplane.com**.

ACKNOWLEDGMENTS

Thanks to our agents, Carolyn Forde at Westwood Creative Artists and Martin Perelmuter, Farah Perelmuter, Bryce Moloney and all the team at Speakers' Spotlight. At HarperCollins we thank our ever-wise, wonderfully encouraging and perennially patient editorial director Jim Gifford, managing editorial director Noelle Zitzer and copyeditor Patricia MacDonald, along with Douglas Richmond for first approaching us with the project. Thanks to all our TRUTH-PLANE team for providing the most solid sounding board and feedback throughout this process: virtuosos Bronwyn Page, Michael Turnbull, Cathryn Naiker, Josephine Aguilar, Rakhee Morzaria; researcher Rob Kenigsberg; drivers Danny and Michael. This book is made possible by the constant love, unwavering support, friendship, mentorship, idea sharing and creativity over the years of all the Thomson and Bowden families, John Wright, Shaun Prendergast, Jennifer La Trobe, Den, Dina Haeri, Trish and Nick Del Sorbo, Tamara and Kieran Conroy, "Crowlympians" Julie Soloway and Brian Facey, Ilana Jackson and Mike Sereny, Michael Leckie (it's either you, me or you and me), Bruce Van Ryn-Bocking for the appreciation of critical thinking, and Michael Bungay-Stanier for cocktails, the book title and the power of asking "What else?" Contributions from our friends, our colleagues, our heroes and some of the giants of body language and behavior: Anderson Carvalho, Jamie Mason Cohen, Janine Driver, Vanessa Van Edwards, Dr. Lillian Glass, Eric

Goulard, Gregory Hartley, Danielle Libine, J. Paul Nadeau, Cathryn Naiker, Joe Navarro, Saskia Nelson, Allan Pease, Robert Phipps, Tonya Reiman, Eddy Robinson, Scott Rouse, Alyson Schafer, Victoria Stilwell and Kanan Tandi. As well as being an expert contributor, Scott Rouse helped hugely by giving his great knowledge as expert reader. Support of friends and followers on Facebook, LinkedIn, Twitter, YouTube and Instagram, including Scott and Alison Stratten's speakers community of Speak and Spill and Mitch Joel's writers community of Write and Rant. Thanks, John Foulkes, for your insight. Cheers to the neighbors for checking in. Big love to our kids, Lex and Stella, whose love, patience and cheering us on, no matter what, made this book possible.

NOTES

CHAPTER 1: BODY LANGUAGE LIES
1. Aaron T. Beck, *Prisoners of Hate: The Cognitive Basis of Anger, Hostility, and Violence* (New York: Harper Perennial, 2000), 42–43.

CHAPTER 5: THEY'RE TOTALLY CHECKING ME OUT!
1. MR, "Adore Me Is Setting Out to Disrupt the Lingerie Space with Style . . . and Data," Digital Innovation and Transformation: A Course at Harvard Business School, November 22, 2015, https://digit.hbs.org/submission/adore-me-is-setting-out-to-disrupt-the-lingerie-space-with-styleand-data.

2. Melissa Hogenboom, "There Is Something Weird about This Gorilla's Eyes," BBC, August 7, 2015, www.bbc.com/earth/story/20150808-gorillas-with-human-eyes.

3. Gillian Rhodes, "The Evolutionary Psychology of Facial Beauty," *Annual Review of Psychology* 57 (2006): 199–226, doi:10.1146/annurev.psych.57.102904.190208.

4. Albert T. Mannes, "Shorn Scalps and Perceptions of Male Dominance," *Social Psychological and Personality Science* 4, no. 2 (2013): 198–205, http://opim.wharton.upenn.edu/DPlab/papers/publishedPapers/Mannes_2012_%20Shorn%20scalps%20and%20perceptions%20of%20male%20dominance.pdf, doi:10.1177/1948550612449490.

CHAPTER 6: PLAYING HARD-TO-GET
1. D.T. Hsu et al., "Response of the μ-opioid System to Social Rejection and Acceptance," *Molecular Psychiatry* 18 (November 2013): 1211–1217, doi:10.1038/mp.2013.96.

2. Gurit E. Birnbaum and Harry T. Reis, "When Does Responsiveness Pique Sexual Interest? Attachment and Sexual Desire in Initial Acquaintanceships," *Personality and Social Psychology Bulletin* 38, no. 7 (2012): 946–958, doi:10.1177/0146167212441028.

3. Kerstin Uvnas-Moberg, *The Oxytocin Factor: Tapping the Hormone of Calm, Love and Healing* (Cambridge, MA: Da Capo Press, 2003).

CHAPTER 7: JUST FEELING SORRY FOR ME

1. Neil A. Harrison et al., "Pupillary Contagion: Central Mechanisms Engaged in Sadness Processing," *Social Cognitive and Affective Neuroscience* 1, no. 1 (2006): 5–17, doi:10.1093/scan/nsl006.

2. Sarah D. Gunnery, Judith A. Hall, and Mollie A. Ruben, "The Deliberate Duchenne Smile: Individual Differences in Expressive Control," *Journal of Nonverbal Behavior* 37, no. 1 (2013): 29–41, doi:10.1007/s10919-012-0139-4.

CHAPTER 8: I'M BEING GHOSTED

1. Miss Twenty-Nine, "The Henley Boy," The 30 Dates Blog, July 8, 2013, https://30datesblog.com/2013/07/08/the-henley-boy.

2. Edward T. Hall, *The Hidden Dimension* (New York: Doubleday, 1966).

CHAPTER 9: WHAT A COMPLETE PSYCHO!

1. Robert D. Hare, *Manual for the Revised Psychopathy Checklist*, 2nd ed. (Toronto: Multi-Health Systems, 2003).

2. Joe Navarro and Toni Sciarra Poynter, *Dangerous Personalities: An FBI Profiler Shows You How to Identify and Protect Yourself from Dangerous People* (Emmaus, PA: Rodale, 2014).

CHAPTER 10: THEY ARE RUNNING THE SHOW

1. Charles Darwin, *The Descent of Man and Selection in Relation to Sex* (London: John Murray, 1871).

2. Jane Goodall, *The Chimpanzees of Gombe: Patterns of Behavior* (Cambridge, MA: Belknap Press of Harvard University, 1986), 130.

3. American Psychiatric Association, *Diagnostic and Statistical Manual of Mental Disorders*, 4th ed., 1994 (commonly referred to as *DSM-IV*).

CHAPTER 11: I'M GOING TO PAY FOR THAT!

1. Paul Ekman and Wallace V. Friesen, *Facial Action Coding System: A Technique for the Measurement of Facial Movement* (Palo Alto, CA: Consulting Psychologists Press, 1978).

2. Ekman and Wallace, *Facial Action Coding System*.

3. Albert Mehrabian, "Silent Messages": A Wealth of Information about Nonverbal Communication (Body Language)," *Personality & Emotion Tests & Software: Psychological Books & Articles of Popular Interest* (2009).

4. Liam Satchell et al., "Evidence of Big Five and Aggressive Personalities in Gait Biomechanics," *Journal of Nonverbal Behavior* 41, no. 1 (2017): 35.

CHAPTER 12: THEY ARE *SO* MAD AT ME
1. Albert Mehrabian, *Nonverbal Communication* (New Brunswick, NJ: Aldine Transaction, 1972), 108.

CHAPTER 13: A LYING CHEAT?
1. Paul Ekman, *Telling Lies: Clues to Deceit in the Marketplace, Politics, and Marriage*, 3rd ed. (New York: Norton, 2009), 169–170.

CHAPTER 14: DEFINITELY INTO MY FRIEND
1. Nicola Binetti et al., "Pupil Dilation as an Index of Preferred Mutual Gaze Duration," *Royal Society Open Science* (2016), doi:10.1098/rsos.160086.

CHAPTER 15: A MATCH MADE IN HEAVEN?
1. Thomas Lewis, Fari Amini and Richard Lannon, *A General Theory of Love* (New York: Vintage, 2001), 63.

2. Catalina L. Toma, Jeffrey T. Hancock and Nicole B. Ellison, "Separating Fact from Fiction: An Examination of Deceptive Self-Presentation in Online Dating Profiles," *Personality and Social Psychology Bulletin* 34, no. 8 (2008), doi:10.1177/0146167208318067.

3. Match.com and Chadwick Martin Bailey, "2009–2010 Studies: Recent Trends; Online Dating," accessed September 11, 2017, http://cp.match.com/cppp/media/CMB_Study.pdf.

4. Eli J. Finkel et al., "Online Dating: A Critical Analysis from the Perspective of Psychological Science," *Psychological Science in the Public Interest*, S13, no. 1 (2012): 3, doi:10.1177/1529100612436522.

CHAPTER 16: THEY ARE *SO* BREAKING UP!
1. Ernest A. Haggard and Kenneth S. Isaacs, "Micro-Momentary Facial Expressions as Indicators of Ego Mechanisms in Psychotherapy," *Methods of Research in Psychotherapy* (New York: Appleton-Century-Crofts, 1966), 154–165.

2. Paul Ekman and Wallace V. Friesen, "A New Pan-cultural Facial Expression of Emotion," *Motivation and Emotion* 10, no. 2 (1986): 159–168, doi:10.1007/BF00992253.

3. Malcolm Gladwell, *Blink: The Power of Thinking without Thinking* (New York: Little, Brown, 2005), chapter 1, section 3.

CHAPTER 17: THICK AS THIEVES

1. Diego Gambetta, *Codes of the Underworld: How Criminals Communicate* (Princeton, NJ: Princeton University Press, 2009).

2. Paul Ekman, "Emotional and Conversational Nonverbal Signals," *Language, Knowledge, and Representation; Proceedings of the Sixth International Colloquium on Cognitive Science* 99 (2004): 40, doi:10.1007/978-1-4020-2783-3_3.

3. Vickiie Oliphant, "What Does Trump's Hand Sign Mean? Conspiracy Theorists Left Stunned over 'Secret Signal,'" *Express*, last modified January 20, 2017, www.express.co.uk/news/world/756924/What-do-Donald-Trump-hand-signals-mean-Illuminati-okay-devil.

CHAPTER 18: MY NEW BFF?

1. Kenneth Levine, Robert Muenchen and Abby Brooks, "Measuring Transformational and Charismatic Leadership: Why Isn't Charisma Measured?" *Communication Monographs* 77, no. 4 (2010): 576, doi:10.1080/03637751.2010.499368.

2. American Psychological Association, "Recognizing the Signs of Bipolar Disorder," accessed September 11, 2017, www.apa.org/helpcenter/recognizing-bipolar.aspx.

CHAPTER 19: FOMO

1. Wayne Hanley, *The Genesis of Napoleonic Propaganda, 1796–1799* (New York: Columbia University Press, 2002), www.gutenberg-e.org/haw01/frames/fhaw04.html.

2. J. Mark Powell, "Mon Dieu! The Real Story Behind Napoleon's Famous Pose," J. Mark Powell, Author (blog), September 4, 2015, www.jmarkpowell.com/mon-dieu-the-real-story-behind-napoleons-famous-pose.

3. Sam Webb, "Red Chalk Self Portrait of Leonardo da Vinci Said to Have Mystical Powers and Hidden from Hitler during World War II Goes on Rare Public Display," *Mail Online*, October 31, 2014, www.dailymail.co.uk/news/article-2815328/Red-chalk-self-portrait-Leonardo-Di-Vinci-said-mystical-powers-hidden-Hitler-World-War-II-goes-rare-public-display.html.

4. Katie Notopoulos, "'Fingermouthing' Is the New Hot Pose for Selfies," BuzzFeedNews, July 1, 2016, www.buzzfeed.com/katienotopoulos/fingermouthing-is-the-new-hot-pose-for-selfies?utm_term=.kt2dVdb0Z7#.jiZBJBP50E.

5. Bianca London and Toni Jones, "How to Squinch, Teeg and Smize: The Art of Selfie Posing Put to the Test," *Mail Online*, last updated November 27, 2013,

www.dailymail.co.uk/femail/article-2514437/How-squinch-teeg-smize-The-art-selfie-posing-test-NeverUnderdressed-com.html; Jennifer Choy, "Here Are the Instagram Poses That Will Get You the Most Likes," HuffPost, last updated April 22, 2016, www.huffingtonpost.ca/2016/04/22/instagram-poses_n_9760570.html; Notopoulos, "'Fingermouthing.'"

6. Andrea Arterbery, "Why the Kardashian-Jenner's Hairstyles Are Cultural Appropriation," *Teen Vogue*, August 11, 2016, www.teenvogue.com/story/kardashian-jenners-cultural-appropriation-hair.

7. Laura Smith-Spark, "Protesters Rally Worldwide in Solidarity with Washington March," CNN Politics, January 21, 2017, www.cnn.com/2017/01/21/politics/trump-women-march-on-washington/index.html.

8. Nolan Feeney, "Facebook's New Photo Filter Lets You Show Solidarity with Paris," *Time*, November 14, 2015, http://time.com/4113171/paris-attacks-facebook-filter-french-flag-profile-picture.

CHAPTER 20: CONTROL FREAK

1. Matthew J. Hertenstein et al., "Touch Communicates Distinct Emotions," *Emotion* 6, no. 3 (2006): 528–533, doi:10.1037/1528-3542.6.3.528.

2. Steven B. Karpman, "The Karpman Drama Triangle," Coaching Supervision Academy, accessed September 11, 2017, http://coachingsupervisionacademy.com/the-karpman-drama-triangle.

3. María José Álvarez et al., "The Effects of Massage Therapy in Hospitalized Preterm Neonates: A Systematic Review," *International Journal of Nursing Studies* 69 (2017): 119–136, doi:10.1016/j.ijnurstu.2017.02.009.

CHAPTER 21: TOO CLOSE FOR COMFORT

1. Juulia T. Suvilehto et al., "Topography of Social Touching Depends on Emotional Bonds between Humans," *Proceedings of the National Academy of Sciences of the United States of America* 112, no. 45 (2015): 13811–13816, doi:10.1073/pnas.1519231112.

2. Judith Horstman, *The Scientific American Book of Love, Sex and the Brain: The Neuroscience of How, When, Why and Who We Love* (Hoboken, NJ: Wiley, 2011).

3. Rafael Wlodarski and Robin I.M. Dunbar, "What's in a Kiss? The Effect of Romantic Kissing on Mate Desirability," *Evolutionary Psychology* 12, no. 1 (2014): doi:10.1177/147470491401200114.

CHAPTER 22: THEY'LL NEVER FIT IN WITH MY FAMILY

1. Ray L. Birdwhistell, *Kinesics and Context* (Philadelphia: University of Pennsylvania Press, 1970).

2. Paul Ekman, "Emotional and Conversational Nonverbal Signals," *Language, Knowledge, and Representation: Proceedings of the Sixth International Colloquium on Cognitive Science* 99 (2004): 40, doi:10.1007/978-1-4020-2783-3_3.

3. James J. Nolan, "Establishing the Statistical Relationship between Population Size and UCR Crime Rate: Its Impact and Implications," *Journal of Criminal Justice* 32 (2004): 547–555, doi:10.1016/j.jcrimjus.2004.08.002.

CHAPTER 24: I AM BORING THE PANTS OFF THEM

1. Leon Watson, "Humans Have Shorter Attention Span Than Goldfish Thanks to Smartphones," *The Telegraph*, Science, May 15, 2015, www.telegraph.co.uk/science/2016/03/12/humans-have-shorter-attention-span-than-goldfish-thanks-to-smart.

2. Natalie Wolchover, "Why Do We Zone Out?" *Live Science*, June 24, 2011, www.livescience.com/33357-why-we-zone-out.html.

CHAPTER 25: LYING THROUGH THEIR TEETH

1. Richard Wiseman et al., "The Eyes Don't Have It: Lie Detection and Neuro-Linguistic Programming," *PLoS One* 7, no. 7 (2012): doi:10.1371/journal.pone.0040259.

CHAPTER 26: PERSONA NON GRATA

1. Rosalyn Shute, Laurence Owens and Phillip Slee, "'You Just Stare at Them and Give Them Daggers': Nonverbal Expressions of Social Aggression in Teenage Girls," *International Journal of Adolescence and Youth* 10, no. 4 (2012): 353–372, doi:10.1080/02673843.2002.9747911.

2. Adrienne Lafrance, "Why 13-Year-Old Girls Are the Queens of Eye-Rolling," *The Atlantic*, May 11, 2016, www.theatlantic.com/science/archive/2016/05/puhlease/482154.

3. Ellie Lisitsa, "The Four Horsemen: Contempt," The Gottman Institute, May 13, 2013, www.gottman.com/blog/the-four-horsemen-contempt.

4. Marianne Lafrance and Julie Woodzicka, "No Laughing Matter: Women's Verbal and Nonverbal Reactions to Sexist Humor," in *Prejudice: The Target's Perspective*, ed. Janet K. Swim and Charles Stangor (San Diego: Academic Press,1998).

5. Justin H. Park and Florian Van Leeuwen, "Evolutionary Perspectives on Social Identity," *Evolutionary Perspectives on Social Psychology* (2015): 119, doi:10.1007/978-3-319-12697-5_9.

CHAPTER 27: INVISIBLE ME

1. Amy Cuddy, "Your iPhone Is Ruining Your Posture—and Your Mood," *New York Times*, December 12, 2015, www.nytimes.com/2015/12/13/opinion/sunday/your-iphone-is-ruining-your-posture-and-your-mood.html.

2. David Biello, "Inside the Debate about Power Posing: A Q & A with Amy Cuddy," Ideas.TED.com, February 22, 2017, http://ideas.ted.com/inside-the-debate-about-power-posing-a-q-a-with-amy-cuddy.

CHAPTER 28: I ACED THAT INTERVIEW—SO WHERE'S THE JOB OFFER?

1. Great Place to Work, "Research for 2017 Fortune 100 Best Companies Reveals Great Places to Work for All Will Be Key to Better Business Performance," press release, March 10, 2017, www.greatplacetowork.com/press-releases/845-great-place-to-work-research-for-2017-fortune-100-best-companies-reveals-great-places-to-work-for-all-will-be-key-to-better-business-performance.

2. Idan Frumin et al., "A Social Chemosignaling Function for Human Hand-shaking," *eLife* (2015): doi:10.7554/eLife.05154.

CHAPTER 29: THEY HATE MY WORK

1. Katy Steinmetz, "Oxford's 2015 Word of the Year Is This Emoji," *Time*, updated November 16, 2015, http://time.com/4114886/oxford-word-of-the-year-2015-emoji.

2. Hannah Miller et al., "'Blissfully Happy' or 'Ready to Fight': Varying Interpretations of Emoji," GroupLens Research, University of Minnesota (2016), retrieved September 11, 2017, www.users.cs.umn.edu/~bhecht/publications/ICWSM2016_emoji.pdf.

3. Sharlyn Lauby, "How Company Values Protect Culture in Times of Growth," Great Place to Work (blog), February 1, 2017, www.greatplacetowork.com/resources/blog/803-how-company-values-protect-culture-in-times-of-growth.

CHAPTER 30: BIG DOG

1. Eric Hehman, Jessica K. Flake and Jonathan B. Freeman, "Static and Dynamic Facial Cues Differentially Affect the Consistency of Social Evaluations," *Personality and Social Psychology Bulletin* 41, no. 8 (2015): 2, doi:10.1177/0146167215591495.

2. Hehman, Flake and Freeman, "Static and Dynamic Facial Cues."

3. Danielle Libine, *A Photographer's Guide to Body Language* (CreateSpace Independent Publishing Platform, 2015).

4. Victoria Stilwell, *The Secret Language of Dogs: Unlocking the Canine Mind for a Happier Pet* (Berkeley, CA: Ten Speed Press, 2016).

CHAPTER 31: NEVER GOING TO SEE EYE TO EYE

1. Miriam Kunz, Kenneth Prkachin and Stefan Lautenbacher, "Smiling in Pain: Explorations of Its Social Motives," *Pain Research and Treatment* (2013): doi:10.1155/2013/128093.

2. Martin Brokenleg et al., *Reclaiming Youth at Risk: Our Hope for the Future* (Bloomington, IN: National Educational Service, 1996).

CHAPTER 32: COLD FISH

1. Adam Smith, "The Empathy Imbalance Hypothesis of Autism: A Theoretical Approach to Cognitive and Emotional Empathy in Autistic Development," *Psychological Record* 59, no. 2 (2009): 273–294, accessed September 11, 2017, http://opensiuc.lib.siu.edu/tpr/vol59/iss3/9.

2. Paul Ekman, "Facial Expression and Emotion," *American Psychologist* 48, no. 4 (1993): 384–392, doi:10.1037/0003-066X.48.4.384.

3. Jerry Adler, "Smile, Frown, Grimace and Grin—Your Facial Expression Is the Next Frontier in Big Data," Smithsonian.com, December 2015, www.smithsonianmag.com/innovation/rana-el-kaliouby-ingenuity-awards-technology-180957204.

4. Brian K. Rundle, Vanessa R. Vaughn and Matthew S. Stanford, "Contagious Yawning and Psychopathy," *Personality and Individual Differences* 86 (2015): 33–37, doi:10.1016/j.paid.2015.05.025.

CHAPTER 33: THEY'RE GONNA BLOW!

1. Adam K. Fetterman, Michael D. Robinson and Robert D. Gordon, "Anger as Seeing Red: Perceptual Sources of Evidence," *Social Psychological and Personality Science* 2, no. 3 (2010): 311–316, doi:10.1177/1948550610390051; Adam K. Fetterman, Tianwei Liu and Michael D. Robinson, "Extending Color Psychology to the Personality Realm: Interpersonal Hostility Varies by Red Preferences and Perceptual Biases," *Journal of Personality* 83, no. 1 (2015): 106–116, doi:10.1111/jopy.12087.

2. "Color Red Increases the Speed and Strength of Reactions," University of Rochester, June 2, 2011, http://rochester.edu/news/show.php?id=3856.

3. "Diseases and Conditions: Intermittent Explosive Disorder," Mayo Clinic, August 25, 2015, www.mayoclinic.org/diseases-conditions/ intermittent-explosive-disorder/basics/definition/CON-20024309?p=1.

4. Stephen A. Diamond, "Anger Disorder: What It Is and What We Can Do about It," *Psychology Today*, April 3, 2009, www.psychologytoday.com/blog/ evil-deeds/200904/anger-disorder-what-it-is-and-what-we-can-do-about-it.

CHAPTER 34: THIS MEETING IS A WASTE OF TIME

1. Irenaus Eibl-Eibesfeldt, *Ethology: The Biology of Behavior* (New York: Holt, Rhinehart and Winston, 1975).

2. Ramiro M. Joly-Mascheroni, Atsushi Senju and Alex J. Shepherd, "Dogs Catch Human Yawns," *Biology Letters* 4, no. 5 (2008): doi:10.1098/rsbl.2008.0333.

3. Derks Daantje, Arjan E.R. Bos and Jasper von Grumbkow, "Emoticons in Computer-Mediated Communication: Social Motives and Social Context," *CyberPsychology & Behavior* 11, no. 1 (2008): 99–101, doi:10.1089/ cpb.2007.9926.

4. Jaram Park et al., "Emoticon Style: Interpreting Differences in Emoticons Across Cultures," *Proceedings of the Seventh International AAAI Conference on Weblogs and Social Media*, accessed September 11, 2017, www.aaai.org/ocs/ index.php/ICWSM/ICWSM13/paper/viewFile/6132/6386.

CHAPTER 35: LOOKS LIKE A WINNING TEAM

1. Michael W. Kraus, Cassy Huang and Dacher Keltner, "Tactile Communication, Cooperation, and Performance: An Ethological Study of the NBA," University of California, Berkeley, accessed September 11, 2017, http:// socrates.berkeley.edu/~keltner/publications/kraus.huang.keltner.2010.pdf.

CHAPTER 36: SO, YOU THINK YOU'RE THE BOSS

1. Kensy Cooperrider, Rafael Nunez and James Slotta, "The Protean Pointing Gesture: Variation in a Building Block of Human Communication," *Proceedings of the Cognitive Science Society* 36 (2014), http://escholarship.org/uc/ item/6sd477h8.

2. Paul Ekman, "Emotional and Conversational Nonverbal Signals," *Language, Knowledge, and Representation: Proceedings of the Sixth International Colloquium on Cognitive Science* 99 (2004): 40, doi:10.1007/978-1-4020-2783-3_3.

3. Sharlyn Lauby, "How Company Values Protect Culture in Times of Growth," *Great Place to Work* (blog), February 1, 2017, www.greatplacetowork.com/resources/blog/803-how-company-values-protect-culture-in-times-of-growth.

CHAPTER 37: HAND IN THE COOKIE JAR

1. Susan A. Bandes, "Remorse and Criminal Justice," *Emotion Review* 8, no. 1 (2015): 14–19, doi:10.1177/1754073915601222.
2. Guy Winch, "Feeling Guilt Increases Our Subjective Body Weight," *Psychology Today*, October 4, 2013, www.psychologytoday.com/blog/the-squeaky-wheel/201310/feeling-guilt-increases-our-subjective-body-weight.
3. Aldert Vrij, *Detecting Lies and Deceit: Pitfalls and Opportunities* (Chichester: Wiley, 2008).